HARVARD HISTORICAL STUDIES

PUBLISHED UNDER THE DIRECTION OF
THE DEPARTMENT OF HISTORY

FROM THE INCOME OF
THE HENRY WARREN TORREY FUND

VOLUME LXXV

NAPOLEON III
AND THE
GERMAN CRISIS
1865 — 1866

E. ANN POTTINGER

HARVARD UNIVERSITY PRESS
CAMBRIDGE · MASSACHUSETTS

Second Printing, 1968

Distributed in Great Britain by Oxford University Press, London

Library of Congress Catalog Card Number 66–18253

Printed in the United States of America

ACKNOWLEDGMENTS

THIS STUDY was made possible by grants from the American Association of University Women, the History Department, Harvard University, and the Massachusetts Society for the University Education of Women. It is impossible to cite all those who have helped to bring the work to completion; but a few names must be mentioned. Professor William L. Langer directed this inquiry; Professor Herbert Michaelis of the Free University of Berlin, Professor Pierre Renouvin of the Sorbonne, and Professor Mack Walker of Harvard University have given valuable opinions and advice. Several conversations with Father John Bush of Le Moyne College, the author of "Napoleon III and the Redeeming of Venetia," were informative and stimulating. In connection with the process of obtaining microfilm and photostats, thanks are due especially to André Cambier of the Archives du Ministère de la Guerre. Martha François and Mary R. Lefkowitz, both of Wellesley College, were kind enough to read the manuscript in its first form. Without the unstinting aid of all these and many more this study would have been far more imperfect than it actually is.

E. Ann Pottinger

Greensboro, North Carolina
September, 1965

CONTENTS

NAPOLEON III
AND THE
GERMAN CRISIS
1865-1866

ABBREVIATIONS

The following abbreviations have been used in this work. For full citations, see the bibliography.

AN	Archives Nationales
Annales (1866)	*Les Annales du Sénat et du Corps Législatif (1866)*
APP	*Die auswärtige Politik Preussens*
BN	Bibliothèque Nationale
GW	Otto von Bismarck, *Die gesammelten Werke*
HHSA	Haus- Hof- und Staatsarchiv
Merseburg	Deutsches Zentralarchiv, Abteilung Merseburg
Oncken	Hermann Oncken, *Die Rheinpolitik Kaiser Napoleons III*
PRO	Public Record Office
Quai d'Orsay	Archives des Affaires Etrangères, Ministère des Affaires Etrangères
Quellen	*Quellen zur deutschen Politik Österreichs*
Vincennes	Archives du Ministère de la Guerre, Château de Vincennes

All translations, unless otherwise noted, are the author's own.

PROLOGUE

THE FRENCH NATION may be said to have faced a "German Question" throughout the first three quarters of the nineteenth century; indeed, an observer determined to generalize might extend the problem backwards to Louis XIV and forwards at least to Hitler. Elementary facts of geography and power politics required that every French government take a vital interest in German organization. Should Central Europe be a power vacuum composed of small states competing with each other, or should it be unified under strong leadership? As long as the Germans themselves thought in terms of local loyalties, ill-defined imperial dreams, or cosmopolitan idealism, it was natural for the French to accept and exploit their divisions. Obvious benefits for French diplomacy were implied in the existence within the Holy Roman Empire in fact if not in law of the so-called "Three Germanies": Austria, Prussia, and the Third Germany of the small states. But in the nineteenth century when the growth of nationalism led to an important movement for unification in Central Europe, the question became more complex. The desirability of keeping Germany disunited had to be weighed against the disadvantages of arousing hostility by intervention in "German" affairs and opposition to "German" ambitions. Such considerations can be traced in French policy toward Germany throughout the nineteenth century; but the problem reached a head in the period designated in the present work as the German Crisis, running from the signing of the Convention of Gastein (August 14, 1865) to the signing of the Preliminary Peace of Nikolsburg (July 26, 1866). When Bismarck concluded the Gastein agreement with the Austrians, he had a dream of a German state unified under Prussia, but little power to implement it. He commanded, rather insecurely, the foreign policy of the weakest of the five European great powers. It is obvious that if a strong neighbor, such as France, had chosen to challenge his maneuvers within Germany toward unification, the results might have been disastrous. In fact, there is ample evidence that one of Bismarck's more important motives in entering into the Gastein agreement was the desire to gain time to determine the French attitude vis-à-vis his ambitious projects.[1] It was at this point that the French role became crucial in the advance of German unification. The decisive phase of this involvement lasted until the Peace of Nikolsburg. This treaty, in crowning the spectacular Prussian victory in the Seven Weeks' War with Austria, enabled the Prussian government to consolidate influence among the small states north of the Main River and to sign defensive alliances with the South German small states. With this significant increase in Prussian strength, involving either annexation or extended influence over all of the Third Germany, the "power gap" had been decisively narrowed, and, as result, the policies of French statesmen could have little effect either in halting or in hastening the definitive formation of the new state.

The present study, then, surveys the months during which French policy was a vital determinant in German history and surveys them from the French point of view. The background of events in Germany has been largely assumed, except insofar as occurrences in Germany directly stimulated French decisions. German unification has been the subject of much excellent work, and the rehearsal of the story here could accomplish little except the swelling of the present volume to an unmanageable size. It will also be noticed that this treatment of French policy concentrates on the period just before and during the Seven Weeks' War. Obviously, this emphasis stems from the fact that French policy was a response to the tensions which reached the surface only in the war. French policy toward Germany during the autumn of 1865 is more correctly described as a collection of attitudes; the definition and elaboration of a specific program was the work of the spring and summer of 1866. This

---

[1] For a full discussion of this point, see Chapter I.

development is reflected in the relevant documents, which, scanty for the autumn of 1865, became very numerous during 1866.[2]

The other focus proposed in the very title of this work is Napoleon III himself. It is the contention of this study that French policy in this question was principally the work of the Emperor. This statement is not intended to imply that Napoleon III imposed a policy ready-made upon willing subordinates. It is a commonplace of recent scholarship that Napoleon III was not the political power his imperial title suggests. At times, as in the autumn of 1865, lack of general interest in or information about a given diplomatic issue might conspire with confidence in the Emperor's competence to give Napoleon limited freedom of action.[3] But in the decisive months of 1866, French policy was debated by ministers, diplomats, generals, legislators, journalists, and the general public, and every shade of opinion was exhibited, from partisanship of German unification to active hostility. If Napoleon managed to guide France in a policy more or less consonant with his own beliefs and schemes, it was only in part because he held a position of power. Another reason was his recognition and astute manipulation of the opposing and potentially self-neutralizing tendencies of French opinion; and finally, it must be recognized, he was served by a very large element of chance. To reconstruct his policy, the historian must consider a broad range of incidents and arguments and examine the way in which French society as a whole met a time of profound change.

[2] The relative lack of sources for 1865 deserves further comment. Metternich, Austrian ambassador to Paris, was on leave in Vienna, and the chargé d'affaires sent unusually brief and uninformative reports to the Ballplatz. Evidently, the Austrians considered this period a lull in relations with France. Bismarck, on the other hand, was actively concerned with French reactions, but he spent a considerable part of the autumn on French soil in connection with the famous Biarritz meeting, and much of the Foreign Office business usually carried on by letter was transacted verbally. On the French side, Napoleon III was notorious for writing nothing down at any time; and as the problem had not yet aroused widespread debate in France, there is little material either from his entourage or from prominent figures outside the government.

[3] Cf. Jean Maurain, *Un Bourgeois français au XIXe siècle: Baroche* (Paris, 1936), pp. 311, 313.

I

THE CONVENTION
OF GASTEIN

THE CRIMEAN WAR made France pre-eminent in Europe through the defeat of Russia and the breakup of the alliance of the three Eastern powers. Napoleon III had become the first statesman of Europe. It is true that his predominance was a consequence of the disarray among the powers rather than an evidence of French strength. There was to be no Age of Napoleon III in the sense that there had been an Age of Metternich and would be an Age of Bismarck. Still, Napoleon marked the next fifteen years decisively—marked and also muddled them. Not for nothing was he called the Sphinx of the Tuileries: he wrote down almost nothing, contradicted himself regularly to ambassadors, and kept secrets from his ministers. The Emperor's innate love of mystery-making, the absence of documents coming directly from his hand, his need, given the domestic conflict of opinion, to keep in favor with both sides in the war, and the relative lack of decisive actions, all are factors combining to obscure his motives and goals. Contemporaries and historians alike have been baffled by the contradictions in which he shrouded his policy. Many derogatory names plagued him in his time and many interpretations have been offered since, but the debate remains open.

One line of analysis, which will be considered at length in this study, suggests that Napoleon was sincerely interested in the programs and proposals of Europe's increasingly self-conscious and articulate nationalist groups. The growth of nationalist sentiment that took place in late nineteenth-century diplomacy was foreshadowed, in mid-century, in the Italian peninsula, in the German states, and in the Balkans. Already it had become a factor in diplomatic developments. Napoleon, in his too often neglected work, *Napo-*

leonic Ideas, had taken a stand in favor of his so-called "principle of nationalities," that is, the contention that European boundaries should ultimately be modeled along the lines of national groupings. Yet the gap between theory and practice is notorious; and it is difficult to trace any consistent championing of the nationalist cause in Napoleon's foreign policy. His support of Cavour and the kingdom of Sardinia in the crisis of 1859 seemed to suggest that he favored the nationalist innovators. Through secret meetings at Stuttgart and at Plombières the Franco-Sardinian agreement was concerted, Russian neutrality guaranteed, and the stage set for the quick and ultimately decisive victory of the Sardinians aided by the French at the expense of the Austrians. Yet, despite this nationalist success, dramatically highlighted by the proclamation of the Kingdom of Italy in 1861, doubt remained as to whether Napoleon was on the side of the angels. His almost unseemly haste in signing the Villafranca Agreement with Franz Joseph, which abruptly ended the war in the north, could be explained by the fear of Prussian intervention; or it could reveal a lukewarm commitment. Again, the annexation by France of the two Italian provinces of Nice and Savoy raised the possibility that Napoleon's policy had been merely a new form of the old game of balance-of-power politics.

Events in the sixties did little to clarify the basic ambiguity surrounding Napoleon's purpose. On the one hand, his support of the Polish revolt in 1863 improved his image as a liberal and a nationalist. Restrained by British pleadings from any direct action in aid of the Poles, he finally suggested a congress, a project which severely embittered Anglo-French relations since Palmerston vetoed it decisively. Yet the embattled champion of the Poles was simultaneously responsible for the expedition destined to set a junior Hapsburg over the Spaniards, Indians, and half-castes of Mexico, while he had supported the Pope against the Italians and, as late as 1864, seemed to desire, through the September Convention, to prevent or modify Italian seizure of Rome.

Even a cursory survey shows that Napoleon's nationalism was a very complex matter. Many scholars have maintained that he was not a nationalist at all, but rather a typical politician in the Machiavellian tradition whose cynical manipulations of the balance of power were marred only by his lack of astuteness. It is true that in retrospect a policy which resulted in the creation of powerful and ultimately threatening neighbors appears as the height of folly. But at the time there was ample reason to hope that the unification movements would end with the creation of small, weak states which would gladly follow the leadership of France and become, as Napoleon wrote, "satellites." [1] Furthermore, Napoleonic France and the emerging national groups had a common opponent, the Hapsburg monarchy. As long as the Hapsburgs continued to hold even a modicum of the power that had lasted for centuries, an alliance between Bonaparte and the agitators might seem natural, quite independently of the question of ideological affinities.[2] These arguments suggest that Napoleon's nationalism stopped at the French border; yet there are many indications that Napoleon was attracted by the broader implications of the Revolutionary and Napoleonic heritage.

It is the contention of this work that in Germany the goals of nationalism and the requirements of the balance of power seemed, at least in Napoleon's eyes, to be complementary.[3] Of course, Napo-

---

[1] For a full explanation of the principle of nationalities, see Napoleon III, *Des Idées napoléoniennes* (Paris, 1860).

[2] Cf. John W. Bush, "Napoleon III and the Redeeming of Venetia, 1864–66," unpubl. diss. (Fordham University, 1961), p. 123; for a contrasting discussion, cf. C. W. Hallberg, *Franz Joseph and Napoleon III, 1852–64* (New York, 1955), pp. 342–4.

[3] Professor Herbert Michaelis of Berlin expressed similar views to this author. Professor Michaelis, however, emphasizes the importance of Napoleon's desire to overturn the 1815 settlement, while the present author's independent evaluation stresses the principle of nationalities.

The author's interpretation given in the above paragraph differs from that given by many scholars in the field. For clarity, it seems best to postpone discussion of the traditional accounts and to ask the reader, in the poet's terms, for a "willing suspension of disbelief" until the story has been told, persuasively or unpersuasively, from the present vantage point. The classic interpretation of Napoleon's German diplomacy is Hermann Oncken, *Napoleon III and the Rhine,* trans. Edwin H. Zeydel (New York, 1928). This is the English edition of Oncken's Introduction to his collection of documents, *Die Rheinpolitik Kaiser Napoleons III. von 1863 bis 1870,* 3 vols. (Berlin, 1926), and where possible it is cited in preference to the German version.

leon's views assumed enormous importance as events moved into a state of open crisis. With the benefit of hindsight, it seems probable that Bismarck had formulated at least a sliding scale of goals for Germany as early as 1862 when he became Prussian Minister-President. He hoped to unify German states under Prussia, if necessary through the exclusion of Austria from this newly constituted nation. This was a solution which the Austrians might refuse to accept, except at the point of the sword. To further his plans, Bismarck cleverly took advantage of the situation in Schleswig-Holstein. These provinces, located side by side in the Danish peninsula and northern Germany, respectively, had been ruled by the King of Denmark as a personal possession since 1815. The principle of their administrative independence had been supported by a series of international agreements; it was threatened, in the case of Schleswig, by a new Danish constitution. Bismarck engineered an Austro-Prussian rescue operation. A rapid campaign ended with the cession of the provinces to Austria and Prussia jointly. This situation was, of course, impossible for the conduct of government. The arrangement which superseded it, that laid down by the Convention of Gastein by which Austria ruled Holstein and Prussia Schleswig, was not much better. Bismarck had found the perfect means of irritating and even rupturing Austro-Prussian relations at will, and the intransigence with which he greeted all international proposals for a final settlement augured correctly that he intended to use his advantage to the full in connection with his unification plans.

These events created a situation in which Napoleon's attitude could be crucial and Bismarck recognized this fact. There is considerable evidence to show that an important reason why the masterful calculator used the Gastein Convention to postpone a possible war with Austria in 1865 was his need for time to adjust the international situation in his favor. His major concern, of course, was intervention by France or Italy, in that order of importance. He could probably overlook England, for her role in the earlier stages of the Schleswig-Holstein question made it seem likely that her action would be limited to diplomatic representations. He also had little to fear from Russia, although the St. Petersburg government was not a Prussian captive as many scholars have suggested.[4] It would be France and Italy under French influence whose roles would be decisive; and the measure of this anxiety is clear from Bismarck's dispatches. On August 4 he instructed Goltz, the Prussian ambassador at Paris, to find out all he could about French views on the German crisis. He also wanted to know whether Napoleon had any formal control over Italian policy and whether the Emperor would veto cooperation between Italy and Prussia. Finally, in a revealing comment, he pointed out that while the negotiations with Austria for the Gastein Convention were still pending, information about the probable future thinking of the French and Italian governments would be welcome.[5] On August 16, after the signing of the Convention, Bismarck in fact stated that "uncertainty over the attitude of France and of Italy influenced the decisions at Gastein." [6] And in an unusually explicit letter to Goltz, in which he summarized the situation created by the Gastein accord, he again listed anxiety about French policy as a factor in the agreement. He said that the Prussian government now faced a choice between maintaining the Gastein settlement or using its insufficiencies to precipitate a new crisis; and he added:

Our position . . . however, the goals, which we . . . set ourselves, and the whole direction, which we ought to give to our policy, will be principally conditioned by the greater or lesser trust which we may place in the attitude of France at any given moment. . . . The consideration of France

---

[4] For an excellent revisionist discussion of Russo-Prussian relations in this period, see W. E. Mosse, *The European Powers and the German Question, 1848–71* (Cambridge, England, 1958). Mosse proves, quite conclusively in the opinion of the present author, that Russia was by no means irrevocably committed to Prussia even after the Polish crisis of 1863; that the possibility that Russia might turn against Prussia was always present although never imminent.

[5] Bismarck to Goltz, August 4, 1865 (Historische Reichskommission, *Die auswärtige Politik Preussens, 1858–71*, 10 vols., Berlin, 1932–45, VI, 308, and n. 3 to no. 225, pp. 308–9).

[6] Bismarck to Usedom, August 16, 1865 *(APP, VI, 336).*

will provide . . . a fundamental, and in a specific moment perhaps the deciding factor in the decisions of his Majesty, the King.[7]

Bismarck even declared himself ready to bribe France with compensations.

Bismarck signed the Convention of Gastein, then, because he feared French intervention in any large-scale development of his unification plans. It is difficult to say whether French policy justified this anxiety. Napoleon's views, as outlined above, were as yet largely theoretical, and his subordinates, although they too had their predilections, had not yet elaborated detailed policies toward the German nationalist movement. The resultant picture is confused, although many of the courses of action later urged by French statesmen were already in the air. According to Metternich, the Austrian ambassador, there was a good chance that France would conclude an alliance with Austria if the Hapsburg monarchy was willing to accept the consequences.[8] Goltz, while unable to dismiss this contingency, emphasized that Napoleon admired William of Prussia, favored the Prussian cause, and might conceivably sell his support to the Prussian side. There was also a possibility that Napoleon might try to settle the German question, by bringing together a congress in which he would play a predominant role.[9] In any event, the idea of compensations seems to have been foremost, for the Foreign Minister, Drouyn de Lhuys, felt obliged to tell his ambassador to the Diet of the German Confederation to contradict such rumors officially.[10]

Along with these general suggestions about French policy, each of which was to be amplified in the ensuing months, several fairly

---

[7] Bismarck to Goltz, August 16, 1865 (Otto von Bismarck, *Die gesammelten Werke*, ed. Friedrich Thimme, 19 vols., Berlin, 1924–35, V, 271–3).

[8] Metternich to Mensdorff, July 31, 1865 (Oncken, *Die Rheinpolitik*, I, 48, n. 1 to no. 20).

[9] Goltz to Bismarck, August 4, 1865 (Oncken, I, 49–50).

[10] Drouyn de Lhuys to Reculot, August 7, 1865 (Ministère des Affaires Etrangères, *Les Origines diplomatiques de la guerre de 1870–71*, 29 vols., Paris, 1910–32, VI, 382).

specific positions emerge in the period just before the Gastein agreement. One problem was presented by Bismarck's attempts to make an agreement with the Italian government. The Quai d'Orsay informed the Italians firmly that they would cooperate with Bismarck on their own responsibility and should expect no help from France if the scheme misfired. (The official French phrase, "à ses risques et périls," has a ring that no translation can render.)[11] This line was approved by both Napoleon and Eugénie.[12] Although Napoleon usually championed the Italian cause, he apparently believed that the situation was not yet clear and feared that Italian impetuosity might lead to a disaster attended by embarrassing international implications. The other point which emerges clearly in early August, 1865, was related specifically to the fate of Schleswig and Holstein: the Quai d'Orsay urged that the ultimate possession of the duchies be determined in accordance with the principle of nationalities.[13] This proposition, which involved the retrocession to Denmark of northern Schleswig, was a commonplace of French diplomacy,[14] and was probably uttered as much from a desire to keep a finger in the pie as from a profound conviction.[15]

Beyond these two specific points, official statements were hazy. Manifestly, French statesmen were temporizing. Some days before the signing of the Gastein Convention, Drouyn de Lhuys received Metternich, Goltz, and the Italian ambassador Nigra and formally communicated his views to them. The remarks, as later reported to Bismarck by the Prussian ambassador in Florence, ran in part:

The Emperor still believes in the possibility of a peaceful compromise between Prussia and Austria; only with unhappiness would he see a war

[11] Drouyn de Lhuys to Gramont, August 1, 1865 (*Origines*, VI, 367).
[12] Metternich to Mensdorff, August 5, 1865 (Oncken, I, 54, n. 1 to no. 21).
[13] Goltz to Bismarck, August 4, 1865 (Oncken, I, 49).
[14] Annexe to Dotézac to Drouyn de Lhuys, September 3, 1865 (*Origines*, VII, 25).
[15] For further protests made shortly after the Gastein Convention, presumably with the same motives, see Goltz to Bismarck, August 20, 1865 (Oncken, I, 64); Lefebvre de Béhaine to Drouyn de Lhuys, August 21, 1865 (*Origines*, VI, 428); Lefebvre de Béhaine to Drouyn, September 1, 1865 (*Origines*, VII, 8); Cadore to Drouyn, September 1, 1865 (*Origines*, VII, 11).

break out. Should this happen however, the Emperor would find no reason to intervene as long as it was simply a question of a decision by force of weapons over Schleswig-Holstein itself. But should the war assume such a character that greater objects and European-French interests were to be played for, then he must reserve the right to act according to the measure of these interests. Specific comments cannot be made before the event.[16]

This vein could hardly be reassuring to the Prussian government, since the emphasis on neutrality was largely negated by the warning of its possible limitations. Goltz could not be called alarmist for his conclusion that, in order to win a pledge of neutrality from the French, the Prussian government would have to promise no action beyond the Schleswig-Holstein question.[17] This prospect would certainly not be attractive to Bismarck, and it is not surprising that he decided in mid-August, 1865, that the time had come to concentrate on arranging matters with Napoleon. Nonetheless, although the French had taken official note of the German question and evidently expected to be consulted in the event of major changes, it is difficult and perhaps even misleading to attempt to determine French reactions to the problem in detail. Definite proposals would emerge only under the pressure of specific developments in Central Europe.

A very real challenge was presented by the Convention of Gastein itself.[18] In an attempt to keep the French informed, Bismarck wrote two letters to Goltz on August 16 in which he explained the Gastein settlement, offered reassurances as to the possibility of eventually returning northern Schleswig to Denmark, and instructed Goltz to work for closer relations between France and Prussia with the ultimate hope that France would support the formation of a strong German state north of the Main River. Unfortunately, Goltz wanted the Prussian government to keep all of Schleswig. Furthermore, he was no friend to the unification plans he suspected Bismarck of

[16] Usedom to Bismarck, August 15, 1865 (*APP*, VI, 333–4).

[17] Goltz to Bismarck, August 15, 1865 (Oncken, I, 57).

[18] It assigned the administration of Schleswig to Prussia and that of Holstein to Austria and further stipulated that Prussia receive outright possession of the small neighboring province of Lauenburg through a compensatory money payment to Austria. The full text may be found in *Origines*, VI, 463–5.

nourishing; nor, for that matter, did he wholeheartedly like or trust Bismarck himself. So he kept his instructions to himself and even neglected to tell the Quai d'Orsay about the conclusion of the agreement, not to mention Bismarck's interpretation of it. The result, as Emile Ollivier picturesquely put it, was that the "convention fell on Paris like a bomb." [19] Metternich, who communicated the signature of the agreement, had been instructed not to give explanations;[20] and the reaction on the part of Napoleon, Drouyn de Lhuys, and the French public in general was one of fury and disappointment.[21]

The violence of the French reception of the Gastein Convention was accentuated by the suspicion, ascendant throughout the last two weeks in August, that the published text did not tell everything. Reculot, from Frankfurt, the seat of the German Diet, was reporting a general belief that the arrangement was so unfavorable to Austria that the Hapsburg monarchy would never have accepted it unless it were balanced by compensating secret articles. There was a widespread idea that Prussia had offered, possibly through the agency of the Federal Diet, some sort of guarantee of the Austrian Empire, notably Venetia. On the other hand, many people believed that Gastein simply marked a stage in eventual Prussian annexation of both of the disputed duchies.[22] These suspicions must have been in the minds of French statesmen as they first attempted to work out a policy toward the Gastein settlement, for it was not until September 1st, more than two weeks after the conclusion of the agreement, that Drouyn de Lhuys was able to write to Lefebvre de Béhaine, the chargé d'affaires at Berlin, that he had received official word from Goltz that no secret articles existed.[23] Bismarck's reassurances, which emphasized the purely temporary nature of the Gastein Convention,

---

[19] Emile Ollivier, *L'Empire libéral*, 18 vols. (Paris, 1895–1918), VII, 450–2.

[20] Goltz to Bismarck, August 14, 1865 *(APP*, VI, 333, n. 2 to no. 249); HHSA: Mensdorff to Metternich, August 14, 1865 (telegram).

[21] Oncken, *Napoleon III and the Rhine*, p. 36.

[22] Reculot to Drouyn de Lhuys, August 23, 1865 *(Origines*, VI, 436–7); a second dispatch reporting secret articles was sent by Reculot to Drouyn on August 25, 1865 *(Origines*, VI, 442).

[23] Drouyn de Lhuys to Mosbourg and Lefebvre de Béhaine, September 1, 1865 *(Origines*, VII, 6).

had to be repeated throughout the second half of August; as late as September 1, Bismarck was writing to Goltz that "the mistrust in France of the Gastein Convention is unfounded." [24] It was only very gradually that French official circles accepted the idea that the Convention of Gastein represented, in the contemporary phrase, " 'a replastering.' " [25]

This confusion and suspicion must have impeded the formulation of an official reaction. Certain alternatives were impossible from the start. It was officially accepted from the first that the settlement represented an Austrian defeat; and the governmental press was instructed to take this line in the days immediately following the agreement.[26] In view of the many reports to this effect from the embassies in the German states,[27] it would have been difficult to think otherwise. This meant that the problem presented by the Gastein Convention was essentially a problem of what to do about Prussia. And, in solving it, it was soon to become clear that no reliance could be placed on France's traditional allies, the small states. According to accounts received early in September, the key countries of the Third Germany, the small German states, were thoroughly demoralized.[28] France's friendly relations with these states were always subject to sudden chills because they were notably suspicious of French ambitions. Later dispatches pointed up the ease with which Bismarck could picture French protests against Gastein as unwarrantable foreign intervention.[29] Such charges were so widely believed that, in

---

[24] Bismarck to Goltz, September 1, 1865, Abeken's draft (APP, VI, 366). For earlier communications emphasizing the same theme, see Bismarck to Goltz, August 14, 1865 (APP, VI, 332); Bismarck to Goltz, August 16, 1865 (APP, VI, 336, n. 3 to no. 251); Bismarck to Goltz, August 23, 1865, Abeken's draft (APP, VI, 350).

[25] Reiset to Drouyn de Lhuys, August 17, 1865 (Origines, VI, 418).

[26] Goltz to Bismarck, August 29, 1865 (APP, VI, 361–2, n. 9 to no. 272).

[27] See Mosbourg to Drouyn de Lhuys, August 27, 1865 (Origines, VI, 451); Forth-Rouen to Drouyn, August 30, 1865 (Origines, VI, 457); Cadore to Drouyn, September 5, 1865 (Origines, VII, 38).

[28] Gabriac to Drouyn de Lhuys, September 4, 1865 (Origines, VII, 34–5); Forth-Rouen to Drouyn, September 12, 1865 (Origines, VII, 62).

[29] Forth-Rouen to Drouyn de Lhuys, September 17, 1865 (Origines, VII, 74); Forth-Rouen to Drouyn, September 28, 1865 (Origines, VII, 93); see also Goltz to William, August 29, 1865 (Oncken, I, 67–8).

October, a group of deputies from the Parliaments of the German
states meeting at Frankfurt was to condemn French opposition to
Gastein.[30]

French policy, then, focused on Prussia. Fortunately it is possible
to trace the actions of the major figures with some certainty. On
August 19, Drouyn de Lhuys talked at length with Goltz. The
Foreign Minister's remarks were in part a recapitulation of the
position adopted before Gastein. Drouyn said that France would be
neutral in the Schleswig-Holstein question but could not give a
definite pledge of neutrality because the problem of the duchies
might spread to involve wider interests. He assured Goltz that the
French government tended to favor the Prussians, especially if they
would apply the principle of nationalities to Schleswig-Holstein.
Then, in a new disclosure, Drouyn added that there was little incen-
tive for the French to aid the Austrians, since the only thing they
were likely to gain was the completion of Italian unification through
the cession of Venetia. This hardly seemed a sufficient motive for
French action. On the other hand, there were many possible compensations which might be arranged with Prussia. Goltz, rather
alarmed, asserted that the Prussian government could not be expected
to cede Prussian territory; but he admitted that there were other
areas where agreement might be reached. Drouyn concurred.[31]

This attitude is strange for Drouyn de Lhuys, since, though he was
always interested in the idea of compensations, he took a strongly
pro-Austrian line throughout these years. The most likely explanation is that he was acting under direct orders from Napoleon. Although there is no evidence of a meeting in this period, it seems
inconceivable that Drouyn would not have told Napoleon in person
about the news of the conclusion of the Gastein accord as communicated by Metternich on August 14.[32] This would have given Napoleon an opportunity to instruct Drouyn on the appropriate attitude

---

[30] Reculot to Drouyn de Lhuys, October 1, 1865 (*Origines,* VII, 109).
[31] Goltz to Bismarck, August 20, 1865 (Oncken, I, 63–4).
[32] See Goltz to Bismarck, August 14, 1865 (*APP,* VI, 333, n. 2 to no. 249).

to take toward the ambassadors of the foreign powers. Furthermore, Drouyn's remarks closely paralleled Napoleon's own comments to Goltz. On August 28, Napoleon held a dinner party at Fontaine-bleau, to which the Prussian ambassador was invited. In a private conversation in the garden Napoleon seemed willing to give broad assurances of neutrality. On the other hand his public and hence more official comments emphasized the impossibility of definite pledges but mentioned his interest in seeing the Prussian state strengthened. He even gave Goltz a full explanation of the Plombières agreement, although he cautioned that he would never enter into such an arrangement again unless he felt certain that it would work.[33] Napoleon and Drouyn were following much the same line, which may safely be assigned to Napoleon's inspiration: a preference for aid of some sort to Prussia, perhaps only benevolent neutrality, at the price of compensations.

Against this background of cordiality to Prussian ambitions, the next official step seems surprising. On August 29, Drouyn de Lhuys issued a circular to the French ambassadors in which he condemned the Gastein settlement in harsh terms. He declared that it violated existent treaties, the legitimate order of succession in the duchies (whatever that may have been), the wishes of the German Confederation and of the duchies themselves, and the principle of nationalities. He further stated that it was based solely on the right of the strong and so was directly contrary to the practice of civilized nations. French ambassadors were instructed to express this protest to the governments to which they were accredited when their opinion of the Gastein agreement was solicited.[34]

This circular needs explanation. Since Drouyn de Lhuys was inclined to favor Austria over Prussia, it is possible that he took this step on his own initiative, in opposition to Napoleon's more con-

---

[33] Ollivier, VII, 454; Goltz to William, August 29, 1865 (Oncken, I, 65–9).

[34] Drouyn de Lhuys to the French ambassadors to Austria, Prussia, the German Confederation, England, Russia, Bavaria, Saxony, Hanover, Württemberg, Baden, the Netherlands, Belgium, Italy, Denmark, Sweden, Hamburg, August 29, 1865 (Origines, VI, 453–4).

ciliatory approach to Prussia. Evidently, though, it was not an unauthorized gesture on Drouyn's part. Goltz later learned that Drouyn had gone to Fontainebleau to see Napoleon on August 27, two days before the communiqué was sent out. He concluded that the two men had worked out at least the main lines of the document during this visit.[35] Napoleon himself later confirmed this story when he told Bismarck at Biarritz that he had approved the circular.[36] This means that Napoleon planned the protest on August 27 and then, on August 28, dined with Goltz and addressed him in the most encouraging terms. The only plausible explanation is that Napoleon was indulging in a "mailed fist" strategy: he gave the Prussian government every reason to believe that he would receive overtures favorably, but he made it clear that if no offers were made he would not hesitate to take a strongly hostile line. This approach tends to be risky, but it afforded certain advantages at that point. First, it gave Napoleon a chance to throw a sop to Drouyn de Lhuys, who cannot have been pleased by the pro-Prussian direction of French policy. Secondly, it was a tougher gesture than a vague threat of eventual renunciation of neutrality would have been. The mystery surrounding Bismarck's plans might have made the more positive step preferable.

If this analysis of Napoleon's intentions is correct, it must be admitted that his policy was relatively successful. As early as September 1, Lefebvre de Béhaine had learned from Eulenburg, the Minister of the Interior, that the Prussian government regarded Gastein as the first step toward consolidation in the area north of the Main. Eulenburg added that if the Austrian government opposed further developments in this direction, Bismarck would have to consider again the attitudes of France and Italy.[37] More complete information was forthcoming when the French chargé d'affaires

---

[35] Goltz to Bismarck, September 20, 1865 (*APP*, VI, 388).

[36] Oubril to Gortschakov, October 29/November 10, 1865 (*APP*, VI, 457).

[37] Lefebvre de Béhaine to Drouyn de Lhuys, September 1, 1865 (*Origines*, VII, 8–10).

was able to present the French stand directly to Bismarck.[38] Bismarck acknowledged that he viewed the Gastein arrangement as the preliminary to Prussian annexation of both Schleswig and Holstein and to the eventual conquest of the primary place in Germany. He recognized that the convention was unclear at many points and impracticable at others and confessed that he had planned it that way so that he would have a continuing excuse for a quarrel with Austria that he would force "the day when the general state of things in Europe would permit Prussia to follow a still more clearly defined policy." [39] In a further conversation on September 14, Bismarck became more explicit. Lefebvre de Béhaine, who now had had ample time to think over the implications of the Prussian revelations, suggested that Bismarck's schemes might upset the balance of power. In reply, Bismarck assured him that his plans were limited to the regions north of the Main. He had no intention of annexing lands south of that division. The Prussian statesman also hinted that France and Italy might simultaneously acquire additional territories in those areas which shared a common "tongue and race" with them. For Italy, this obviously meant Venetia; as for France, Bismarck was evidently trying to turn Napoleon's interests away from the German Rhineland toward the French-speaking parts of Belgium. Lefebvre de Béhaine concluded from this talk that Bismarck was hardly eager to give compensations to France, but that he was well aware that the French had a certain claim to them and that he would not oppose any compensations that the French chose to seize by force.[40]

The strategy of the Fontainebleau dinner and the August 29 circular had achieved substantial results. Among other things the mystery surrounding Bismarck's intentions at the time of the Ga-

---

[38] Lefebvre de Béhaine to Drouyn de Lhuys, September 12, 1865 (*Origines*, VII, 55).

[39] Lefebvre de Béhaine to Drouyn de Lhuys, September 12, 1865 (*Origines*, VII, 57-8).

[40] Lefebvre de Béhaine to Drouyn de Lhuys, September 14, 1865 (*Origines*, VII, 64-5).

stein Convention had been partially dispelled; but the relatively frank disclosure of the profundity of Bismarck's interest in unification could only alarm the group of French officials who favored a policy designed either to maintain Austria's position or to build up the small states. The next development appears to be a direct expression of this anxiety. In mid-September, the August 29 circular, which had originally been directed to the French ambassadors abroad, was published in the *Indépendence belge* and in the *Gazette d'Augsbourg*.[41] This was a serious step. In the first place, it brought the French protest to a wider public. In the second place, it presented the French views in the harshest possible form, unmitigated by the unconscious softenings of a verbal communication. The result was dramatic. Bismarck naturally was thoroughly puzzled. King William, always dubious about Bismarck's schemes, was still more upset and ordered Bismarck to give up his plan, formulated during the Gastein negotiations, for a stay in Biarritz.[42] Since Bismarck's trip had been timed to coincide with Napoleon's sojourn at the resort, it is clear that the Prussians had been thinking in terms of high-level conferences. William's insistence on the cancellation of the projected visit meant the abandonment, at least for the moment, of summit negotiations.

Who was responsible for the announcement in the press? It seems unlikely that Napoleon was implicated. He specifically denied complicity in a talk later with Bismarck at Biarritz. The Emperor explained that he had approved the original circular to the French ambassadors, but stated that he had not agreed to its release to the press.[43] Such an assertion, coming at the moment when Napoleon was carrying on personal negotiations with Bismarck, is open to doubt; it is possible that Napoleon was merely trying to smooth his relations with Bismarck, but it does fit very well with the rest of Napoleon's actions. It seems implausible that the advocate of nego-

[41] Forth-Rouen to Drouyn de Lhuys, September 17, 1865 (*Origines*, VII, 71); Méloizes to Drouyn de Lhuys, September 18, 1865 (*Origines*, VII, 75).

[42] Alfred Stern, *Geschichte Europas [1815–71]*, 10 vols. (Berlin, 1894–1924), IX, 429; Ollivier, VII, 460–1.

[43] Oubril to Gortschakov, October 29/November 10, 1865 (*APP*, VI, 547).

tiations with the Prussians would have sponsored a step so dangerous to those negotiations, especially at the moment when his previous efforts were on the point of success. And Napoleon's later reactions give the impression that he was upset by the Prussian remonstrances to the published circular and embarrassed by the whole incident. It seems most likely that the unauthorized publication of the circular came from someone within the Foreign Office who wished to sabotage the pro-Prussian drift of French policy and suppress Bismarck's ambitions. Dramatic unity would assign this role to Drouyn de Lhuys,[44] whose Austrian sympathies might have led him in this direction; but there were many others who felt that French interests could best be realized through support of Austria or of the small states.

The first evidence of Napoleon's reaction comes from Goltz. On September 20, Napoleon probed him as to the Prussian government's opinion of the document. Goltz admitted that the impression had been most unpleasant. Napoleon's attitude was soothing. He assured Goltz that he had never considered the August 29 circular very important.[45] As soon as Goltz had left he showed his concern by ordering Drouyn de Lhuys to soften the circular in some way.[46] The result was Drouyn's letter of September 23 to the French chargé d'affaires at Berlin: Drouyn instructed his emissary to answer Prussian objections to the circular by saying that "that dispatch is in effect only the summary of all our former declarations."[47] It is doubtful that anyone believed this statement; but at least the unfortunate circular was tied to previous, more pacific expressions of French policy. The Prussian Foreign Office had received reassurance that the publication of the document did not herald new and threatening developments.

With this letter in hand, it was possible for Lefebvre de Béhaine to

[44] This guess was made by Stern, IX, 428.
[45] Goltz to Bismarck, September 21, 1865 (APP, VI, 389).
[46] Goltz to Bismarck, September 22, 1865 (APP, VI, 390, n. 4 to no. 300).
[47] Drouyn de Lhuys to Lefebvre de Béhaine, September 23, 1865 (Origines, VII, 80).

arrange things in Berlin. A talk with Bismarck made it clear that immediate action was necessary. Bismarck explained the extent of King William's worry and revealed to Lefebvre that he might not go to Biarritz. Lefebvre, quite shaken, took the extraordinary step of giving Bismarck the text of the September 23 letter to show his sovereign. The upper echelons of the Prussian government attended the Opera that evening. Bismarck was there with the letter and he managed to hand it to the King. William, who read it immediately, declared himself mollified. Bismarck was able to assure Lefebvre after the performance that all was well and that the Biarritz meeting would proceed as planned.[48]

This thaw made it possible to settle other differences between the two governments. On September 24, Bismarck had explained to Lefebvre that he had been surprised and pained by the French reaction to the Gastein Convention because he had thought that he had given them a fair picture of his intentions. As proof, he read Lefebvre the text of at least one of his explanatory dispatches to Goltz on August 16. Lefebvre pointed out that, as far as he knew, Goltz had never communicated these disclosures to Drouyn de Lhuys.[49] This conversation clarified French suspicions considerably for Bismarck. In another talk on September 27 Bismarck returned to the theme of compensations, suggesting a grandiose exchange of territories in which France would "eventually" receive all French-speaking territories.[50] His proposals were both too indefinite and too sweeping to constitute a basis for negotiation; but at least it was encouraging for the French to know that he was thinking once again of agreement on fairly flexible terms.

Against this background Drouyn's second circular, written on September 29, appeared. Directing himself once again to the French

[48] Lefebvre de Béhaine to Drouyn de Lhuys, September 25, 1865 (*Origines,* VII, 82–3); Ollivier, VII. 463.

[49] Lefebvre de Béhaine to Drouyn de Lhuys, September 25, 1865 (*Origines,* VII, 84–7).

[50] Lefebvre de Béhaine to Drouyn de Lhuys, September 27, 1865 (*Origines,* VII, 89–91).

ambassadors abroad, Drouyn excused the circular of August 29 by calling it a kind of commentary. He stated that the French government wished to respect the sovereignty of the German states, but thought it possible at the same time "to express our opinion on the principles" involved in the Schleswig-Holstein question; he reiterated that the position held since Gastein was intended simply as a continuation of the line taken before that agreement. Finally, he declared that since the Gastein arrangement was temporary, the French hoped that the eventual settlement would be closer to the wishes which the Quai d'Orsay had enumerated in the course of the crisis.[51] This represented a substantial weakening of the very vigorous protest of August 29, and it was influenced by Napoleon III. The September 23 letter, which he had ordered, was a hasty, informal means of reassuring the Prussian government; now it might be desirable to confirm this stand by a formal instrument. After Bismarck's disclosures to Lefebvre following his perusal of the letter, there would be no question of losing face by seeming overanxious. Instead, the confirming circular would appear to be a gracious recognition of Bismarck's return to a cooperative attitude and a sensible way of preparing the ground for future negotiations at Biarritz.

During the first month and a half of the French "year of crisis," Napoleon had moved cautiously toward a time of bargaining between France and Prussia. The initiative in creating a situation designed for discussions came from Bismarck; on the French side, Napoleon seems to have been the one responsible for the willingness to discuss the German problem with the Prussians and to explore some kind of arrangement with them instead of rejecting this alternative out-of-hand and taking refuge in the prospect of ultimate support of Austria, the other likely ally. In formulating and implementing this policy, Napoleon did not go unchallenged. The publi-

[51] Drouyn de Lhuys's circular to the French ambassadors to England, Austria, Russia, Prussia, the German Confederation, Baden, Württemberg, Bavaria, Saxony, Weimar, Hesse-Darmstadt, Hanover, Belgium, and the Netherlands, September 29, 1865 (*Origines*, VII, 95).

cation of the August 29 circular is evidence of an active opposition, which presumably included his Foreign Minister. But at this stage, the crisis had not assumed proportions sufficiently grave to interest many people, even in the government. Napoleon was able to counter the relatively small number of his opponents. At the end of September, the Emperor was in fairly complete control of French policy, which he was shaping in a pro-Prussian direction.

II

THE FIRST
NEGOTIATIONS

NAPOLEON'S REACTIONS to the Convention of Gastein showed his nationalistic and pro-Prussian predilections. He apparently shared the prevailing belief that the accord represented a Prussian victory and an Austrian defeat. He hoped that, with calm restored in Germany for the moment, Bismarck could be induced, by a suitable ambiguity in France's attitude, to offer the basis for some sort of working arrangement, even alliance. His expectations were not far from Bismarck's intentions. Efforts to stimulate Bismarck were rather successful, and a definite effort at rapprochement between France and Prussia filled the last months of 1865. It would be a mistake to overemphasize its seriousness, for Bismarck had many worries besides Napoleon and was not yet ready to welcome an Austro-Prussian crisis; the conversations, as result, lack the feverish immediacy of the discussions on the eve of the war. Yet it would not be accurate to assume, since both sides were well aware that a later bargain might be a better bargain, that the efforts made in 1865 were not sincere. Absence of pressure affects intensity, not intentions. And this early effort to cement understanding makes an illuminating prelude to the events of 1866, because many of the later problems and solutions are foreshadowed. The Biarritz meeting between Bismarck and Napoleon exposed some of the diplomatic difficulties. A study of the agitation within France, which reached a height in November, reveals the internal difficulties created by pacifist public opinion, tense economic conditions, and unruliness in the Corps Législatif. Finally, the government's policy in December, 1865, marks an attempt to find another answer. A pattern emerges here which was to be repeated, with variations, throughout the year.

The first questions were raised by Bismarck's visit to Biarritz during Napoleon's vacation there in October. The conference had been preceded and prepared by the conversations in Berlin between Bismarck and Lefebvre de Béhaine.[1] In the last of these, on September 27, Bismarck had spoken fairly specifically. In describing a wide-ranging exchange of territories, he had mentioned that France might one day receive all French-speaking areas.[2] The consideration of compensations as bait was already in the forefront of Bismarck's mind. Further indications of his intentions can be gleaned from the events of his stay in Paris on the way to Biarritz.

The Prussian minister talked with Drouyn de Lhuys and Napoleon's minister of state, Rouher. The conversations were largely a formality and an uncomfortable one for the French; but Bismarck did bring up compensations again and received the impression that his formula of "tout ce qui parle français" was heard with interest by both men.[3] According to Bismarck, Drouyn went so far as to disclaim any intention on the part of France of acquiring German-speaking lands,[4] an assertion which is important if true. Further details about the talk between Bismarck and Drouyn can be gathered from the report of Lord Cowley, the English ambassador to France, who inquired as to Bismarck's plans for Germany. Drouyn admitted

---

[1] See pp. 17–8.

[2] Such was the story reported to Paris by Lefebvre (Lefebvre de Béhaine to Drouyn de Lhuys, September 27, 1865 [*Origines*, VII, 89–91]); it was later confirmed by the Prussian ambassador Goltz on the basis of a talk with Bismarck. See a memorandum by Goltz (Otto zu Stolberg-Wernigerode, *Robert Heinrich Graf von der Goltz* [Berlin, 1941], pp. 403–4). Stolberg-Wernigerode assigns this document, which is undated, to October 10, 1865. Bismarck's own version was rather different: in a report to King William, he portrayed the French as eager for compensations and said that Lefebvre had demanded "sections of Prussian or German land." The weight of the evidence seems to be against Bismarck here, however, and the interpretation offered by Friedrich Frahm gives a plausible explanation of his dishonesty; Frahm points out that King William was extremely dubious about the wisdom of negotiating with France and he suggests that the Prussian monarch might have been more willing to accept a bargain had he felt that the original French price had been high and that his minister had successfully brought it down. See Friedrich Frahm, "Biarritz," *Historische Vierteljahrschrift*, 15:348–9 (1912).

[3] Memorandum by Goltz (Stolberg-Wernigerode, p. 404).

[4] Bismarck to William, October 11, 1865 (Oncken, I, 70).

that "the tone of M. de Bismarck's remarks indicated an intention of carrying matters as far as he dared." [5] The French minister limited his opposition to the comment:

You ask us for ready money and you offer us a long-term note or even a note whose maturity is entirely uncertain; and, what is more, I must keep this note in my pocket, without showing it to France, to the journalists, to the deputies, to all those, in a word, who could pay me the money which you have received. [6]

Apart from this speech, Drouyn's conduct seems to have been uncharacteristically encouraging. It is a temptation to conclude with Bismarck that Napoleon had given him firm instructions as to what to say. [7] The Emperor could hardly afford to allow his Foreign Minister to ruin important negotiations by a word out of turn at the start.

Meanwhile Napoleon was already at Biarritz with his court. The mood was relaxed and gay. Mérimée, the tame author, tells the story of how, one day, he amused himself by making a dummy head of Bismarck. Eugénie saw it and decided that it was too good to waste, so she, Napoleon, and Mérimée conspired to hide it in the bed of one of the ladies-in-waiting. [8] Against this background, conversations commenced between Napoleon and Bismarck. The negotiations, which were held secret, at once became the focus of passionate interest, for it was widely suspected by contemporaries, and later by some historians, that the two statesmen intended to work out an arrangement along the lines of the Plombières agreement between Napoleon and Cavour. Although no one has discovered exactly what did happen, it soon became evident that it was less spectacular than this model.

Napoleon afterwards summarized the meeting with Bismarck negatively: "He [Bismarck] talked a great deal . . . but in general and vague terms; I couldn't untangle exactly what he wanted, and he

---

[5] PRO: Cowley to Foreign Office, October 3, 1865 (F. O. 519/13).
[6] Goltz to Bernstorff, October 22, 1865 (Stolberg-Wernigerode, p. 412).
[7] Bismarck to William, October 11, 1865 (Oncken, I, 71).
[8] Prosper Mérimée, Lettres à M. Panizzi, 2 vols. (Paris, 1881), II, 142.

didn't make me any formal proposition. On my side I didn't express to him any personal desire whatsoever."[9] On the surface, it is unlikely that Bismarck would have traveled so far without some plan for negotiation in mind. It is hard to imagine that he could have conversed with Napoleon at length without hinting at some proposals, however seriously he intended Napoleon to take them. In view of the preliminary discussions with Lefebvre de Béhaine, Drouyn de Lhuys, and Rouher, the likely suggestion would have been exchange of French support of Prussia in Germany for Prussian support of France in Belgium. Friedrich Frahm has reached the same conclusions on the basis of the contemporary impressions of Nigra, the Italian ambassador to Paris and an unusually astute observer. Frahm believes that Bismarck thought that Napoleon wanted the German left bank, but at the same time hoped to effect a treaty of alliance at little cost by diverting Napoleon's interests northwards toward the independent but weak state of Belgium and perhaps ultimately to the tiny area of Luxemburg, tied very loosely to the German Confederation.[10] Such a bargain would offer the minimum offense to German national feeling and the minimum harm to German potential power; it would have been a logical approach from Bismarck's viewpoint. It is impossible, however, to document this interpretation. Surviving dispatches give outlines of the conversations that seem to lack nothing except the point of the performance.

The first important discussion, on October 4,[11] took place over a splendid luncheon.[12] The menu included turbot with a Genoese sauce which so impressed Bismarck that he remarked: "For a sauce like that, I would give twenty banks of the Rhine."[13] This beginning

---

[9] Ollivier, L'Empire libéral, VII, 475.

[10] Frahm, "Biarritz," pp. 339, 345.

[11] Bismarck to William, October 5, 1865 (APP, VI, 403).

[12] Memorandum by Goltz (Stolberg-Wernigerode, pp. 406-9) gives us the nearest thing we have to a schedule of Bismarck's meetings with Napoleon. Although Goltz does not say that the first conference took place over lunch, it seems impossible on the basis of his timetable to assign to any other occasion the luncheon story related by Forth-Rouen (Origines, VII, 163-4).

[13] Forth-Rouen to Drouyn de Lhuys, November 2, 1865 (Origines, VII, 163-4).

sounds propitious, but Bismarck was apparently rather reserved. He did express, in general terms, Prussian eagerness for an alliance with France and admitted that he had seriously considered war with Austria before the Gastein Convention. Napoleon's response was evasive.[14] He offered "assurances of unchanged friendship and sympathy." Talk ranged over the August 29 circular and the possibility that Prussia might purchase the province of Holstein from Austria. Napoleon's attitude was encouraging throughout and Bismarck came away ready to declare, for the benefit of King William at least, that Napoleon was prepared to cooperate with Prussia.[15]

The second meeting occurred some days later on October 7 and afforded an opportunity for nearly an hour of private conversation. This time the conference took place over breakfast and Bismarck fortified himself with "one glass of Madeira, one ditto of sherry, one whole flask of Yquem," and "a glass of cognac." The conversation touched on a variety of subjects, including the Prussian constitutional situation, the Gastein agreement, and the question of Moldavia and Wallachia.[16] It was probably at this time that Napoleon, perhaps with tongue in cheek, broached the problem of the control of cholera, which was being spread by the Holy Pilgrimages to Mecca. Bismarck, feeling as though he had wandered into a nightmare, foresaw the whole Near East in flames, but in the interests of the immediate situation, he felt he had to say, to be sure unspecifically, that King William would cooperate.[17] However, despite this fencing on irrelevant issues, the bulk of the discussion centered around Bismarck's German ambitions and the need of French support for them.[18]

These reports, while they seem at first glance to offer a wealth of detail, are not entirely satisfying, and a haze of speculation has con-

---

[14] Memorandum by Goltz (Stolberg-Wernigerode, p. 406).

[15] Bismarck to William, October 5, 1865 (*APP*, VI, 403-4).

[16] Memorandum by Goltz (Stolberg-Wernigerode, p. 406); Goltz to Bernstorff, October 22, 1865 (Stolberg-Wernigerode, p. 412).

[17] Bismarck to William, October 11, 1865 (Oncken, I, 73).

[18] Memorandum by Goltz (Stolberg-Wernigerode, p. 408). For a parallel and confirmatory description of the Biarritz conversations, see Bismarck to William, October 11, 1865 (Oncken, I, 71-2).

tinued to surround the episode. It is possible that the meetings were limited to this general and commonplace level, but such an explanation seems unconvincing in view of the timing of the visit, the previous eagerness of both statesmen to explore an arrangement, and the demonstrable fact that Bismarck had been considering possible bases for negotiation, such as the Belgian plan.[19] It is tempting to imagine that Bismarck did suggest, perhaps very inexplicitly, some sort of French offensive in the Belgian area, and that Napoleon, probably with equal vagueness, brushed the plan aside. There is no need to postulate a formal discussion which was afterwards hushed up; since the ground had been well prepared by Bismarck's initial conversations in Berlin and Paris, the merest hint on both sides should have been sufficient. Such an exchange, if it took place, would of course have remained secret. Bismarck would have had little desire to publicize an abortive attempt to bribe the traditional enemy; from Napoleon's standpoint, the mere mention of the subject might have been expected to precipitate the international crisis which his refusal was designed to avoid.[20] It is undeniable that the lack of direct evidence of such a discussion at Biarritz is a serious objection to this interpretation, or indeed to any interpretation positing clear-cut and important propositions. But perhaps this is not in the last analysis very important. If indeed the exchange at Biarritz was limited to vague or irrelevant conversation, it is nonetheless indisputable that Bismarck had indicated a compensation plan involving

[19] P. Bernstein, in his interesting discussion of Bismarck's trip to France in "Les Entrevues de Biarritz et de Saint-Cloud (Octobre-Novembre 1865)," *Revue d'histoire diplomatique*, 78: 330–9 (1964), describes the visit as uneventful but satisfactory, on the basis that Bismarck learned little at Biarritz but much at St. Cloud on his way home to Berlin. The reference is to Napoleon's protestations of neutrality (see p. 33 below). However, even R. Fester in "Biarritz," *Deutsche Rundschau*, 113:212–36 (1902), although particularly impressed by Napoleon's attitude, admits that Bismarck did not believe that Napoleon would hold to it unless he had committed himself to a definite agreement, with compensations for France.

[20] Ollivier (VII, 475–80) draws a similar conclusion: he speculates that Napoleon neglected to take up Bismarck's hints made prior to his arrival in Biarritz and that Bismarck correctly interpreted this reticence as a refusal. A meeting of minds of this sort would undoubtedly, as Ollivier believes, leave Napoleon free to tell Ollivier and others that nothing had happened.

Belgium in his earlier negotiations with Lefebvre, Rouher, and Drouyn; and these proposals, whether repeated at Biarritz or not, can stand as the most definite statement of the Prussian position in the autumn of 1865.

It is in the light of these remarks that the Prussian plan must be evaluated. A proposition involving Belgium was of dubious value to the French. There were certain obvious things in its favor. The Belgian region was geographically and historically a logical theater for French expansion and had attracted Napoleon's interest at least since 1860. In fact, in April of that year, Napoleon had approached the Prussians with suggestions of mutual support which closely fore-shadowed Bismarck's line in 1865. There is no doubt that an arrange-ment centered on Belgium would look tempting to Napoleon, but temptation was not enough. There was the further problem of whether or not such a bargain would be practicable, and this ques-tion turned on the attitude of the English government. The British were not much worried by the possibility of French annexations on the upper Rhine, but Belgium was another matter. This anxiety had already influenced English policy in the Schleswig-Holstein question. In 1864, when the problem had reached an acute phase, the English had held back partly because they dreaded a general European war which might give Napoleon an excuse for taking over Belgium and the Low Countries. And as the German crisis developed, the British continued to emphasize their interest in Belgium and in the main-tenance of its neutrality. These warnings were particularly revelant because the Belgian ruler, King Leopold, was dying. If the transfer of power in Belgium coincided with disturbances in Germany, Napoleon might see a golden opportunity. The British ambassador, Lord Cowley, who grasped these possibilities, said in September, 1865, that he did not think that England would reply with anything more severe than diplomatic steps,[21] but rumors had reached the French government that in private Cowley had termed French

---

[21] Herbert James Moss, "Napoleon III and Belgium 1866–70," unpubl. diss. (Harvard, 1937), pp. 2, 32–49, and 70 (note).

annexation of Belgium a *casus belli* for England.[22] Since the British did eventually adopt a rather strong line about Belgium when the German crisis was breaking in April and May,[23] Cowley may indeed have expressed himself unofficially in such terms.

How did the French government react to the threat of English intervention? There is evidence that English warnings were seriously considered. Eugénie, in talking to Metternich, is reported to have said that the French would not try to take over Belgium because of their fear of British opposition.[24] Such a reaction would be logical, since British intervention was not to be dismissed lightly. If France were to try to seize Belgium as part of a war between Austria and Prussia, and if England were to enter the war in consequence, a general European war might be unleashed; the Russians might do as they liked in the Black Sea; and the results could be incalculable. The surprise seems to lie in the fact that in his initial conversation with Bismarck Drouyn de Lhuys, as Foreign Minister, should have strongly implied that France would be willing to settle for French-speaking, rather than German-speaking lands. However, it is well to remember that Drouyn had almost certainly been carefully briefed by Napoleon for this occasion. Caution and pique may have combined to produce an overacquiescent attitude. It seems fair to conclude that the expectation of active hostility from England led Napoleon to reconsider his Belgian ambitions and to decide that Bismarck's alliance for mutual gain, whatever its attractions, was a very risky proposition.

This examination of French motives raises the question as to how Bismarck estimated these factors. Did he think that his position offered a potential basis for agreement or was he manufacturing a pretext to study the situation in France in person? He had received information which tended to cast doubts on Napoleon's eagerness to annex Belgian territory. On October 4, while the conversations with

---

[22] Dotézac to Drouyn de Lhuys, September 27, 1865 (*Origines,* VII, 92).
[23] Moss, pp. 49–50.
[24] Moss, p. 36.

Bismarck were in progress, Goltz had a talk with Napoleon in which the Emperor detailed his prerequisites for moves against Belgium. The conditions included troubles with the succession and a popular desire on the part of the Belgians to unite with France.[25] Perhaps Napoleon was trying to forestall proposals based on French action in Belgium, without renouncing his ambitions in that area. However, Goltz was at that point outranked by the presence of his superior, and Bismarck might have concluded that Napoleon had wished to avoid a searching discussion with Goltz rather than to avoid the subject per se. Nonetheless, Goltz's indications on this topic had been disquieting for some time. At the end of August, after a conversation with Eugénie, Goltz had written that the British would not permit the French government to take over Belgium and that the French were well aware of this potential opposition. Goltz added that Eugénie did not expect the British to proceed to active steps,[26] an observation which rather took the edge off his report. In any case, Bismarck was not accustomed to set great store by Goltz's worries, which were many; he is even supposed to have remarked that "Goltz was a nervous old woman." [27] Against these discouraging reports, Bismarck could set the long history of French interest in Belgium, which was still active in 1865,[28] and the obvious advantages of the gamble should it be successful. For one of Bismarck's optimistic and scheming nature, the plan would have great appeal, and it is not surprising that he should tend to underrate the difficulties. Looking back in 1870, he declared that Napoleon had missed a great chance; had he marched into Belgium and Luxemburg as soon as the Austro-Prussian War broke out, he could probably have succeeded in calling England's bluff. Whether he held on to his acquisitions or used them as bargaining pieces, he would have won some tangible gains from the crisis.[29]

[25] Memorandum by Goltz (Stolberg-Wernigerode, pp. 405–6).
[26] Goltz to Bismarck, August 23, 1865 (APP, VI, 351–2).
[27] PRO: Cowley to Russell, October 3, 1865 (F. O. 519/232).
[28] Introduction, Bismarck to Balan, September 12, 1865 (GW, V, 295).
[29] Frahm, pp. 344–5.

Evidently, then, Bismarck's approaches were quite sincere. The Biarritz meeting, which according to any interpretation did little to advance matters, left the Prussian minister disgruntled. He stayed in Biarritz for the rest of October and on his return stopped in Paris for further conversations with Rouher, Drouyn de Lhuys, and Napoleon. But little or nothing of moment seems to have occurred. Bismarck did leave France with certain positive impressions. In their last talk, on November 3, Napoleon remarked that he regarded an alliance with the Hapsburgs as "an impossibility";[30] this meant, in effect, that Napoleon would either remain neutral or would ally with Prussia. Bismarck also gathered that Napoleon would not ultimately oppose an alliance between Prussia and Italy; this gave the Prussian statesman another approach which he was not slow to develop.[31] In general, however, Bismarck's conclusions were not optimistic; disappointed by Napoleon's attitude, he decided that the Emperor was hoping for a long war which would achieve the Italians' goals while it exhausted Prussia and left Napoleon as the mediator of Europe.[32]

This picture of Napoleon's intentions has survived hardily in historical scholarship. Yet it is possible that the truth was far simpler. The Emperor did not think that the autumn of 1865 was the last occasion to bargain with Bismarck. He believed that the Prussian statesman needed him to complete his cherished and ambitious plans and might make more attractive offers later.[33] These expectations would encourage him to scrutinize the Prussian offers carefully. And such scrutiny could only emphasize the element of risk, created by the English interest in Belgium. This was reinforced by considerations of internal policy. Napoleon faced two questions: he had to ponder not only the gamble involved in Bismarck's offers but also French readiness to take such a risk. Further light can be thrown on

---

[30] Introduction, Bismarck to Foreign Office, November 3, 1865 (GW, V, 315); Bismarck to Foreign Office, November 3, 1865 (GW, V, 316).

[31] Frahm, p. 355.

[32] [Jean] de Persigny, Mémoires, ed. H. de Laire, Comte d'Espagny, 3rd ed. (Paris, 1896), pp. 376–7.

[33] Frahm, pp. 352–3.

his rejection of the offers by an examination of this second question.

While the French government was facing the problems raised by the Convention of Gastein and the meeting at Biarritz, there were even more immediate difficulties on the domestic scene. The bad harvest of 1865 had led to widespread distress.[34] The situation was complex, as is suggested by a report from the Procureur Général at Colmar in Alsace. He wrote on October 20, 1865, that the grain crops had been overabundant, with the consequence that the price had crashed; much discussed famine conditions existed not in the grains but in the forage crops. Because of deficiencies here, farmers had been forced to slaughter their domestic animals on a large scale. This action had drastically lowered the price of meat and the inevitable shortage of animal power and products would be serious.[35] Whatever the agricultural technicalities of the situation, the discontent was real and well founded. It assumed the form of demands for tax reductions. The farmers, whose incomes had suddenly shrunk, hoped that their expenditures could be contracted also. The favorite target was the army. Public opinion became suddenly enthusiastic for cuts in the military budget. Such steps offered the prospect of twofold relief to agriculture: taxes could be lowered, while more men could be released to work in the fields.[36] The result was a wave of popular feeling which, joined with the agricultural depression, created pressures that the government could not afford to overlook.

As early as the summer of 1865, key government figures had concluded that something would have to be done in accord with popular opinion. The Finance Minister, Achille Fould, wanted to cut military expenditures by twelve million francs. This saving would necessitate a significant reduction in the size of the army. On July 17, Napoleon wrote a letter to the Minister of War in which he suggested

---

[34] Egon Caesar, Count Corti, *The Reign of the House of Rothschild 1830–71,* trans. Brian and Beatrix Lunn (New York 1928), p. 368.

[35] AN: Colmar, Report of October 20, 1865, "Situation agricole" (BB[30] 376 Colmar 1865–66).

[36] Cf. PRO: Cowley to Foreign Office, May 12, 1866 (F. O. 519/13).

that two companies be dropped from each infantry regiment. At the same time, the number of cavalry squadrons would be reduced.[37] This was merely a preliminary plan and not a very sophisticated one; rather than expecting its adoption, Napoleon probably hoped to stimulate his minister, Marshal Randon, who had a tendency to pigeonhole plans he disliked.

As the autumn wore on, plans for army reduction were prominent on government agendas, and their scope increased. This development was the result of a new anxiety, the possible use of the difficult fiscal situation by the government's opponents in the Corps Législatif. The small group of politically minded intellectuals who opposed the Second Empire had become increasingly active and vociferous during the Sixties. Headed by legislators like Adolphe Thiers and Emile Ollivier and by journalists like Prévost-Paradol, they were able to make an impact out of all proportion to their real strength. The movement was originally centered on Paris and within Paris was focused on certain bourgeois Orleanist circles. Essentially, the group was made up of the dispossessed leaders of the Second Republic and of the July Monarchy who shared mildly libertarian sentiments and wanted to recover their old position. Their skillful exploitation of the minor inconveniences and major blunders of the Napoleonic regime was a significant factor in the government's grant of the reforms summed up in the title "Liberal Empire." This movement was well under way in 1865–66. The Tiers Parti, or Third Party, Adolphe Thiers' organization of his followers in the Corps Législatif, was formed in 1866. Up to that point, the principal target of the movement had been the system of censorship. This rallying cry had certain disadvantages. In the first place, it was becoming monotonous;[38] secondly, although the censors certainly were active, they often took steps only after the offending article had been published,

---

[37] Maréchal [Jacques] Randon, *Mémoires,* 2nd ed., 2 vols. (Paris, 1875–77), II, 107–8.

[38] Mérimée, *Panizzi,* II, 151.

so that opposing views, while discouraged, were by no means entirely stifled.[39] It was time for a new slogan, and the government's fiscal embarrassment could not have occurred more opportunely for the opposition group.[40]

In an effort to answer these three pressures, economic distress, popular demands, and the hostility in the Corps Législatif, Napoleon and his advisers devoted considerable thought to the budget and the army during the autumn. On October 13, Napoleon addressed the Council of Ministers and emphasized the need for economies in the next budget, that for the year 1867. He was followed by the Finance Minister, who declared that the budget must be cut by thirty-five million francs. Fould hoped that the major part of this sum, thirty millon francs, could be saved through reductions in the army and navy budgets. The remainder, a mere five million francs, would be taken out of civilian expenses.[41] This plan did not please the War Ministry. On October 15, Napoleon informed the Council that Randon thought that he could not manage a cut of even twenty million francs.[42] The plan ultimately presented to the Corps Légis-latif and passed into law on November 15, 1865, represented a victory for Randon and his military colleagues, for the reduction in the military budget amounted to only nineteen and a half millions.[43] Translated into soldiers, this meant a drop in manpower of about twelve thousand men. The French army in 1865 had numbered 402,824 men; in 1866, after the decree which went into effect on January 2, 1866,[44] the army included 390,771 soldiers. With the re-

---

[39] For a good example of the degree of latitude allowed, see Prévost-Paradol, *Quelques Pages d'histoire contemporaine: Lettres politiques,* 2nd ed., 4 vols. (Paris 1862–67), vols. III and IV.

[40] Mérimée, *Panizzi,* II, 151.

[41] AN: Rouher's notes on the meeting of the Council of Ministers, October 13, 1865 (45 AP1, cahier 1).

[42] AN: Rouher's notes on the meeting of the Council of Ministers, October 15, 1865 (45 AP1, cahier 1).

[43] Vincennes: "Relevé du montant des budgets depuis 1815 jusqu'à 1881" (Mé-moires-Supplément Préval 1986). The War Ministry's budget for 1866 was 380,695,-851 francs; that for 1867 was 361,224,797 francs. The cut amounted to 19,471,054 francs.   [44] Randon, II, 126.

serve, the total figure for 1866 was 631,305, on paper at least a sizable fighting force.[45]

What difference did these changes make in the effectiveness of the French military establishment? The cuts involved a relatively small number of men. The reduction, stated proportionately, was about three percent. This does not seem drastic; and the impression is confirmed by a more detailed survey of the statistics.

In the first place, this was not a cut across the board: the reductions were irregular and presumably calculated. Many sections of the army, the Cent-Gardes de l'Empereur, the Gendarmes d'Elite, and the Garde de Paris, for instance, were unaffected by the decree. They retained their old organization and manpower intact. A few groups, such as the Gendarmerie, the Gendarmerie d'Afrique, and the Train des Equipages Montés, gained or lost a few men, but the numbers involved were so slight that the change may be discounted. A cut involving a somewhat larger number of men appears in the figures for the Ouvriers d'Administration: this body lost one hundred and forty-nine men. The only significant drops appear in the ranks of the Garde Impériale, the infantry, and the cavalry. Here important qualifications are necessary.

The Garde Impériale and the infantry present parallel cases and may be considered together. It is noteworthy that in each instance the number of soldiers was reduced, but the number of regiments, battalions, companies, and so on, remained the same and was even increased for the infantry. The corps as a whole was thinned out, but its organizational skeleton was preserved. It was necessary to release some officers from the staff of each unit, since the smaller group required a smaller command;[46] but as long as the structural frame-

[45] Vincennes: "Effectifs moyens . . . depuis l'année 1841" (Mémoires et Reconnaissances: 2121). Of course a sizable proportion of these were stationed in Algeria, Mexico, and Rome. For a full discussion of the effects of these commitments, see Epilogue. For full figures on the army cut, see Vincennes: Mémoires et Reconnaissances: 2121, dossier Second Empire.

[46] The number of officers dropped from the infantry was 677. See Vincennes: "Infanterie: Officiers à la suite au 1 9ᵇ 1866" (Mémoires et Reconnaissances: 2139, dossier 1866). The total number dropped from the army was 1,193. See Vincennes:

work was maintained, it should have been relatively easy to bring the regiments, battalions, and companies up to their full strength.[47]

The cavalry represents a somewhat different problem. Two regiments and forty-two squadrons were dropped. It would not have been possible, as in the infantry and the Garde Impériale, to bring new recruits into pre-existent bodies; new units would have to be set up. On the other hand, the War Ministry had been careful to retain the services of a considerable number of trainers, so that in case of emergency, new recruits could be whipped into shape rapidly.[48] Furthermore, the cavalry, unlike the infantry, is traditionally an offensive weapon; unless the French had been planning a surprise attack, it should have been possible, theoretically, to hold the line with the infantry and the more strictly defensive sections of the army while the cavalry was being developed as a striking force.

This possibility is underlined by the provisions concerning the groups primarily useful for protection, namely the engineers and the artillery. Although one company of engineers was abolished, the number of men was increased by two hundred and twenty-two. A far more impressive addition was made to the artillery: 1,961 new soldiers were enrolled, though the number of units remained the same. These figures show an important exception to the reduction of the army and suggest the government's concern with maintaining French military strength. At the same time, significant shifts were being made in the allocation of funds for the upkeep of French fortifications. According to a draft memorandum by Colonel Colson, Randon's second-in-command, the War Ministry was diverting money from many fortifications in order to concentrate on building up the defense at certain key frontier posts, notably Metz, Strasbourg, and Belfort. This program, which must have been secret since

---

Guerre, "Organisation et Recrutement. Réduction des cadres de l'armée, 2e Epreuve 22 Janvier 1867," p. 3 (Mémoires et Reconnaissances: 2139, dossier 1866).

[47] Cf. [Friedrich] Freiherr von Loë, *Erinnerungen aus meinem Berufsleben 1849–67,* 2nd ed. (Stuttgart, 1906), pp. 73–4. The present author has discounted von Loë's figures in favor of the official records.

[48] Vincennes: Mémoires et Reconnaissances: 2139, dossier 1866; Randon, II, 112–3.

Colson's description was carefully edited before circulation even within the Ministry, was followed throughout 1865 and 1866 and in the latter year required an expenditure of 620,000 francs.[49]

What conclusions can be drawn from this survey as to the power that stood behind Napoleon's political pronouncements? There are two parts to the answer. On the purely military side, it appears that the decree meant a minimal reduction of French strength. The experts at the War Ministry planned carefully and successfully to provide a blueprint which would permit lessened expenditure while causing the least possible loss in effectiveness. Through the concentration on the fortification of key points and the increases in the personnel of the Engineer and Artillery Corps, the French defenses could actually have been improved. At the same time, the retention of staff units in the infantry and the Garde Impériale and the provision of trainers should have made it possible to man these defenses with a force which could quickly have reached its 1865 levels. Since the cut was also very small, one must conclude that it had relatively little effect on French power. Of course the French army was not a perfect machine before the cut: events in 1870, after several years of army improvement, made this clear. But at least it was about the same in 1866 as it had been in 1865.

The disquieting part of the decision as a key to French military strength is the nonmilitary aspect. As has been discussed, in the fall of 1865 the French government was approaching the crucial phase of perhaps the most important international question to beset the Second Empire, the unification of Germany. Historians have seen in the events of 1866 the turning point—and the beginning of decline—of Napoleon's regime. Evidence of the significance of the impending crisis had reached the French government and Napoleon at least was already concerned. The decision against a wholesale cut in the army's manpower is further proof of the seriousness with which the government viewed the international situation. Yet it did

---

[49] Vincennes: Mémoires et Reconnaissances: 2139, dossier 1866. See also Appendix A.

not adopt the obvious alternative and refuse outright to reduce the army. The elaboration of the plans shows both official solicitude over foreign problems and official anxiety before the pressures of economic distress, popular pacifism, and liberal agitation in the legislature. Napoleon must have believed he could find military backing for a vigorous policy, but may have doubted that he could muster support in the country at large.

His position was very delicate as of mid-November, 1865. The domestic situation symbolized by the army reduction law offered many cautions to an active policy, although the state of affairs was not sufficiently grave to put a stop to French diplomatic maneuvering. The German question seemed to have entered a phase of relative quiet after Gastein; but a more virulent outbreak of the problem seemed probable in the near future, both because of the importance of the issues involved and because of the restless and scheming personality of Bismarck. It seemed likely that the French would sooner or later have to take a stand; but Napoleon's first preference, an arrangement with the Prussian minister, seemed impracticable for the moment at least. The risks involved in a French attempt to conquer Belgium while the Prussians were fighting the Austrians were too great to make such a plan viable: from Cowley's attitude, it could be deduced that the English would presumably enter the war on Belgium's behalf; and a general European war would result, over which, even if the French army fought adequately, French public opinion might create serious problems for the government.

What were the alternatives to a pro-Prussian policy? One obvious possibility was an agreement with the small German states. Such a course seemed relatively feasible in November and December, 1865, to judge by the attitude of the Bavarians, who were the natural German leaders of such a combination. It was widely believed in Bavaria that Bismarck's inactivity during these months was the result of French indifference at Biarritz. The Bavarian government made it evident that it was correspondingly grateful to France,[50] and the French ambassador, Méloizes, surmised that this predisposition

[50] Méloizes to Drouyn de Lhuys, December 13, 1865 (*Origines*, VII, 220).

would tend to increase as tension developed between the two German great powers.[51] Furthermore, there was some evidence in December that the Bavarian government was trying to create a loose union of the small states under Bavarian leadership.[52] Such a grouping would have facilitated French relations with the Third Germany, for French diplomacy had always been hampered by the many governments and personalities involved. The big obstacle to such a policy was created by German national feeling. Too often, French attempts to work with the small states were denounced by the Germans as intervention; and it had frequently seemed likely that the result of a French effort toward such a union would be a combination directed against France, rather than one cooperating with her. Because of this, both Drouyn de Lhuys and Méloizes believed that it was wisest to adopt a restrained attitude toward the Bavarians in the period immediately following the Biarritz meeting.[53] This caution was perhaps exaggerated. In December, a rumor from Weimar suggested that French involvement in the German question would no longer necessarily provoke a hostile alliance;[54] and the Bavarian Foreign Minister, Ludwig von der Pfordten, was evidently disappointed that his tentative overtures to France had not been more warmly received.[55] Nonetheless, the hostile reaction to the publication of the August 29 circular on the Convention of Gastein remained a warning to the French. It was probably sensible to avoid negotiations with the Bavarians. There was a further, incidental advantage to this course of action: the French could and did tell Bismarck about their cool response to von der Pfordten's approaches.[56] It was an easy way of winning favor,[57] which might work to French advantage in the event of further discussions with the Prussian government.

Once the possibility of closer relations with the Third Germany

[51] Méloizes to Drouyn de Lhuys, November 22, 1865 (*Origines*, VII, 193).
[52] Méloizes to Drouyn de Lhuys, December 25, 1865 (*Origines*, VII, 231).
[53] Drouyn de Lhuys to Méloizes, November 22, 1865 (*Origines*, VII, 189–90); Méloizes to Drouyn de Lhuys, November 22, 1865 (*Origines*, VII, 193).
[54] Belcastel to Drouyn de Lhuys, December 14, 1865 (*Origines*, VII, 225).
[55] Méloizes to Drouyn de Lhuys, November 29, 1865 (*Origines*, VII, 208).
[56] Drouyn de Lhuys to Benedetti, December 1, 1865 (*Origines*, VII, 211).
[57] Benedetti to Drouyn de Lhuys, December 14, 1865 (*Origines*, VII, 221).

was dismissed, the only alternative was a rapprochement with Austria. This is the policy toward which French efforts were directed during the winter of 1865–66. This movement had such a decidedly tentative quality that the word "rapprochement" is perhaps an over-statement. The crisis had not yet reached that pitch of intensity when definite commitments were desirable; but the German question was a thorny one and the French could hardly have avoided preliminary maneuvers designed either to prevent trouble in Central Europe or to make sure that they were not completely isolated in case of an overt crisis or war involving French interests. The incidents of this period contrast strongly with Napoleon's pro-Prussian predilections of the autumn. It does not seem necessary to conclude, as some scholars have done,[58] that Napoleon's policy was premeditatedly two-faced. In view of circumstances already adduced, it is difficult to see what other course he could have pursued at this juncture. It is well to remember also that this policy was not irreconcilable with an eventual return to pro-Prussianism: the wily Emperor might have reasoned that Bismarck might offer more inducements as obstacles arose. Finally, it is probably not out of place to suspect here the fine hand of Drouyn de Lhuys. No records of conversations or "conver-sions" exist; but Metternich's dispatches reveal how congenial Drouyn found the new French orientation. One incident seems worth detailing: when Metternich returned to France in November after an extended leave he presented himself to Drouyn in Paris before traveling to Compiègne to pay his respects to the Emperor. In the course of their talk, Drouyn remarked: "You will find the Emperor very well disposed *and such a good boy (et si sage)* that you will be astonished." [59]

What was the tangible shape of this rapprochement? The first and in many ways most important aspect was the French loan to Austria. The Austrian government regarded the uneasy détente created by the Convention of Gastein as a vital opportunity to build up Austrian

[58] Cf. Oncken, *Napoleon III and the Rhine.*
[59] HHSA: Metternich to Mensdorff, December 2, 1865, no. 49C.

power. This effort necessitated money from some source. The government turned first to the Austrian branch of the House of Rothschild, but this institution, under no illusions as to Austrian credit, offered conditions which were judged exorbitant by the Emperor Franz Joseph. The next step was to try to raise the money outside the banking hierarchy by selling shares directly to the public. This expedient was a dismal failure. It became necessary to turn to foreign banking houses. The English branch of the Rothschilds proved unyielding, despite a personal appeal by Lord John Russell.[60] At first the situation seemed equally unpromising in Paris. The French Rothschilds were willing to discuss a loan, but their conditions were heavily weighted in their own interest through special concessions for their large railroad holdings. The Austrian emissaries calculated that this one requirement would have meant a loss to the Austrian government of 1.4 million gulden a year. Considering these terms impossible, they opened additional negotiations with another group of banks, including the Haber concern, the Crédit foncier, and the Comptoir d'Escompte. The disclosure of Austrian readiness to pay high interest rates led the Habers to raise their demands at the last minute, but the Austrians were so desperate that, after a final and again abortive attempt to reach an agreement with the English Rothschilds, they were forced to close with the Habers. As finally negotiated, the amount of the loan at face value was ninety million gulden. It was to run for a term of thirty-seven years. The interest, however, was so high that the Austrian government received only 61¼ gulden out of every 100.[61]

However harsh the conditions, the Austrians had raised the money; all they needed now was the approval of the French Finance Ministry which would permit the loan to be listed for subscription

[60] C. W. Clark, *Franz Joseph and Bismarck* (Cambridge, Mass., 1934), pp. 298–9.

[61] Ernst von Plener, *Erinnerungen,* 2 vols. (Stuttgart, 1911), I, 47–8; for an excellent discussion of the dealings with the Rothschilds, see Lawrence D. Steefel, "The Rothschilds and the Austrian Loan of 1865," *Journal of Modern History,* 8:27–39 (March 1936).

on the Paris Bourse. This request was made by Mülinen in a letter to Drouyn de Lhuys.[62] Drouyn, naturally, was in favor of the loan and sent Metternich's letter to Fould in the Finance Ministry with the recommendation that it be given "favorable consideration." [63] This was by no means a foregone conclusion, since one of Fould's principal anxieties was the condition of the French gold reserves. On the other hand, there were certain countervailing factors: these included the public desire to invest abroad, the governmental desire to lessen the influence of the Rothschilds, and Fould's own personal financial connections.[64] Fould finally referred the matter to the meeting of the Council of Ministers on November 17, 1865. It was Napoleon himself who decided that the Austrian demand should be granted.[65] The notes kept unofficially by Rouher, Minister of State, do not reproduce any of the discussion on this occasion; but the measure was undoubtedly viewed in the light of its political implications, for Drouyn's official communication of the decision to the Austrians read in part: "The Cabinet of Vienna will see, I do not doubt, in the facilities granted to it for the conclusion of this loan, a new proof of our desire to be benevolent toward it." [66] Metternich, not to be outdone, replied that he regarded the French government's action as "a new and precious proof" of kindness toward Austria;[67] the subscription was opened on November 27;[68] and the incident closed in a general display of goodwill.

What were the effects of this loan to Austria? How important was Napoleon's concession to Austrian interests? These questions seem inseparable from any consideration of the loan as a stage in the policy of Franco-Austrian rapprochement. In the first place, the loan did little to aid the Austrian fiscal position. The sum of ninety

[62] HHSA: Drouyn de Lhuys to Metternich, November 18, 1865 (copy), no. 49B.
[63] Drouyn de Lhuys to Gramont, November 18, 1865 (*Origines,* VII, 182).
[64] Goltz to Bismarck, November 26, 1865 (*APP,* VI, 477–9).
[65] AN: Rouher's notes on the meetings of the Council of Ministers, 1865–68, November 17, no year given (45 API, cahier 1).
[66] HHSA: Drouyn de Lhuys to Metternich, November 18, 1865, no. 49B Annexe.
[67] HHSA: Metternich to Drouyn de Lhuys, November 21, 1865, no. 49B Annexe.
[68] HHSA: Metternich to Mensdorff, December 2, 1865, no. 49B.

million gulden was a mere drop in the bucket. The arrangement might make it possible for the Austrians to evade, for the moment at least, still more unattractive measures; but it did not allow for any large or lasting readjustment of the Austrian financial situation.[69] Yet the loan did have some indirect, beneficial effect on the Austrian economy, since the French banking firms participating in the loan now had an interest in that economy.[70] In addition, these firms were eager to portray Austria as a fertile field for French money. As the result presumably of certain carefully placed bribes, the French press published a series of glowing pro-Austrian articles.[71] The wave of enthusiasm was strong enough that Metternich optimistically calculated that further French investment in Austria and even further loans to the government might be forthcoming.[72]

But these prospects were purely speculative; in the winter of 1865–66 the effect of the French loan on the Austrian economy was not very great. Its real impact was upon Austrian prestige. It was widely hailed in the small states as a direct blow to Bismarck, and the estimation of Austria's position rose accordingly.[73] As a matter of fact, Bismarck shared this view of the significance of the loan; his dispatches of the time reveal a certain anxiety as to the import of recent developments in Franco-Austrian relations.[74]

Finally, the loan had a certain probably unintended influence on specific Austrian policies. One area affected was the Schleswig-Holstein question. In a moment of discouragement after his lack of success at Biarritz, Bismarck had set afoot a plan to buy out the Austrian rights in Holstein. He apparently took this scheme quite seriously, for he had discussed it early in November with Napoleon[75] and also had sounded out the Rothschilds about the necessary finan-

---

[69] Clark, p. 300.
[70] Gramont to Drouyn de Lhuys, November 29, 1865 (*Origines*, VII, 210).
[71] Goltz to Bismarck, January 4, 1866 (*APP*, VI, 521).
[72] HHSA: Metternich to Mensdorff, December 2, 1865, no. 49B.
[73] See, for a sample, Forth-Rouen to Drouyn de Lhuys, December 14, 1865 (*Origines*, VII, 224–5).
[74] Bismarck to Goltz, November 26, 1865 (Oncken, I, 79).
[75] Bismarck to Foreign Office, November 3, 1865 (*GW*, V, 316).

cial arrangements. The project was finally proposed informally to a minor figure at the Austrian embassy in Paris who lost no time in suppressing it once and for all.[76] But despite this uncompromising reception, there is a certain plausibility to Goltz's speculation that had the Austrians not been achieving success in their efforts to negotiate a loan in Paris, they might have found themselves so hard pressed for ready cash that they would have been obliged to accept the Prussian offer, unattractive as this expedient might have been.[77]

The coincidence in time between Napoleon's approval of the Austrian loan and the Prussian plan to purchase Austrian claims in Holstein raises interesting conjectures as to Napoleon's intentions. Clearly, the Austrian fiscal situation, and the German problem as well, were too complicated for Napoleon's action to represent a simple response to the Prussian plan. He had no assurance that the Austrians would refuse the Prussian advance if they received a loan from France, and it was even less certain that they would accept the Prussian offer if they did not receive French money. Furthermore, given Bismarck's fertile brain and persistent nature, there was no reason to believe that the solution of the Schleswig-Holstein question would mean the liquidation of the German problem. On the contrary, there was every likelihood that Bismarck and the German nationalists would find a new pretext within a few months or years. In short, Napoleon's agreement to the Austrian plan cannot be explained by a desire to prevent Prussian acquisition of Holstein; but it seems justifiable to see in the interrelationship of the two events evidence of the ambivalence of Napoleon's turn toward Austria. Austria was the German power most interested in the maintenance of the status quo, and those Frenchmen who advocated support of Austria usually did so because they favored the status quo; Napoleon, however, while helping the Austrian government, was quite willing

---

[76] Mérimée, *Panizzi*, II, 154–5. The minor figure was presumably Count Mülinen: see Steefel, "Austrian Loan," pp. 28–32.

[77] Goltz to Bismarck, November 26, 1865 *(APP, VI, 478).*

to take actions which would at the same time keep the German question open.[78]

In the more calculable matter of Austrian policy toward France, the loan authorized by Napoleon III had a definite and beneficial effect. The exuberance of the Austrian ambassador can be taken for granted, for Metternich sincerely believed that some sort of an arrangement with France was Austria's best hope, and he lost no opportunity to expound his hopes and expectations at the Ballplatz. It is noteworthy that a warmer attitude toward France was manifested by the government in Vienna. One may take as an example the report made by Gramont of a dinner with Franz Joseph and the Empress on December 7. The Emperor received him most kindly, alluded to "the commercial and other negotiations" which were then in progress between France and Austria, and ended by assuring Gramont that the Austrian government would show "the most favorable dispositions toward a reciprocal accord, whose prompt conclusion he ardently desired." [79] The implementation of this wish forms the rest of the story of the Franco-Austrian rapprochement.

It soon became clear that the French were eager to pursue the rapprochement through a wide range of measures in the economic and commercial fields. There was talk of a series of agreements covering commercial relations, navigation laws, copyrights, railroads,

---

[78] Another complication about the Austrian loan can be dismissed more easily: it also coincided in time with the Italian-sponsored Malaguzzi Mission (see p. 55 below). The latter was an attempt by the Italian government to achieve close relations with Austria through the preliminary measure of a purchase of Venetia from the Hapsburgs. The winning of Venetia for the Italians was close to Napoleon's heart; but the complete failure of the plan, which was evident by November 11, must have been known in Paris before Napoleon approved the loan on November 17 (Bush, "Napoleon III and the Redeeming of Venetia," pp. 59–60; cf. Alfonso [Ferrero del] la Marmora, *Un peu plus de lumière,* trans. Niox and Descourbès, 4th ed. [Paris, 1874], pp. 64–70). There is, therefore, no question of helping or harming the Italians as a factor in Napoleon's decision, although, as Steefel observes ("Austrian Loan," p. 39), Napoleon presumably had no wish to see the Schleswig-Holstein question liquidated except as part of a general European settlement.

[79] Gramont to Drouyn de Lhuys, December 9, 1865 (*Origines,* VII, 216–7).

and inheritance provisions as they were administered by the consulates. This was an impressive program. Most of it came to nothing; but as evidence of the scope and sincerity of the French wish to achieve closer relations with Austria, its significance cannot be overlooked.

The only one of these measures to be discussed at sufficient length for consideration here was the commercial treaty. The project was not new. It had been considered intermittently at least since 1860; after the Austrian government decided in 1864 on the general policy of tariff revision through treaties of commerce, these thoughts had taken more concrete shape. It was only upon completion of the arrangements for the French loan to Austria, however, that the plan was finally adopted as an immediate goal by the Austrian government. The Austrians believed, according to D. C. Long, the historian of the treaty, that it offered political and diplomatic advantages as well as strictly economic ones. It is plausible that similar political motives activated the French statesmen, although economic factors were presumably paramount, since the Austrian protective wall of high tariff barriers had proved very galling to the more liberal western nations.

In November, the French took a preliminary step designed to facilitate conclusion of a treaty by laying before the Corps Législatif a proposal to abolish the surtaxes levied by the French customs on foreign vessels carrying trade between French ports and other countries. The existence of these surtaxes was a principal Austrian grievance, for despite French efforts to keep transportation in their own hands, Austrian ships carried an impressive bulk of merchandise between France and the Near East. This commerce accounted for a far from negligible part of Austria's trading economy. There was conviction in Austrian circles that were the surtaxes abolished a lucrative opportunity would open up for Austrian merchants. The French bill, then, represented an encouragement to the Austrian government and shows the seriousness with which the French regarded improvement in Franco-Austrian relations.

In December, talks began. The incident has a comic-opera tinge. The first step consisted in unofficial soundings; these took place in the early part of the month. On December 20, all was ready for the first "official preparatory conferences." These were held on December 20 and December 22. At this point, the negotiations were adjourned to allow for further study.[80] Gramont was later to remark: "The progress of our negotiations . . . reminds me a little of the libretto of the ballet in which one sees constantly: 'Three steps forward—three steps backwards—posture erect.' " [81] Despite this pessimistic judgment, the making of the commercial treaty was not without significance. The talks did not result in an agreement until December 11, 1866;[82] but it did form part of the French desire to move closer to Austria in the winter of 1865–66. Through its timing the treaty achieved diplomatic importance, an importance which it was only later to assume on purely economic grounds.

Simultaneously, the Ballplatz made an effort to improve commercial relations with Italy. Again there were political as well as economic motives. Tentative moves were made in mid-November by Metternich in a conversation with Drouyn de Lhuys.[83] The Austrian offer was limited, however, in a way that would impede its implementation. Gramont reported from Vienna that although the Austrians wanted to remedy the trade situation, they were not willing to recognize the Italian government.[84] With typical Austrian slowness, it was not until the end of December that definite proposals were forthcoming. These were expounded by Count Mensdorff to Gramont, in the hope that the French government would assume the role of go-between.[85] This was a service which the French were quite willing to perform. On January 2, Drouyn de Lhuys forwarded the

[80] Dwight C. Long, "The Austro-French Commercial Treaty of 1866," *American Historical Review*, 41: 475–80 (April 1936).

[81] Gramont to Herbet, April 13, 1866, Quai d'Orsay, Dir. Commer., C–3B–1, quoted by Long, p. 482, n. 26.

[82] Long, p. 474.

[83] Drouyn de Lhuys to Gramont, November 18, 1865 (*Origines*, VII, 182).

[84] Gramont to Drouyn de Lhuys, November 29, 1865 (*Origines*, VII, 208–9).

[85] Gramont to Drouyn de Lhuys, December 28, 1865 (*Origines*, VII, 233–4).

Austrian request, as reported by Gramont, to the French ambassador at Florence, the Baron de Malaret.[86] The Italian reception was mixed. La Marmora, the Italian Prime Minister, was quite ready to extend commercial privileges to the Austrians which would establish the desired conditions of lowered tariffs through unilateral concessions; but he was displeased by Vienna's effort to side-step the obvious opportunity to accord diplomatic recognition to Italy. He proposed a face-saving device: Austria, while not recognizing Italy, could yet refer to that nation as the Kingdom of Italy during the negotiations.[87] This, however, was precisely what the Austrians were not willing to do. In his dispatch of February 5, Drouyn indicated to Gramont that the Italians were, nevertheless, granting most-favored-nation treatment to the Austrians unilaterally; the Austrians proceeded to accord these privileges to the Italians in the hope of prompt reciprocity. In fact, the Italians did not follow suit, and the whole incident came to nothing.[88]

What were the motives behind these negotiations and how do they fit into the total picture of Franco-Austrian rapprochement? Certainly one aspect of the Austrian approach to Italy was the desire to curry favor with the Quai d'Orsay. In this goal, the Austrians were more or less successful: Metternich was able to report, after telling Drouyn about the Austrian overtures, that the French Foreign Minister "finds our proceedings very noble and very skillful." [89] Since one of the greatest, if not the greatest, of obstacles to a comprehensive Franco-Austrian agreement was the total dissimilarity, or even hostility, in the two powers' policies toward the Italian question, the Austrian initiative was a well calculated step. Furthermore, in view of its carefully limited nature, it did not cost the Austrians very much diplomatically while it carried positive economic benefits.

---

[86] Drouyn de Lhuys to Malaret, January 2, 1866 (*Origines,* VII, 239).

[87] Malaret to Drouyn de Lhuys, January 10, 1866 (*Origines,* VII, 250–1).

[88] Drouyn de Lhuys to Gramont, February 5, 1866 (*Origines,* VII, 280); Heinrich von Sybel, *The Founding of the German Empire,* trans. Marshall Livingston Perrin and Gamaliel Bradford, Jr., 7 vols. (New York [1890–98]), IV, 317–8 and Clark, pp. 300–1 give brief accounts of the episode.

[89] HHSA: Metternich to Mensdorff, February 17, 1866, no. 7E.

After all, the motive of winning favor with the French was not the sole, or even the primary factor in the Austrian attempt to better commercial relations. The most important motive for these negotiations was the desire to lessen tension with Italy. This was particularly important because it came at a time when Bismarck seemed to be making effective use of similar weapons in an effort to improve Prusso-Italian relations. The implications of any relaxation of tension in this quarter were too ominous for the Austrians to overlook, and the need for countermeasures could hardly be denied by the most stiff-necked of Franz Joseph's entourage. Bismarck's overtures included the award of the Prussian Order of the Black Eagle to Victor Emmanuel,[90] but the most significant step was the conclusion of a treaty of commerce between Italy and the Zollverein. This expedient, first brought forth by Bismarck in the spring of 1865 and then shelved after Gastein, became prominent again during November, 1865.[91] The Prussian minister had to face the opposition of some of the small German states based on economic grounds and the hesitation of Bavaria and Saxony over the requirement, built into the agreement, that the Italian government be given recognition.[92] However, an arrangement was reached during December. A treaty was drawn up on the basis of most-favored-nation treatment[93] and signed on December 31.[94] This chain of events, which can only be briefly summarized here, was the principal factor behind the Austrian desire to reach a commercial agreement with Italy;[95] but whatever its larger perspective, the move did contribute, and was presumably intended to contribute, to the Franco-Austrian rapprochement.

This description of the economic side of the Franco-Austrian rapprochement is the heart of the story. It is this which gives the whole incident its tentative and indirect quality. Economic moves

[90] Benedetti to Drouyn de Lhuys, January 11, 1866 (Origines, VII, 252–3).

[91] Forth-Rouen to Drouyn de Lhuys, November 28, 1865 (Origines, VII, 202–3).

[92] Benedetti to Drouyn de Lhuys, November 26, 1865 (Origines, VII, 197).

[93] Méloizes to Drouyn de Lhuys, December 13, 1865 (Origines, VII, 220).

[94] Benedetti to Drouyn de Lhuys, December 30, 1865 (Origines, VII, 235).

[95] Drouyn de Lhuys to Gramont, November 18, 1865 (Origines, VII, 181–2).

were by no means solely based on the desire to improve relations: the loan to Austria offered Napoleon a chance to further his campaign against the Rothschilds; the commercial treaty opened positive trade advantages; while the Austro-Italian readjustments were only secondarily designed to influence France. The same double focus appears when one looks at the results of these maneuvers. Economic concessions, while they might contribute substantially to a lessening of tension, do not form a very impressive instance of rapprochement unless they are reinforced by political measures. In this sphere, the Franco-Austrian rapprochement appears significantly weak. To be sure, in the dispatches of December, particularly, there are many fine statements of mutual good will. On December 2, Metternich wrote: "I didn't believe, before my return to France, that I would find as satisfying a state of affairs. One would say that people here have an imperious need of our benevolence, they are accommodating, polite and they express toward us an interest which I have not been accustomed to meet up to now under the regime of the democratic Caesar." [96] Mensdorff responded with expressions of hope for a political agreement. Metternich duly communicated these sentiments to Drouyn de Lhuys, who reacted pleasantly but noncommitally. The Foreign Minister brushed aside the Italian question by minimizing its importance and emphasizing its delicacy, but he did state that France wanted "mutual good will" in relation to Austria.[97] A more flowery statement from Drouyn was reported by Metternich on December 22. Drouyn had said: "We are harassed . . . here we are become *frankly conservatives*—that is to say that we resemble you very much. Those who resemble each other assemble . . ." [98] Metternich had answered, in the great tradition of meaningless diplomatic courtesy, that "the Emperor Napoleon would find us always ready to place ourselves on his ground provided that this ground is that of good principles." [99]

[96] HHSA: Metternich to Mensdorff, December 2, 1865, no. 49C.
[97] HHSA: Mensdorff to Metternich, December 12, 1865; Drouyn de Lhuys to Gramont, December 19, 1865 (*Origines*, VII, 227–8).
[98] HHSA: Metternich to Mensdorff, December 22, 1865, no. 52C.
[99] HHSA: Metternich to Mensdorff, December 22, 1865, no. 52C.

This exchange of fair phrases was continued in the area most perfectly designed for the purpose, the awarding of foreign orders. A rash of ribbons marked the Franco-Austrian rapprochement. One candidate for a decoration was Achille Fould, who, as Finance Minister, had been responsible for the formal authorization of the Austrian loan. He was given the Grand Cross of the Imperial Order of Leopold of Austria, and Metternich took advantage of the conferment of this trinket to write a letter in which he emphasized the diplomatic significance of the award. Fould replied in tones which showed that he had been moved by the gift, and the incident was generally regarded, in Metternich's words, as "a new proof of the good relations" between France and Austria.[100]

A still more impressive display of amity marked the grant of the Grand Order of St. Stephen to Napoleon's son, the Prince Imperial. Metternich, who reverenced these traditional ceremonies, described the event at length:

The Emperor received me today at one-thirty at the Palace of the Tuileries.

His Majesty was surrounded by the officers of the crown in full uniform—I noticed among the personages who were grouped around the Emperor in the throne room the Master of the Horse and the Master of the Hunt—the Generals Fleury and the Prince de la Moskowa . . .

The Emperor thanked me warmly, . . . told me that He would write Himself to our August Master in order to convey to Him all his gratitude . . . and to assure Him that the Prince Imperial would never forget this proof of solicitude on the part of a Sovereign for whom his father felt a sincere friendship.[101]

Perhaps the Austrians outdid the French in this round of diplomatic courtesies. The scale was balanced to some extent when Napoleon conferred the Grand Cross of the Legion of Honor on the Austrian Crown Prince, with the usual statements about "cordial relations." [102] If an exchange of medals had meant an alliance, the Franco-Austrian combination would have rested by then on the firmest foundations.

---

[100] HHSA: Metternich to Mensdorff, December 22, 1865, no. 52B.
[101] HHSA: Metternich to Mensdorff, December 31, 1865, no. 54A.
[102] Drouyn de Lhuys to Gramont, February 10, 1866 (*Origines*, VII, 287).

There was very little progress in the discussion and resolution of mutually important political problems and in decision on common lines of action. Some effort was made during the winter to investigate areas of international tension, but the conversations all too often turned on matters of secondary importance. Drouyn de Lhuys was interested in promoting agreement with Austria in the Eastern question.[103] His inquiries bore fruit in assurances from Mensdorff that Austria would consult France and England before initiating any moves in the Danubian principalities.[104] There were similar efforts to explore the rather more important question of Schleswig and Holstein. Metternich was able to report that the Austrian position seemed to be regarded more favorably by the Quai d'Orsay than was the Prussian attitude. But there was a certain curious unrealism in French utterances on the subject. Both Napoleon and Drouyn talked unofficially of elaborate schemes for resolving the question of the duchies by finding a ruler of German origin who would enjoy some kind of popular sanction; this plan was to be crowned with the retrocession of northern Schleswig to Denmark. Metternich listened carefully but could not resist pointing out that the Prussian government would hardly allow the implementation of such a scheme, at least under purely Austrian auspices. To this well-founded hint, the French Foreign Minister had no response.[105]

This vagueness is still more noticeable in relation to the major question dividing France and Austria, the problem of Italy. This fact is hardly surprising; for the achievement of a détente between Austria and Italy, upon which any solution satisfactory to Napoleon must have rested, would have been very difficult at that point. The Italian government, supported with unusual unanimity by public opinion, desired above all things to gain control of the province of Venetia, which, although clearly Italian in population and culture, had remained under Austrian domination after the war of 1859,

---

[103] Drouyn de Lhuys to Gramont, January 7, 1866 (*Origines*, VII, 249–50).
[104] Gramont to Drouyn de Lhuys, January 20, 1866 (*Origines*, VII, 265–6).
[105] HHSA: Metternich to Mensdorff, January 14, 1866, no. 2E.

when the rest of the peninsula, with the exception of Rome, had been freed from foreign rule and unified as a nation-state. This plan was anathema to the Austrians, who saw in such proposals not only a threat to a rich and strategically located territory, but also the elevation of the principle of nationalism, the thorough-going application of which would have meant the destruction of the Hapsburg Empire. Napoleon himself was deeply involved in this problem on at least three grounds. First, he felt a sentimental desire, as a former Italian conspirator, to see the Italian people completely freed; secondly, he had committed his prestige through aid to the Italian nationalists in 1859; and finally, if we are to believe Father Bush's highly plausible interpretation, he had definitely promised support in 1864 at the time of the Franco-Italian September Convention.[106] As result, it was extremely difficult for Napoleon to conclude agreements with Austria upon any matter which might involve Italy, either directly or as one of the European powers, until Austro-Italian hostility had been appeased through resolution of the Venetian question.

The Italian government had taken advantage of the desire for the relaxation of international tensions evidenced by the Convention of Gastein to try a new approach to the Ballplatz. La Marmora had hoped that it might be possible for the Kingdom of Italy to buy Venetia from the Austrians. A mission under Malaguzzi had been sent to Vienna on an unofficial basis. Nonetheless, the fact that detailed information was provided for the emissaries regarding "financial," "politico-administrative," and "international" requirements leaves no room for doubt that La Marmora regarded this attempt as a serious effort to end the differences separating the Austrian and Italian governments. The apparent failure of this overture was discernible by the end of the autumn;[107] and on November 25, 1865, La Marmora issued a circular in which he said that both commercial and diplomatic relations between Austria and Italy were out of the

[106] Bush, pp. 31–45.

[107] La Marmora, pp. 60–71. Clark notes Franz Joseph's refusal in November; although the offer remained open, technically, until April, 1866 (Clark, p. 307), the Italians had little reason to be encouraged.

question as long as Austria retained Venetia.[108] This statement was a serious diplomatic step, and one which might give pause to French statesmen eager to promote a détente between Italy and Austria. It must have seemed evident that such a solution could only be implemented through a prolonged and tactful approach in which the first goals would be relatively small ones. As a matter of fact, the Duc de Gramont, commenting on the circular, pointed out that there seemed to be some hope that commercial relations, the lesser objective, could be considered separately from the more important and more difficult question of diplomatic relations;[109] and it is noteworthy that the Quai d'Orsay followed exactly this policy. Commercial relations were promoted, with some success, while diplomatic questions were minimized. As result, conversations about Italy between the Austrians and the French in the winter of 1865 were infrequent and inconclusive. Still the differing attitudes of Napoleon and of his Foreign Minister emerge and should be noted. Napoleon, embarrassed by the contradiction of supporting Austria in Germany while supporting Italy against Austria in Venetia, would have liked to separate the Italian question entirely from affairs in Germany. Metternich reported a talk with the Emperor at the end of November in which Napoleon broached the topics of both Italy and of Rome. Metternich exposed his own hopes frankly. He was of the opinion that Austria's real danger lay in the possibility that activist politicians might win power in Italy and reopen the Italian question by a campaign to conquer Venetia. Metternich's preventive measure was a definite agreement between France and Austria. Napoleon's reply shows, among other things, how well he deserved his reputation for mysteriousness; he said:

That is not impossible, and if one could provoke a war in one corner of Europe without setting fire to the gunpowder elsewhere that would perhaps be the best way of putting an end to the matter. I would prefer, however that, once the hatreds and defiances have been calmed, one

---

[108] *Origines*, VII, 226, n. 2.
[109] Gramont to Drouyn de Lhuys, December 18, 1865 (*Origines*, VII, 227).

could remain one beside the other tranquilly, but we are not there yet . . .[110]

Exactly what this meant would be difficult to say; even Metternich was bewildered. Apparently Napoleon preferred a peaceful solution of the Italian question; he saw no likelihood of such an arrangement at present; he would not object in principle to an alliance between Austria and France designed to discourage the Italians from taking active steps; but in practice, he felt that such an alliance would almost certainly be the prelude to war in Germany, an eventuality which would offer the Italian activists an irresistible opportunity. The result of such an intermingling of the Italian and German questions would be a war in which Napoleon would find himself supporting the Hapsburgs against the Italian patriots, a virtually impossible position.

Drouyn de Lhuys was hardly more successful than his master in grappling with this problem, although he was more explicit. Drouyn liked Metternich's suggestions of a Franco-Austrian entente. Since he was never particularly partial to the Italians he was not much worried about the results in case of war. He was quite willing to contemplate an Austrian campaign against Italy in which, while France maintained a position of benevolent neutrality, the Austrians would defeat the Italians decisively and then regulate the Venetian question by a grant of autonomy in line with the plans then under consideration for a decentralization of the Empire on the basis of national groups.[111] Later in the winter, Drouyn went even further; he remarked: "I repeat it solemnly, if things were to go worse in Italy and if you were one day attacked in Venetia—not only would we leave you freedom of action, but a complete entente could be established between us on a definitive solution of the Italian question."[112]

An important although hardly unexpected difference emerges here between the Emperor and his Foreign Minister. Napoleon presum-

---

[110] HHSA: Metternich to Mensdorff, December 2, 1865, no. 49C.
[111] HHSA: Metternich to Mensdorff, December 2, 1865, no. 49D.
[112] HHSA: Metternich to Mensdorff, December 17, 1865, no. 51.

ably did not want to see the Italians abandoned to the Austrians; and so he found it difficult to envisage cooperation with the Austrians in the German question unless the Italian question had been put aside, either through a peaceful diplomatic arrangement or through some miraculous localization of the German conflict. Drouyn, on the other hand, felt no such scruples. He was a strong proponent of the Austrian alliance and was quite prepared to see Italy suffer the consequences if she chose to provoke them. At any rate, the Mala-guzzi Mission had made it clear that the time was not ripe for negotiations between Austria and Italy. Napoleon placatingly informed Metternich that the Ballplatz must wait until the Italians were ready to offer overtures toward better relations. This moment had not yet come and Napoleon added: "unhappily things are not going as I would wish." [113] Drouyn reassured Metternich by saying that, in the light of the existing state of Austro-Italian relations, Austrian national honor would not permit Austrian advances to the Italian government at this time. Metternich was delighted to hear this, as the Austrian government always feared that the French would make extensive Austrian concessions to Italy the price of Franco-Austrian rapprochement.[114] Later in December, when Metternich disclosed that Mensdorff was ready to consider a Franco-Austrian agreement which would take note of the Italian problem, Drouyn again discouraged Austrian action. He did not preclude Franco-Austrian discussions designed to lessen the tension, but, pointing to the extreme sensitivity of Italian nationalism, he cautioned that any direct Austrian moves toward Italy were apt to be misconstrued.[115]

The intense hostility between Austria and Italy, which made conversations concerning the Venetian question a virtual impossibility at this time, implied in turn strains between the Austrian government and the pro-Italian Napoleon. With these tensions, it was vir-

[113] HHSA: Metternich to Mensdorff, December 2, 1865, no. 49C.
[114] HHSA: Metternich to Mensdorff, December 2, 1865, no. 49D.
[115] Drouyn to Gramont, December 19, 1865 (*Origines,* VII, 227–9).

tually impossible for the Franco-Austrian rapprochement to assume anything more than the most tenuous and superficial guise. In fact, the policy of overtures to Austria proved as unproductive of a solution as the Biarritz meetings. However, the events of the autumn and winter of 1865 merit study, for they show the limits within which French statesmen moved and the problems which beset them. Napoleon's preferred policy, an arrangement with nationalism as exemplified by Prussia, was complicated by the practical desirability of winning compensations for France and by the difficulty of finding an area whose transfer would be acceptable to both German and non-German powers. In pursuing such a relatively active course, with the risk of war entailed, Napoleon was hampered by the thoroughly pacifist turn of French public opinion. This trend had led the government to make reductions in the army as late as November, 1865. Careful calculations held these cutbacks to minimal military significance; but as an index of popular feeling and of the seriousness with which the government regarded this popular feeling, the changes are disquieting indeed. However, the obvious alternative, which Napoleon was forced to adopt during the winter, a rapprochement with Austria as the status quo power, was also difficult to implement, for it presupposed the resolution of the Venetian question in which Napoleon was engaged against the Austrians. These problems form the indispensable background to an understanding of the attempts of Napoleon and his advisers to shape policy during the open crisis of 1866.

III

THE MARCH FLURRY:
RENEWED ATTEMPTS
AT ALLIANCES

THE SITUATION in France and in Europe at the end of January, 1866, was highly unstable. Napoleon, ably supported by the pro-Austrian Drouyn de Lhuys, had been following a policy of rapprochement with Austria. This program, however, had two serious drawbacks: in the first place, it would be difficult if not impossible, in the existing state of affairs, to bring the Hapsburg government to an accord over Venetia which would enable Napoleon to cooperate with Austria without violating moral, sentimental, and perhaps even practical commitments to Italy; secondly, this policy implied opposition to the changes in Germany which Napoleon tended to favor through faith in the principle of nationalities, need for *la gloire,* and the possibility of compensations. The pro-Austrian line had many disadvantages, and it seems unlikely that Napoleon ever regarded it as more than a second-best expedient. He had been forced to adopt this course because his first attempts to negotiate with Prussia had ended in an impasse: Bismarck's offers at Biarritz, if they assumed any tangible shape at all, involved a high risk; and the temper of the French public, as revealed by the agitation for army reductions, was definitely not attuned to gambling. Support of Austria, the champion of the status quo, appeared to be the safe policy, but Napoleon almost certainly retained his hope that agreement with Prussia would eventually prove feasible. New opportunities seemed to open up about the end of January, when Bismarck again took the offensive in the German question. There was every reason to believe that, as the crisis reached greater and greater proportions, Bismarck would become more and more aware of the need for allies, and as result would offer Napoleon new conditions. Events were to bear out these hopes; but in his resumption of the attempt to make an arrangement with Prussia, Napoleon was faced once more with all the problems which had beset his efforts in the autumn and winter: the difficulty of getting attractive offers from the Prussians; the opposition to an active or pro-Prussian policy within France; and the impracticability of turning to Austria as an alternative ally, given the unresolved Venetian question.

The first approaches came from Bismarck himself. Early in February, the French ambassador at Berlin, the later famous or infamous Benedetti, had an interesting conversation with the Prussian Minister. Benedetti asked Bismarck what he intended to do if relations with Austria took an unfavorable turn. Bismarck's answer, which the ambassador hastened to report, was highly revealing. Bismarck said: "We will move quickly . . . and perhaps we will move far." He added that his first step would be to recall Goltz to Berlin for conferences.[1] For a time it seemed as though the storm which had been brewing at the end of January might blow over temporarily;[2] but shortly afterwards Goltz was indeed recalled to Berlin. Before leaving, he took the precaution of talking at length with both Napoleon and Drouyn de Lhuys. The conversations, which, according to Goltz's report, were substantially the same in content, reveal renewed interest in a pro-Prussian line. French neutrality was emphasized. Assurances were offered as to the impossibility of a Franco-Austrian alliance. Hints were given that the French might approve Prussian annexation of the duchies, while they would be willing to reach an agreement with Prussia in case more extensive annexations were imminent.[3] Drouyn de Lhuys, if his own report is to be believed, went even further: he pointed up France's friendly attitude toward the Prussians and hinted that, in case of war, the French

---

[1] Benedetti to Drouyn de Lhuys, February 11, 1866 (*Origines,* VII, 293).
[2] Benedetti to Drouyn de Lhuys, February 14, 1866 (*Origines,* VII, 297–9).
[3] Goltz to Bismarck, February 17, 1866 (Oncken, I, 89–90).

government would have to re-examine its position of neutrality in light of the "necessities" created by her interests and the "advantages" to be gained from action.[4]

From the rapidity with which Drouyn forgot these remarks, they must have been inspired by his imperial master. Still, they seemed to imply a Franco-Prussian arrangement and doubtless served to encourage Bismarck. The first result of the conferences which took place after Goltz's return to Berlin on February 19,[5] was made evident at a royal dinner party on March 2 to which Benedetti was invited along with Goltz. Already honored by the invitation, Benedetti was overwhelmed when King William, in an unusual overture, said to him after dinner: "We are coming to the moment when we will need to distinguish our true friends." [6] This frank confidence showed the new direction and intensity of Prussian policy; its implementation was entrusted to Goltz, who was sent back to Paris bearing a message from William to Napoleon. In this letter, the Prussian monarch stated in very general terms his desire for closer relations with France and announced that Goltz was authorized to treat with Napoleon in this sense.[7] It would seem that the Prussians were making a definite bid for an alliance.

Simultaneously with this overture to France, the Prussian government was endeavoring to win Italian support. The Italians continued to be eager for Venetia. Just at this juncture, outside developments caused them to push their claims with renewed vigor. At the end of February, Prince Couza, the ruler of the principalities, was deposed by a military coup,[8] and the question of the succession was opened. The Italians had long seen in the two provinces a possible compensation for Austria and had dreamed up the famous exchange plan by which the Austrians would cede Venetia to Italy and would receive Moldavia and Wallachia in return. This scheme, which had seemed

[4] Drouyn de Lhuys to Benedetti, February 22, 1866 (*Origines*, VII, 311–2).
[5] Benedetti to Drouyn de Lhuys, February 20, 1866 (*Origines*, VII, 310).
[6] Benedetti to Drouyn de Lhuys, March 3, 1866 (*Origines*, VII, 368).
[7] William to Napoleon, March 3, 1866 (Oncken, I, 93).
[8] Tillos to Drouyn de Lhuys, February 23, 1866 (*Origines*, VII, 315).

ideal in Italian circles, became more feasible as a result of the revolution. The ambassador to France, the Chevalier Nigra, urged it upon Napoleon at the end of February. It was evident that the scheme formed an alternative (in Nigra's view a second-best alternative) to an alliance with Prussia. Napoleon was impressed by the plan, which was certainly calculated to appeal to his daring imagination and, although he took care to mention all the difficulties which such a suggestion would encounter at the Ballplatz,[9] he pointed out that the Italians might be able to vanquish Austrian opposition by threatening to conclude an agreement with Prussia.[10] Since this trick could presumably be worked in reverse as well, the Italians were in a position to play a very effective game, in which they might further either a pro-Prussian or a pro-Austrian policy on the part of the French Emperor.

By the beginning of March, the situation looked ripe for the realization of a Franco-Prussian entente. Bismarck was planning new overtures; the Italians, while they could move either way, were already in contact with Berlin. At this point, however, Napoleon was faced with an outburst of anti-Prussian sentiment in the Corps Législatif. These debates had to be taken the more seriously because they occurred against a background of popular unrest, which had been gaining in strength throughout the winter. The Latin Quarter was in turmoil as a result of proceedings against some students who had listened to a suspect series of lectures. Furthermore, the inhabitants of the Quarter were bitter because Napoleon intended to take over some of the Jardin de Luxembourg.[11] Claremont, long attached

---

[9] La Marmora, *Un peu plus de lumière*, pp. 131–2. For Austrian sentiments, see HHSA: Mensdorff to Metternich, March 1, 1866, no. 4.

[10] La Marmora (pp. 131–2) quotes a dispatch from Nigra in which the ambassador credits himself with the origin of this plan to sell Italian cooperation; Ollivier (VIII, 42) assigns it to Napoleon III. The present author is in agreement with Bush ("Napoleon III and the Redeeming of Venetia," pp. 64–6), who seconds Ollivier's opinion. In addition to a comment on the Italians' notorious untrustworthiness, which is even greater than Ollivier's, it may be urged that such a scheme was typical of Napoleon III's thinking.

[11] HHSA: Metternich to Mensdorff, December 22, 1865, no. 52H; PRO: Cowley to Foreign Office, March 23, 1866 (F. O. 519/13).

to the British embassy in Paris, reported a talk with the noted Parisian journalist Girardin, in which the conversation turned to the Mexican question. Girardin seemed to feel that this humiliating war might occasion Napoleon's deposition. In retrospect, this seems an extravagant prediction, but it is significant that at the time Girardin sensed that sufficient ill-will had built up against Napoleon that his overthrow, from this one source or from many, was not only possible but even likely.[12] An example of the state of contemporary feelings is provided by the story of Napoleon's visit during March to the Odéon Theater, in the heart of the Latin Quarter. Napoleon and Eugénie had decided to attend the opening performance of a play appropriately entitled "La Contagion." They were hissed throughout the drive to and from the theater and during the performance. Eugénie retired to spend hours grumbling against the democrats, but Napoleon simply remarked "that what he had seen reminded him of the worst days of 1848." [13] The comment, although doubtless exaggerated, gives some measure of the turmoil.

Meanwhile, the Corps Législatif had been working on its reply to the Speech from the Throne with which Napoleon traditionally opened legislative sessions. Since this speech ranged over virtually every problem before the French government, though in guarded terms, the legislators, in replying, were able to record an opinion on the work of practically every administrative department. The speech itself had been delivered on January 22, in an impressive ceremony in the Louvre.[14] As usual, the tone of the address was highly optimistic. With regard to foreign policy, Napoleon remarked: "Abroad, peace seems assured everywhere . . ." The Emperor went on to take up the specific issues of diplomacy in turn. It is worth noting that the paragraph dealing with Italy made no mention of Venetia, while the approving reference to the recent designation of Florence as the capital implied that the Italian govern-

---

[12] PRO: Claremont to Cowley, February 6, 1866 (F. O. 519/168).
[13] PRO: Cowley to Foreign Office, March 23, 1866 (F. O. 519/13).
[14] *Annales du Sénat et du Corps Législatif (1866)*, 10 vols. (Paris, 1866), I, 1.

ment had given up its hopes of obtaining Rome. By these devices, the continuation of peace in the peninsula was strongly implied.

A more delicate problem was raised by the necessity of commenting upon French policy in the German question. Napoleon's declaration read: "With regard to Germany, my intention is to continue to observe a policy of neutrality, which, without preventing us at times from feeling grieved or from rejoicing, will nonetheless leave us uninvolved in those questions in which our interests are not directly engaged." [15]

Napoleon's speech was well received at the time, with cheers from the deputies at appropriate moments;[16] but this mark of favor is easily won by more or less despotic governments, and the reaction of the public at large was not so favorable.[17] As February wore on, it became evident that the opposition was being organized in the Tiers Parti under Adolphe Thiers. Their principal aim was the loosening of governmental control over individual freedoms,[18] but it was soon apparent that this goal did not preclude action on any issue where questions could embarrass the government.

In this atmosphere, the Corps Législatif discussed the reply to Napoleon's statements on Italy and Germany. The debate on the Italian question turned mainly on the presence of French troops in Rome. All the delegates favored the September Convention, which had implied the exclusion of Rome from the Italian nation.[19] This attitude was hardly very encouraging to the Italian nationalists. But the direct challenge to Napoleon's policies came with the debate on the German question. On March 2, the Corps Législatif presented an amendment, introduced by Jules Favre, to the original reply to Napoleon's speech.[20] Favre, who had been an ardent nationalist during the crisis of the Italian question, had reconsidered his views

[15] *Annales (1866)*, I, 2.
[16] *Annales (1866)*, I, 6.
[17] PRO: Cowley to Clarendon, January 23, 1866 (F. O. 519/232).
[18] PRO: Cowley to Clarendon, February 23, 1866 (F. O. 519/232).
[19] *Annales (1866)*, II, 11-2.
[20] *Annales (1866)*, II, 63.

as the German question developed in the 1860's; he had come to the conclusion that the aims of the Prussian government were imperialistic rather than nationalistic and had turned to support of Austria in his disillusionment.[21] His amendment, which embodied his disapproval of the Schleswig-Holstein situation in general and the Gastein Convention in particular, read as follows:

> But to be durable, this peace must rest on respect for justice. We cannot see it violated in Germany without manifesting aloud our lack of approbation.
>
> France, who prides herself on having re-established the dogma of popular sovereignty, owes it to herself to protest against conventions in which force disposes of population.[22]

This statement called forth impassioned speeches which reveal the wide range of opinion among the deputies. Many who did not support Favre's amendment did not support the governmental position either, and the resulting session was frequently chaotic. Several ideas emerge which were fundamentally incompatible with Napoleon's views. One of the less drastic speeches was made by Emile Ollivier. Ollivier, like Favre, was pro-Austrian and in fact was using information supplied by Metternich.[23] He cricitized Favre's amendment on the grounds that it was too weak, although actually the policy which he suggested seems less extreme. Ollivier counseled an attitude of neutrality for the present. He agreed that the Gastein settlement had been unjust, but he pointed out that many Germans also disliked it and suggested that the wisest course was to let the opposition to Bismarck crystallize within Germany. He seemed to deviate from official policy, as expressed in the Speech from the Throne, when he looked ahead. He declared that French action would probably become necessary and he advised that the ground be prepared by a statement removing the issue of the duchies from the

---

[21] Rudolf von Albertini, "Frankreichs Stellungnahme zur Deutschen Einigung während des zweiten Kaiserreiches," *Schweizerische Zeitschrift für Geschichte*, 5:328–9 (1955).

[22] *Annales (1866)*, II, 63–4.

[23] HHSA: Metternich to Mensdorff, March 7, 1866, no. 9B.

sphere of domestic German politics and by insistence that France and England as well be consulted before a permanent settlement was established.[24] Such a step would have meant a change from a passive to an active policy on the Schleswig-Holstein question; but in general, Ollivier's attitude of watchful waiting, with intervention a possibility at the psychological moment, was not on the surface very different from Napoleon's expectations, although questions might arise as to the form and aim of the intervention.

The other significant speech, made by Adolphe Thiers, was not reconcilable with Napoleon's attitude. Thiers objected to the Speech from the Throne on the grounds that it was too compliant; he maintained that the German question already involved French interests, since it was fundamentally a problem in the balance of power. He did not want military intervention in Germany, but he hoped that war might be averted if France took a firm stand and left no doubt as to what she intended to do if war came. He criticized the current French policy as a direct encouragement to "the dangerous quarter, the ambitious quarter." In short, he wanted Napoleon to abandon a policy of neutrality which could only further Bismarck's plans and emerge as the guardian of order and the status quo. These suggestions stood in direct contradiction to everything Napoleon was doing at the time, either officially or unofficially; and to make matters worse, Thiers was able to rally sufficient support to carry, despite procedural difficulties, his proposal that the entire question of the amendment be reconsidered by the committee.[25]

The battle came on March 3. Three new versions of the amendment were laid before the legislature for discussion. The mildest, sponsored by the committee, read: "We give our support to the policy followed by Your Majesty with regard to Germany; this policy of neutrality which does not leave France indifferent to events, is in conformity with our interests." [26] A somewhat harsher version

---

[24] *Annales (1866)*, II, 75–6.
[25] *Annales (1866)*, II, 77–8; 80.
[26] *Annales (1866)*, II, 85–6.

was presented by Morin as a compromise between the committee and the extremists. The third possibility was a new amendment written by Favre and his friends: "In the presence of the events which are agitating Germany, we will be happy to see the Government persevere in the principles expressed by its despatches." [27]

This last statement, with its obvious reference to the August 29 circular, implied a judgment on government policies; as such, it was embarrassing in intent if not in form. As the government spokesman, Rouher discussed all three versions and indicated that the government preferred the one drawn up by the committee.[28] Ollivier then rose to make a conciliatory speech. He said that, in his opinion, the differences between the committee draft and the draft sponsored by Favre were purely verbal; both proposals approved past French policies and both advised for the future the maintenance of the position enunciated in the official dispatches, particularly the protest against the Gastein Convention. The most important point, in Ollivier's own words, was that "France doesn't favor, either in a direct manner or in an indirect manner, the pretensions and the claims of M. de Bismarck." The best way of impressing this wily diplomat with the seriousness of French intentions would be to confront him with a display of French solidarity; for this reason, Ollivier counseled acceptance of the committee's version. Rouher was not slow to press these favorable points. He assured the deputies that despite the compliance read into the Speech from the Throne by the opposition, the government regarded the German situation with deep concern. Ollivier announced that he was satisfied with these assurances; and in the ensuing vote, the committee version was accepted by an overwhelming majority.[29]

These debates could hardly fail to have an effect upon Napoleon, who was even then awaiting Goltz's return with the result of the conferences in Berlin. The speeches did reveal a deep hostility to

[27] *Annales* (*1866*), II, 85–6.
[28] *Annales* (*1866*), II, 86–7.
[29] *Annales* (*1866*), II, 88-9.

many of his ideas in an influential quarter. It would be a mistake to overemphasize the degree of passion animating the discussions. The government-approved draft was finally passed. And the sessions themselves were by no means so tense as some of the later debates on matters directly affecting political rights. Lord Cowley, always an astute observer, wrote on March 6: "The Corps Législatif is wonderfully quiet this year." [30] His reports later in the month became more ominous as he described the crystallization of the Tiers Parti;[31] on March 20, he noted: "The Opposition managed to unite 63 votes yesterday on the paragraph respg [*sic*] the liberties of France and the quidnuncs are throwing up their hands in despair in consequence. Seriously speaking the Emperor will have to look about him at the next general elections." [32] The difficulty, of course, was that political concessions were the last thing Napoleon wished to grant; and many in his entourage (Eugénie, for instance) objected even more strongly. But the government's relatively firm stand in this area made it unwise to be equally unyielding in other matters. In short, Napoleon had received a warning which was significant, first, because the German question, by its comparative unimportance, represented a possible field for conciliation; second, because the opinions of many of the deputies were so directly contrary to his secret plans.

It was at this point that poor Goltz returned from Berlin, bearing King William's letter and full of "mysterious airs." [33] First he paid a courtesy call on Drouyn de Lhuys, but he carefully said nothing to the Foreign Minister, whom he correctly mistrusted, about Bismarck's latest plans. Then later, on March 5, he had a talk with Napoleon.[34] The Emperor agreed that it would be well to say nothing to Drouyn.[35] In this conspiratorial atmosphere, a very frank discussion ensued. Goltz declared that the tension between Austria

<hr/>

[30] PRO: Cowley to Clarendon, March 6, 1866 (F. O. 519/232).
[31] PRO: Cowley to Foreign Office, March 23, 1866 (F. O. 519/13).
[32] PRO: Cowley to Clarendon, March 20, 1866 (F. O. 519/232).
[33] HHSA: Metternich to Mensdorff, March 7, 1866, no. 9B.
[34] Goltz to Bismarck, March 6, 1866 (Oncken, I, 94).
[35] Ollivier, VIII, 23.

and Prussia had reached a pitch so high that the Prussian government believed that the time had come to seek definite agreements. It was planning a double program. The first stage would be a treaty with Italy which would assure combined action. Negotiations were already in progress. The second stage would be a bargain with France which would assure the Prussians of the benevolent neutrality of their powerful western neighbor. Goltz unfolded Bismarck's German goals, which included the formation of a federation north of the Main and, if possible, the establishment of a bridgehead in southern Germany through the insurance of closer cooperation with Bavaria. This settlement, although modest by comparison with the German Empire of 1871, would have established a more or less united Germany whose links could have been drawn closer by time. In return, Goltz asked Napoleon explicitly what he expected by way of compensation.

Napoleon's reply was more definite than any as yet recorded. He expressed approval of Bismarck's plans, but pointed out that, in view of the state of French public opinion, it would be impossible for him to aid Bismarck, even tacitly, unless he received some important and tangible reward. He refused to state exactly what cessions he had in mind, but mentioned a long list of possibilities, including Belgium, the Rhenish Palatinate, Luxemburg, and French Switzerland. Apparently as a trial balloon, he remarked that Marshal Vaillant wanted the left bank of the Rhine on the basis of the restoration of the frontiers of 1814 which had included Saarbrücken and Landau. He said that he hoped that he could shortly make a more specific declaration of French desires and asserted his intention of maintaining a position of benevolent neutrality.[36]

Since French-speaking areas had presumably been discussed at Biarritz, it seems likely that these hints at the Rhineland revealed Napoleon's true hopes at the time. If it could actually have been attained, it would have represented an important extension of French territory, and might have made cooperation with Prussia palatable in opposition circles. On the other hand, neither Napoleon's

[36] Goltz to Bismarck, March 6, 1866 (Oncken, I, 94–6).

vagueness nor his implied desire for the Rhine was likely to appeal to Bismarck, and consequently this approach might serve to extricate Napoleon from an embarrassing position. Bismarck, in his reply to Goltz's original announcement of the French Emperor's terms, made exactly this guess. He noted that Napoleon seemed to be asking for considerably more important compensations than before and concluded that the French sovereign was trying to sabotage the negotiations. In any event, Bismarck was adamant in his declaration that Prussia could not contemplate giving up any German territory.[37]

Meanwhile, Napoleon had apparently decided from Goltz's rather unenthusiastic answer[38] to his demands on March 5, that the negotiations were approaching a standstill and had taken the step of informing Drouyn of the overtures, probably in connection with a cabinet meeting on March 7.[39] Presumably both men drafted the official answer to King William's letter, which was read to Goltz by Drouyn at a meeting in Napoleon's presence on March 7.[40] This reply was couched in the most general terms. Napoleon contented himself with assuring William of his intention of preserving benevolent neutrality and added that he would consult with the Prussians in case of a shift in the balance of power.[41] Since it would have been hard to maintain that Bismarck's schemes meant anything other

[37] Bismarck to Goltz, March 6, 1866 (GW, V, 389).

[38] Goltz to Bismarck, March 6, 1866 (Oncken, I, 97).

[39] Goltz to Bismarck, March 8, 1866 (Oncken, I, 102). Evidently Napoleon did not tell Drouyn at this time about the Prusso-Italian negotiations. All went well for some weeks; but toward the end of March, Nigra tried to ascertain the minister's views on a Prusso-Italian alliance. Drouyn was shocked to learn that the Italians were under pressure from the Prussians to make a definite agreement. He also had reason to think that he had been duped, since, only a few days previously, Napoleon had authorized him to reassure Metternich about the continued cordiality of Franco-Austrian relations. He restrained himself in front of Nigra and gave the ambassador a "very guarded" answer; but no sooner was he alone than he went to see Napoleon. He described the exchange and observed, as Cowley reported, "that he had been somewhat taken by surprise." Napoleon calmed his minister, told him that his remarks to Nigra had been correct, and instructed him to hold the same line in future conversations. See PRO: Cowley to Foreign Office, April 2, 1866 (F. O. 519/13). Despite this apparent reconciliation, the episode must have embittered the relations between master and minister.

[40] Goltz to Bismarck, March 7, 1866 (APP, VI, 635).

[41] Napoleon to William, March 7, 1866 (Oncken, I, 98–9).

than a change in the balance of power, the effect of this document was merely to postpone the negotiations and to leave the Prussians as uncertain as before. The letter was not too badly received by William, but Bismarck made no secret of his own chagrin.[42] He even said that he would have to slow down the tempo of his plans.[43] Goltz endeavored to smooth matters by emphasizing the extent of opposition to Napoleon's plans in the Corps Législatif and in other important circles; as we have already seen, there was ample reason for his picture of Napoleon as the captive of forces hostile to his designs.[44]

Meanwhile, Napoleon found himself embarrassed in another direction. Not only had he been contemplating an arrangement with the Prussians himself, he was also well aware that the Italians were seriously considering an agreement with Berlin. Such a treaty would inevitably have an inflammatory effect upon the situation, making Franco-Austrian relations more difficult. Given the virulent nationalism of large and vocal sections of the Italian population, however, it was quite unrealistic to suppose that the government could be restrained from bargaining with the Prussians unless Venetia was guaranteed to them through some other arrangement. Such thoughts must have motivated Napoleon's championship of the Moldavia-Wallachia exchange plan in mid-March, 1866. Metternich has recorded the Emperor's abrupt resumption of interest in this Italian move. On March 7, the Austrian ambassador wrote Vienna that Napoleon was no longer concerned with plans for an Austrian cession of Venetia. He advised his government to concentrate on handling the crisis as creditably as possible and to forget all thoughts of an agreement with Napoleon until the outbreak of war was imminent.[45] On March 10, the ambassador telegraphed that the French government was urging an Austro-Italian agreement based

[42] Benedetti to Drouyn de Lhuys, March 11, 1866 (*Origines*, VII, 407–11).

[43] Bismarck to Goltz, March 24, 1866 (*GW*, V, 414–5).

[44] See Goltz to Bismarck, March 8, 1866 (Oncken, I, 104–5); Goltz to William, March 17, 1866 (Oncken I, 111–3); Goltz to Bismarck, March 23, 1866 (*APP*, VI, 727–8); and Goltz to Bernstorff, March 26, 1866 (reproduced in Stolberg-Wernigerode, *Graf von der Goltz*, p. 427).

[45] HHSA: Metternich to Mensdorff, March 7, 1866, no. 9B.

on compensations and was holding open the possibility of a Franco-Austrian entente.[46] At the same time, the French were trying to discourage the Italians from closing a bargain with the Prussians.[47]

The first, and perhaps the most hopeful phase of Napoleon's efforts to bring the Austrians and the Italians together entailed the use of the Danubian principalities as compensation. Nigra had already proposed this scheme to Napoleon at the end of February. Napoleon had agreed to try to persuade London to lay the idea before the Austrians. This plan was in line with Nigra's own suggestions;[48] and the answer might have been an attempt to get rid of a controversial matter without offending the Italians. The exchange plan probably did not become really appealing to Napoleon until his negotiations with Bismarck had fallen through. In point of fact, it was on March 6, the day after Napoleon's unsatisfactory conversation with Goltz, that the Quai d'Orsay wrote to the ambassador to England, the Prince de la Tour d'Auvergne, instructing him to broach the plan to Clarendon.[49] La Tour d'Auvergne hastened to carry out this mission, but without success.[50] Clarendon agreed that the scheme was fine in theory, but he pointed to practical difficulties that, in his opinion, rendered the plan impossible. In the first place, this extension of Hapsburg territory would bring the Austrian Empire into contact with the Russians and would create new tensions.[51] (As a matter of fact, the Russians were to term the plan "inadmissible to the point of war.")[52] Secondly, the inhabitants of the principalities hated the Austrians and would certainly oppose such an arrangement. Clarendon concluded that the Austrians probably would not accept Moldavia and Wallachia in any circumstances.[53]

By now, however, with the new revelation of the obstacles to an

[46] HHSA: Metternich to Mensdorff, March 10, 1866, no. 26.
[47] Benedetti to Drouyn de Lhuys, March 11, 1866 (Origines, VII, 410).
[48] Bush, pp. 64–6.
[49] Drouyn de Lhuys to La Tour d'Auvergne, March 6, 1866 (Origines, VII, 380–1).
[50] La Tour d'Auvergne to Drouyn de Lhuys, March 9, 1866 (Origines, VII, 395–6).
[51] Ollivier, VIII, 44.
[52] Talleyrand to Drouyn de Lhuys, March 14, 1866 (Origines, VII, 433).
[53] Ollivier, VIII, 44.

agreement with Prussia, Napoleon had become seriously interested in this exchange plan and he was not content to let the matter rest. Clarendon's answer was received on March 11.[54] On or about March 12, Napoleon tried a more direct step. He had attempted to discuss the Venetian question with Metternich at the time of the Polish crisis and had offended that diplomat so deeply that, in order to mollify him, he had had to promise that he would never mention the subject again. Consequently, it was necessary to work through Eugénie; but since she and the Austrian ambassador were the best of friends, this was no disadvantage. About March 12, Eugénie summoned Metternich to her private cabinet. She laid before him a letter from Talleyrand, the French ambassador to St. Petersburg. In this dispatch, Talleyrand exposed the exchange plan, supposedly on his own initiative. He observed that the Russian government would be greatly upset by such an arrangement, but suggested that at the present time, the Russian state was too weak to take preventive action. Eugénie supported this letter with a genuine oration: she declared that Venetia was the only problem separating France and Austria; and assured the ambassador that if the Ballplatz would adopt a sensible attitude on this matter it would be possible to find a solution which would be the signal for both the French and the Italians to rally to Austria's side. There was a great deal more in the same vein. Metternich listened with a mixture of outrage and stupe-faction. As soon as she had finished, he burst out that "her counsels ... (were) of a nature to ... cut off our arms and legs." He persisted in seeing the suggestion as something closely akin to betrayal and informed Eugénie outright that her husband lacked "that diplomatic finesse, that *instinct for nuances and for opportunities* which in politics, seems to me of the first necessity and the essential condition *for success.*" Metternich was so little master of himself that he proceeded to prove his point with details from the Polish crisis. He finally concluded with a restatement of his opposition to the ex-

[54] La Tour d'Auvergne to Drouyn de Lhuys, March 9, 1866 (*Origines*, VII, 395).

change plan and with only the barest hints of a possible change in attitude in the event of basic revision of the European order.[55]

It might be expected that this conversation would have ended the exchange plan, if not Franco-Austrian relations, but Napoleon was not daunted. A few days later, Eugénie approached the Austrian ambassador again. She made a great joke of Metternich's burst of temper and said she had repeated his comments word for word to Napoleon. She added "that they admitted frankly that they understood nothing of diplomacy and that in effect the Emperor repented of certain mistakes *of bad timing* committed by him." Eugénie then told Metternich about the confidential disclosures of a French spy in Austria. This source credited a member of the Austrian ministry with a variation of the exchange plan in which the loss of Venetia would be compensated by the gain of territory in the area of Bosnia and Herzogovina. This scheme had something to recommend it, since the Bosnia-Herzogovina region was as far from the Russian border as any part of the Balkans and formed a relatively unobjectionable sphere for Austrian expansion, as was discovered the time of the Congress of Berlin. Metternich, however, liked this proposition no better than that of the principalities. He admitted that such an idea was current in Vienna, but attributed it to Gramont, the French ambassador, and added that he had been very much disappointed to learn of the démarche. He concluded "that it was impossible that such a blunder could be committed by an Austrian, everyone in Austria being in agreement in defending the important maritime and military position in Venetia by all possible means." [56] Metternich's reaction made the impossibility of the plan

[55] HHSA: Metternich to Mensdorff, March 22, 1866, no. 12B.

[56] HHSA: Metternich to Mensdorff, March 22, 1866, no. 12B. It is hard to say what was the provenance of this scheme. For evidence to be found in French correspondence that the plan had been circulating in Vienna see Drouyn de Lhuys to Gramont, March 13, 1866 (*Origines,* VII, 420); Mensdorff to Metternich, March 16, 1866 (Oncken, I, 110); Gramont to Drouyn de Lhuys, March 17, 1866 (*Origines,* VIII, 11–2); it was not merely a product of Napoleon's mind. Nigra reported a rumor that Gramont had discussed the principalities exchange plan with

quite evident; and if corroboration were needed, it was soon forth-coming in a firm rejection by Mensdorff.[57]

The attempt to deal with Metternich had been a dismal failure. Napoleon and Eugénie hastened to extricate themselves by turning the negotiations over to Drouyn de Lhuys who was quickly in-formed of Napoleon's proceedings. Drouyn had a long talk with Metternich, in which he tried to calm him. This was a task for which Drouyn was better fitted than anyone else (Eugénie being disqualified for the moment by her earlier overtures) and he seems to have been relatively successful. Metternich asked for and received solemn assurances on two points: first, that the question of Venetia would·not be raised again unless circumstances caused a general redrawing of boundaries; second, that this rejection would not have an adverse effect upon Franco-Austrian relations. Metternich was particularly anxious about the last point, as well he might have been.[58] Although Drouyn was unaware of the Prusso-Italian nego-tiations,[59] he still believed it advisable to consult Napoleon before definitely reassuring Metternich that Franco-Austrian relations would continue unchanged. He received this corroboration and in-formed Metternich of the good news on the morning of March 22.[60] Thus ended this phase of the negotiations—or so Metternich thought.

Napoleon's true reaction to the failure of the exchange plan was

---

the Ballplatz. It is possible that this was the overture Metternich had in mind and that either he or Nigra was mistaken as to the content. Ollivier claims that he had studied all of Gramont's letters and had found no trace of such conversations (Ol-livier, VIII, 44, n. 2); but since Gramont's correspondence with Drouyn indicates that the Foreign Minister was ignorant of the matter (Drouyn de Lhuys to Gra-mont, March 13, 1866 [*Origines*, VII, 420]), such a démarche would have been made either on Gramont's own initiative or through instructions from some source other than the Quai d'Orsay, of which there might be no written record. Gramont himself assigned the project to members of the Austrian ministry (Gramont to Drouyn de Lhuys, March 17, 1866 [*Origines*, VIII, 11–2]). Although he is hardly an impartial witness, this story is probably the most credible.

[57] Mensdorff to Metternich, March 16, 1866 (Oncken, I, 110–1).

[58] HHSA: Metternich to Mensdorff, March 22, 1866, no. 12B.

[59] Goltz to Bismarck, March 8, 1866 (Oncken, I, 102) and see above note 39, this chapter.

[60] HHSA: Metternich to Mensdorff, March 22, 1866, no. 12B.

quite different. Of course, Metternich had left the door ajar for further discussions by saying that the Ballplatz might reconsider the Venetian question if the map of Europe were redrawn. This would be almost inevitable in the case of war. The general idea in Austrian circles at that time was to try by means of war to annex Prussian territory in Silesia in return for which Venetia could be ceded to Italy.[61] This scheme was attractive to the Austrians' *amour-propre,* since the humiliating loss of Venetia would be more than balanced by the triumph over a historic enemy in a historic area of controversy. Even without benefit of hindsight, this contingent arrangement looks insecure, although some politicians, sincerely dedicated to the cause of Italian, though not of Prussian, nationalism felt that it offered a solution. Among those was Napoleon's cousin, Prince Napoleon, better known as Plon-plon.[62] Napoleon did not share his cousin's views. It is possible that he was animated by pro-Prussian sentiment here, for the Silesian exchange would have been a severe blow to the Prussian monarchy. It seems most likely, however, that after his thorny experiences with Metternich, he had simply become irritated past bearing and had given up hope of a negotiated solution. He was to say to Nigra: *"Don't cherish any illusions. Austria will not cede Venetia unless she is forced to it by war."* [63] As result of such thinking,[64] Napoleon secretly told Nigra on March 21 to advise his government to go ahead with the Prussian treaty.[65]

Negotiations had been going on between Berlin and Florence, and it was soon possible for the two governments to agree on a draft treaty. The plan, as communicated to Drouyn de Lhuys by Benedetti on March 27, called for an alliance which was to last for three months or for the duration of the war. The treaty was disadvantageous to the Italians because they promised to aid Prussia if she should declare war, although Prussia did not make the equivalent

---

[61] PRO: Cowley to Clarendon, March 20, 1866 (F. O. 519/232).
[62] PRO: Cowley to Clarendon, March 29, 1866 (F. O. 519/232).
[63] La Marmora, p. 136.
[64] Clark, p. 406.
[65] Goltz to Bismarck, March 23, 1866 (Oncken, I, 121, n. 1).

promise with regard to Italy.[66] This aspect of the treaty worried the Italians and they needed considerable reassurance before they agreed to it.[67] Further articles provided for the acquisition of Venetia by Italy and the assignment of "territories equivalent in population" to Prussia.[68] This draft was eventually to be signed unchanged in any of these major provisions;[69] but, before that event, much maneuvering took place behind the scenes as result of a perplexing change of position by Napoleon III.

The confusion started on March 24 when Nigra telegraphed new information to his chief about French policy. He had heard that Napoleon had said that France could not aid Italy in an offensive attack on Austria. Meanwhile, Drouyn de Lhuys was taking a similarly discouraging line: he had remarked that "if Italy attacks Austria, she will do it upon her own responsibility (à ses risques et périls)." [70] The Foreign Minister had implied that things might be different if the situation were reversed. France might rescue the Italians from an Austrian attack. However, in view of the shape of the projected treaty, this reassurance was not too helpful. La Marmora had reason to feel that Napoleon was abandoning the position implied in his previous advice to accept the treaty. To clarify matters, he decided to send Count Arese, who knew Napoleon personally, on a special mission to Paris.[71]

La Marmora was not the only one mystified by Napoleon's actions. Plon-plon found himself in a similar position. After attending the opening of the Corps Législatif in Paris at the end of January,[72] he had left for Italy in February, free from official worries and responsibilities. What was his surprise on reaching Reggio in March to observe a most unusual busyness among the army. Plon-plon, intrigued and suspicious, hastened to Florence to discover what was

---

[66] Benedetti to Drouyn de Lhuys, March 27, 1866 (Origines, VIII, 75–6).
[67] Ollivier, VIII, 57–8.
[68] Benedetti to Drouyn de Lhuys, March 27, 1866 (Origines, VIII, 76).
[69] Benedetti to Drouyn de Lhuys, April 9, 1866 (Origines, VIII, 200).
[70] La Marmora, pp. 134–8.
[71] La Marmora, pp. 134–8.
[72] Annales (1866), I, 2.

going on.[73] He was received with the courtesy customary to the man who was at once Napoleon's cousin, Victor Emmanuel's son-in-law,[74] and a notorious pro-Italian. La Marmora was only too happy to unburden himself on the progress of negotiations with Berlin and gave the Prince the full story of his anxieties.[75] All this gave Plon-plon something to think about. Although he was a noted champion of Italian nationalism, he did not feel the same sympathy for the German cause. He strongly suspected that Bismarck would be forced from office before he had brought his plans to fruition and, although he had heard rumors in February about Prussian overtures to Italy, he put no faith in them whatsoever.[76] He believed that Italy's true interest lay in support of the Austrians, with the hope that if the Hapsburgs were assured of aid in winning territory in Silesia, they would be willing to promise Venetia to the Italians.[77] It was a shock to the Prince to learn from La Marmora's revelations that Italy was so far advanced on a contrary course, and on March 28 he rushed to Paris to talk to Napoleon.[78]

Napoleon was faced at the end of March with both Count Arese and his cousin. His explanations were not designed to reassure the Italians. Arese was told that Napoleon did indeed advocate the conclusion of a treaty with Berlin, but this advice was "a counsel as a friend and without any responsibility." Meanwhile, Drouyn de Lhuys continued to be indefinite, while in Berlin Benedetti had assumed a dampening attitude.[79] The French commitment was summarized as follows in a telegram from Nigra on March 29: France would aid the Italians in case of need arising from either

---

[73] Ollivier, VIII, 54.

[74] François Berthet-Leleux, *Le Vrai Prince Napoléon* (Paris [1932]), p. 96.

[75] Ollivier, VIII, 54–5.

[76] Prince Napoleon to Queen Sophie of Holland, February 1866 *(Papiers et correspondance de la famille impériale,* 3 vols., Paris, 1870–[72?], I, 389–90).

[77] PRO: Cowley to Clarendon, March 29, 1866 (F. O. 519/232).

[78] Ollivier, VIII, 55. It is possible that Ollivier dates this episode a few days too late, for according to La Marmora's account (pp. 134–8) the Prince was in Paris on March 24.

[79] Bush, pp. 73–4.

of two contingencies: an Austrian attack, or a separate peace between Austria and Prussia.[80] The sum of these implications from the various French sources was certainly disquieting for the Italians. Even if Arese did not manage to extract any more explicit statement from Napoleon, this much seemed clear: the Emperor had thought better of his broad consent to a Prusso-Italian treaty.

The result was hardly surprising. La Marmora, who had always regarded Bismarck's enticements with suspicion, made a new effort in Vienna. At the end of March, he had a long talk with Landauer, a banker connected with the Rothschilds. La Marmora expressed serious doubts as to Italian chances in a war and pleaded again for the cession of Venetia. In return, he offered either a sum of money or diplomatic aid in working out one or another of the exchange plans already suggested. The proposals in short contained no major new suggestions, and the Austrians proved no more receptive than before. On March 30, Baron Anselm Rothschild brought the propositions to the attention of Mensdorff and Esterhazy in Vienna, but his overtures were firmly refused.[81] With this new evidence of Austrian recalcitrance, there was nothing La Marmora could do, in light of the overwhelming popular desire for Venetia, except to go ahead with the Prussian treaty as planned and to hope for the best. There is no direct evidence as to what Napoleon thought about the project at this date. It seems quite likely that he continued skeptical. Plon-plon on his mission to Italy of April 1[82] may or may not have carried negative advice; but it is certain that in Berlin Benedetti, who was presumably in communication with Napoleon, made a last-minute attempt to forbid the treaty.[83] This proved impossible,

---

[80] La Marmora, pp. 139–41.

[81] Bush, pp. 74–5.

[82] Oncken, I, 123, n. 2.

[83] It is impossible to do more than record without resolving the conflicting tales of this incident. Napoleon told Arese that Plon-plon's trip had no political objective (La Marmora, p. 139), but this seems barely credible; it is more likely that Napoleon suppressed his cousin's real purpose to avoid insulting Arese by suggesting that a second mission was necessary, parallel to his own. Ollivier reports that the Prince was charged with a double message: to assure Victor Emmanuel that France

and the Prusso-Italian Treaty was finally signed on April 8, 1866.[84] Even before the conclusion of the alliance, Bismarck had demonstrated his increased confidence by drawing up a plan for reform of the German Confederation for submission to the Diet.[85] There can be no doubt that the new agreement greatly increased the likelihood of war and the situation began to assume an ever more ominous cast. Meanwhile, Napoleon chose this moment to divert himself with the youthful Countess Mercy-Argenteau. If Mérimée, the court poet, is to be believed, the countess was not a tribute to the Emperor's taste: Mérimée referred to her as "a beauty of the Olympic variety." [86]

The countess could provide only a temporary diversion. The Prusso-Italian Treaty created a fundamental and inescapable dilemma for the French Emperor. This fact explains the contortions of policy which contemporaries found puzzling. Napoleon had long had a sympathetic attachment to the cause of Italian nationalism, dating from the days of his youthful participation in the movement. In addition to these romantic connections, he had recently, in the events of 1859, gone on record in the arena of European diplomacy as the champion of Italian aspirations. Although balance-of-power diplomats were not noted for their consistency, it is difficult to see how Napoleon could have reversed his pro-Italian stand without suffering a public humiliation, as well as a certain amount of personal

would help Italy if Prussia abandoned her ally through a separate peace and to advise acceptance of the treaty despite the inequality in commitment to aid an attack, which has already been noted (Ollivier, VIII, 57). This may be true. However, it seems possible that Ollivier may have been misled through a misunderstanding of the extent of Napoleon's belated hostility to the treaty. It is worth mentioning that the Landauer overtures, the apparent outcome of this opposition, were so secret that there is no mention of them in the Quai d'Orsay documents. (Bush's account, pp. 74–5, is drawn from Gramont's private papers at the Archives Nationales.) It is unlikely that Napoleon intended to have Plon-plon and Benedetti working at cross-purposes; but it is not inconceivable that Napoleon once again regarded the treaty as inevitable and that Benedetti was acting upon outdated instructions in his simultaneous attempts to stop the treaty (Bush, pp. 76–7).

[84] For the text of the Treaty, see *Origines*, VIII, 462–3.
[85] Benedetti to Drouyn de Lhuys, April 3, 1866 (*Origines*, VIII, 153–4).
[86] Mérimée, *Panizzi*, II, 188.

distress. During the years since the proclamation of the Kingdom of Italy, the question of French support had been largely academic. Troubled only by the perpetually embarrassing Roman question, Franco-Italian relations had suffered no major crises: there had been no moment of decision when Napoleon had been asked to reaffirm or contradict his sponsorship of a free Italy. But, nonetheless, he had created a hostage to fortune, and the Prusso-Italian alliance brought this fact into new prominence. From the entire text of the treaty, the personality and ambitions of Bismarck, and the Prussian minister's immediate initiation of a reform plan for the Confederation, it was clear that the treaty would almost certainly become the basis for a wartime alliance. The question that faced Napoleon was, would this alliance be successful? Or would the Italians, suffering defeat, find themselves at the mercy of an Austrian government whose most cherished wish was to undo the work of unification?

Unhappily for Napoleon's peace of mind, the general expectation in almost all circles in France in the spring and early summer of 1866 was that Austria would win. Such opposing observers as Bismarck and Metternich concluded that Napoleon himself believed in Austrian success.[87] It is possible, as Bapst reports, that Napoleon thought for a brief time in May, 1866, that the Prussians might win. However, if Napoleon wavered, his doubt was short-lived. General Desvaux, who had just toured the Austrian army, was in Paris in May and in three conversations with Napoleon gave him glowing reports of the condition of the Austrian forces. On the basis of this information, Napoleon decided that the war would be a long one,[88] and on the eve of the war, according to Metternich, he once again thought that the Austrians would win.[89]

Napoleon's views as to Austrian superiority must have been the stronger because they were shared by most of the people around

---

[87] For Bismarck's views, see Loë, *Erinnerungen aus meinem Berufsleben 1849–67,* p. 80; for Metternich's, Metternich to Mensdorff, June 29, 1866 (Oncken, I, 285, and n. 4).

[88] Germain Bapst, *Le Maréchal Canrobert,* 5 vols. (Paris, 1898–1911), IV, 35–6.

[89] Oncken, I, 285, n. 4.

him. The most cursory survey indicates the prevalence of this conviction in court circles. Eugénie believed it.[90] Drouyn de Lhuys quoted it as the conclusion of the army experts.[91] Plon-plon remarked to an Italian friend: "I wish, both for the sake of Italy and for the sake of France, that you would be able to get on without us; but I fear either that the Prussians will not fight, or that they will be disastrously beaten, and you may have more Austrians on your back than you can manage." [92]

It would have been difficult for Napoleon to escape the influence of this climate of opinion at court; but the views of the army must have been still more influential. Despite Drouyn's confident assertions, army opinion was apparently divided, for testimony favoring the Prussians as well as the Austrians exists.[93] There were two groups. The Minister of War, Marshal Randon, believed firmly in Austrian success. Randon based his faith not only on traditional Austrian prestige but also on the record of Austrian performance.[94] When Loë, the Prussian military attaché, came to say good-by to him, on the eve of the war, the departing soldier even noticed "a certain pity" in the Minister's manner.[95] Similar opinions were quite generally held in the French army.[96] Ironic as these expectations look in the light of later events, there was reason for holding them at the time, for according to rumor they were shared by important military figures in the Prussian army itself.[97] But Randon and his intimates, however important, represented the old guard. Randon himself was a veteran of the first Napoleon's Russian campaign and had also participated in the disastrous march across Germany and France in 1813–14. Sentimentally speaking, this was fine background for a minister of the Second Empire; but although Randon was

[90] Metternich to Mensdorff, May 16, 1866 (Oncken, I, 204–5).
[91] Goltz to Bismarck, May 18, 1866 (Oncken, I, 213).
[92] Mérimée, Panizzi, II, 202.
[93] Goltz to William, April 21, 1866 (Oncken, I, 138).
[94] Randon, Mémoires, II, 206.
[95] Loë, p. 89.
[96] Bapst, IV, 34.
[97] Fournier to Drouyn de Lhuys, May 9, 1866 (Origines, IX, 84).

generally praised for being "sound," he was elderly[98] and not sufficiently venturesome. In contrast, a group of younger men had
emerged. This circle included young generals like Bourbaki,
Leboeuf, and Trochu. Although they stood in the position of
"coming men," none of them were "coming" as fast as they might
reasonably have expected; Trochu, for example, was notoriously
disgruntled.[99] Probably the ablest was Bourbaki. He was convinced
that the Prussians would win. In this view, he was joined by one or
two others, like Berckheim and Février. Bourbaki was in an especially good position to judge, for he had been sent to observe the
annual maneuvers of the Prussian army at Spandau about two years
previously.[100] Against the picture of Randon's farewell to Loë, one
may set the story of Bourbaki. When Loë came to see him, Bourbaki
remarked that he believed that the Prussians would win the war with
ease. Loë pointed out that this opinion was heresy in French army
circles; Bourbaki represented merely the lunatic fringe. Bourbaki
answered prophetically that France might pay highly for this mis-
conception.[101]

The belief in Austrian success was not limited to high army circles
and to those official quarters of the government where the point of
view was based in large part on official military information. Faith
in Austria's victory seems to have been widespread throughout
France (and indeed Europe). For example, as evidence of the train
of thought of the intelligentsia, Thiers' friend, Duvergier de Hauranne, wrote at the end of June that the Austrians, having already
beaten the Italians, would certainly go on to defeat the Prussians.[102]
And as a sample of sentiment in the country at large one may cite
the July report of the Procureur Général at Colmar: he declared that

[98] Loë, p. 78.
[99] Loë, p. 78.
[100] Bapst, IV, 34.
[101] Loë, pp. 88–9.
[102] BN: Duvergier de Hauranne to Thiers, June 27, 1866 (Nouvelles acquisitions
françaises XIX, 20619).

the smashing Prussian victory at Sadowa was hailed with great astonishment.[103]

How could an entire country, practically without exception, have fallen into a miscalculation so gross in its proportions and so grave in its consequences? This demands examination in specific terms of the knowledge upon which French thought was based and of the direction in which the reasoning proceeded. While the man in the street may have been deluded by past Austrian glories which, unbeknown to him, had developed a bad case of dry rot, the military experts were in possession of full information and were studying it with a logic which is still persuasive, even by hindsight.

The Italian situation was probably the simplest and the least controversial. The chief reporter here was Colonel Schmitz, sent on a special mission to ascertain the state of Italian military preparations at the beginning of April, 1866.[104] Schmitz was a good choice. He had seen long service under Marshal Randon; he was sincere in his efforts, businesslike in his investigations, sober and balanced in his judgments, and obviously dedicated, in a matter-of-fact, unpretentious way, to his duties. Probably the explanation of his relatively simple assignment lies in his poor health. He wrote Colson resignedly at the end of the spring: "My health is bad; I would have needed to take the waters for my frightful kidney ailments; but instead of going to the waters I will go to the fire." [105]

Schmitz's reports were discouraging from the beginning, but this should have surprised no one who had the slightest knowledge of conditions in Italy. It did seem that the Italians had an advantage in the actual number of men in the field. Figures varied from week to week as the processes of mobilization and concentration continued, but the Italians, after a slow start, gathered the more numerous army.

---

[103] AN: Nancy, report of July 28, 1866 (BB³⁰381 Nancy 1866–68).

[104] Vincennes: Ordre de la Division no. 1, April 12, 1866, issued by General Pécard (Correspondance Générale G⁸114).

[105] Vincennes: Schmitz to Colson, June 1, 1866, no. 9.

At the end of April, Schmitz wrote that the Italian army consisted at that time of 260,768 men.[106] Against this, the Austrians had only 80,720 soldiers currently in Venetia, but with the arrival of reinforcements it was expected that Austrian forces would number 450,000 within three weeks.[107] Schmitz calculated that these paper figures would be reduced in an actual engagement. He estimated that at the beginning of May the Austrians would be able to put 150,000 men into the field in case of a pitched battle, while the Italians would be able to muster a force of upwards of 90,000, a ludicrously smaller body.[108] However, at the end of May, Schmitz reported that the Italian army numbered 192,000 men, not counting Garibaldi's 29,000 volunteers, while 145,000 would be available for replacements before January 1, 1867. The Austrians were now definitely outclassed, for Schmitz wrote that they had only 140,000 men in Venetia and could not concentrate more than 90,000 in a specific engagement. These figures seem relatively reliable, since they dealt with existing situations and not with paper estimates or plans for the future. Schmitz commented: "A month ago, no one in Europe believed in a real Italian army; if it were not too rash I would say that the country itself didn't believe in it. Today, the tangible affirmative dissipates the doubt.—One can no longer discuss anything except the intensity of the force." [109]

This was an astute remark, and Schmitz's observations throughout May had not been such as to relieve his anxiety. Early in May, he reported that the government had been lying about the number of men on leave; there were not, as was claimed, a number sufficient to bring the army units up to their full wartime quotas.[110] The next

[106] Vincennes: Schmitz, "Etat approximatif des forces italiennes," April 26, 1866, no. 8; the picture given after the fact by Chiala is more optimistic. See J. V. Lemoyne, ed. and trans., *Campagne de 1866 en Italie* (Paris, 1875).

[107] Vincennes: Schmitz, "Situation des troupes autrichiennes en Vénétie à la date du 15 Avril 1866," no. 10.

[108] Schmitz to Randon, April 27, 1866 (*Origines*, VIII, 355).

[109] Vincennes: Schmitz to Napoleon, May 31, 1866, no. 25.

[110] Vincennes: Schmitz, "Note sur la journée du 7 Mai, à Florence," May 8, 1866, no. 14.

day, he wrote a very discouraging description of the troops he had seen at Bologna, but added that he hoped the situation would have improved by the time the month was over.[111] One of the most serious problems, however, was the lack of horses; Schmitz declared that many were being purchased abroad, but suggested that much time would be necessary before the army would be adequately supplied.[112]

The gist of Schmitz's reports was that the Italians had more soldiers than the Austrians, but that their quality was not as good. Schmitz pointed out that the army lacked esprit de corps, since it was made up of contingents from various parts of a nation so newly unified that, whatever the sentimental ties, specific associations between different areas had not had a chance to develop. This disunity among the men was, incidentally, compounded by the differences between Victor Emmanuel and La Marmora in the top command. Schmitz also suspected that many of the soldiers, who had started off with enthusiasm, would quickly turn against the war if they found that it necessitated a long struggle which would keep them away from their homes for a prolonged period. Unfortunately, an army of this sort was particularly ill-qualified to fight in the campaign ahead, since the Austrians, although they might have to deploy a certain number of troops to police the restive southern provinces of the Empire, were well placed for a defensive struggle from the famous fortresses of the Quadrilateral. The capture of these key points would require an army of far more professional skill than the Italians possessed. Essentially, success against the Hapsburg Empire required science rather than numbers, and it was clear that in this respect the Italians fell far short.[113]

These facts raise the question as to why the Prussians were so eager to ally with a power whose military weakness seemed patent. Unfortunately, it is impossible at the present time to muster a body

[111] Vincennes: Schmitz to Randon, May 9, 1866, no. 17.
[112] Vincennes: Schmitz to Randon, May 31, 1866, no. 23.
[113] Vincennes: Schmitz, "Aperçu général sur les conditions actuelles des armées italiennes et autrichiennes," May 12, 1866, no. 20; see also Merlin to Randon, April 25, 1866, no. 2.

of Prussian military reports and comments equivalent to those produced by Schmitz. However, the publication of Moltke's military papers does something to fill this gap, especially when these documents are studied in conjunction wtih the hints contained in the published diplomatic correspondence and with the deductions which can be drawn from Prussian actions.

It is justifiable to assume that the Prussians were no more optimistic than the French about Italian strength, that Schmitz was probably right when he said that all Europe shared his doubts. Moltke himself had some opportunity to study the Italian situation at first hand when he was sent to Florence to negotiate the treaty; evidently he was not impressed. He assured Bismarck that though the Italians claimed they could gather from 250,000 to 280,000 men for attack, in actuality only about 200,000 might be available. And, although Moltke did not record his observations as fully as did Schmitz, he did note that the effectiveness of these troops was dubious.[114]

Purely military considerations were only part of the Prussians' concern. Further indications of Italian weakness could be found in the very shaky financial situation, a matter which was no secret to the Prussians. Usedom, the Prussian ambassador in Florence, pointed out that the Italians might serve their interests best if they used the crisis to persuade the Austrians to sell Venetia and then disbanded the army and lowered governmental expenses. He estimated that the strain of buying Venetia outright would be considerably easier to bear than the indefinite long-term pressure of maintaining a large army.[115] Bismarck himself doubted that the Italians could keep their forces at the 1866 level for any length of time.[116] This evidence of a low estimate of Italian power is corroborated by the extreme Prussian reluctance to consider a treaty which would have become

---

[114] Moltke to Bismarck, March 20, 1866 (Helmuth von Moltke, *Militärische Werke*, 13 vols. [Berlin, 1892–1912], vol. I, pt. 2, pp. 54–7).

[115] Usedom to Bismarck, November 4, 1865 (*APP*, VI, 454).

[116] Protocol of the meeting of the Crown Council, February 28, 1866 (*APP*, VI, 615).

operative if the Italians started the war. There were many reasons for the Prussian decision to limit the effectiveness of the alliance to the case of a Prussian declaration of war, but confidence in the Italian military establishment was certainly not one of them.[117]

Yet despite the discouraging caliber of the Italian soldiers, there were sound and obvious arguments in favor of the alliance. The greatest benefit, from the Prussian point of view, was the enormous strategic advantage of engaging the Austrians in a two-front war. Even if the Italian campaign was a mere holding action, it would tie up a sufficient number of Austrian troops to improve Prussian chances in the north by eliminating, at least at the outset, the superiority in manpower which some observers believed the greatest Austrian asset. Bismarck's concern with this factor appears in a marginal note penciled on a dispatch from Usedom. The ambassador had mentioned that the Italians, through a separate peace, might leave the Prussians to fight the Austrians alone; Bismarck, evidently thinking of the consequences for Prussia, scribbled, "and afterwards?" [118] Moltke made elaborate calculations which show clearly how much the Prussians needed Italian aid.[119] He summarized this technical planning for a civilian audience at a meeting of the Crown Council held on February 28, 1866. He asserted that if the Italians attacked in the south, the Austrians would be unable to put more than 240,000 men in the field in the Bohemian theater; the Prussians would be able to match this performance, even if they were forced to hold a small contingent (52,000 men) against Bavaria. Moltke believed, on this basis, that an arrangement with Italy was an "indispensable condition for the war." [120]

Since the Italian contribution was viewed as a holding action, it would be in Bohemia, in the direct conflict between Prussia and

[117] Cf. Sybel, *The Founding of the German Empire*, IV, 330.

[118] Usedom to Bismarck, February 7, 1866 (*APP*, VI, 574).

[119] See, for example, Moltke to Bismarck, March 20, 1866, and Anlagen (Moltke, vol. I, pt. 2, pp. 53–61).

[120] Moltke's notes on the meeting of the Crown Council, February 28, 1866 (*APP*, VI, 618).

Austria, that the major decisions would be made. The real interest, therefore, lay in the evaluation of Prussian strength; and in comparing the two German great powers French estimates became both complex and controversial. The difficulties were compounded by the striking contrast in character between the two attachés whose reports formed the basis for French judgments. Clermont-Tonnerre, the French military attaché in Berlin, was a thoroughly competent observer, whose letters give a completely accurate picture of conditions in the Prussian army. Unfortunately, his presentation did not enhance the credibility of his material. His style was taciturn and matter-of-fact; he did nothing to embellish his information or to underline the more important or ominous details. To the extent that one can trace a consciousness of his audience, servility substitutes for dedication. It would seem that his heart was not really in his work as an attaché.[121] Completely different was the character and approach —and also the accuracy—of the French attaché in Vienna, Merlin. He had had far less experience in his post. While Clermont-Tonnerre had spent several years in Berlin, Merlin arrived in Austria on April 22, 1866. He was very pleasantly received by the Austrians and emphasized throughout his early reports the kind and confidential manner with which he was treated.[122] Unfortunately, Merlin was both vain and trustful; he was almost pathetically inclined to believe anything that was told him, however improbable, by anyone of importance who treated him as a friend. The resultant reports were sometimes rather extraordinary; but they were lent verisimilitude by the fact that the same confiding, eager nature which contributed to his undoubted charm and to his so-called friendships gave his letters a direct, enthusiastic, colorful style, whch, especially in contrast to that of Clermont-Tonnerre, could be highly persuasive.[123]

A tendency to accept information without careful checking was

---

[121] Vincennes: Clermont-Tonnerre to Colson, May 9, 1866, no. 77, reinforces this impression of the attaché's disgruntlement with his work although the letter is too allusive to be completely comprehensible.

[122] Merlin to Randon, April 25, 1866 (*Origines*, VIII, 335); Vincennes: Merlin to Colson, May 5, 1866, no. 4; Merlin to Colson, May 17, 1866, no. 5.

[123] Cf. Loë, p. 80.

probably enhanced by Merlin's worries about his wife. She had been seriously ill when he left Paris. She had followed him belatedly to Vienna; but she did not like her new home. Merlin's concern and his unprofessional candor are exemplified by this extract from a semi-official letter to the War Ministry:

My wife has a lot of trouble getting along in this country. Ignorance of the language makes her life so to speak passive. It is true that in society people often speak French, but there is no more society, everyone has left for the country; now, in daily life there is no French, cabs, shops, porters, all those people speak only German. As for me I am often absent, running about my business, she gets sad and I fear for her health. At least I hope that there will be an improvement in the country where we are going probably to settle in the neighborhood of our chancellor, of M. Brenon and various other French people.[124]

Merlin's preoccupations may have taken up valuable time, but his anxieties, unlike Clermont-Tonnerre's basic distaste for his job, did nothing to hamper the persuasive tone of his reports. So, judged simply from the character and circumstances of the two attachés, the Austrian reports had the virtue of effectiveness, if not accuracy. The difficulty in evaluating the two sets of reports was compounded by the fact that much of the correspondence, in both cases, dealt with details such as organization, morale, composition of the officer staff, and the financial situation of the two countries. These matters were to prove relatively unimportant in the face of the Prussians' great technical advance in the needle gun; but since such considerations had always been vital in the past the French War Ministry could not wisely have discounted them. In these secondary factors the advantage was not always with the Prussians.

Clermont-Tonnerre had been reporting since the winter of 1865–66 that the Prussians were extraordinarily advanced in the training of the new recruits. Maneuvers which usually began in early February or at the earliest in late January were already underway in December, 1865.[125] Not only was the course begun ahead of schedule; it was

---

[124] Vincennes: Merlin to Colson, May 27, 1866, no. 8.
[125] Vincennes: Clermont-Tonnerre to Randon, December 27, 1865, no. 63.

also speeded up, so that the royal review was to be held early in February. At the same time, Clermont-Tonnerre announced that thanks to special steps the army would be completely furnished with the new and far superior cannons with rifled barrels by the summer of 1866; and measures were being taken in some areas to instruct officers in the use of the new weapons.[126] Finally, Clermont-Tonnerre reported at the beginning of May that Moltke had assured him that the Prussian army could be ready to fight in eighteen days. Clermont-Tonnerre cautiously estimated that this figure was overoptimistic; but he did believe that mobilization could be completed in twenty-five days.[127] The advantage which the Prussians derived from the speed and efficiency toward which the General Staff had organized the mobilization plans became a commonplace after 1870; but this tradition had not yet been well established and early efforts to save time through a rationalization of mobilization procedures were not widely understood. Loë noted upon his return to France after the war that Napoleon had difficulty in grasping his description of these plans; both Napoleon and Randon had been surprised by the rapidity with which the Prussian army prepared for action in 1866.[128] Even before the event, however, it should have been evident that the Prussians had the advantage. The ever enthusiastic Merlin, despite some praise for Austrian mobilization procedures,[129] admitted that it was too frequently the Austrian practice "to say . . . no and do yes";[130] and he felt that the Austrians might suffer from the over-complexity of their military plans and from their lack of flexibility.[131]

If, however, reports indicated that the Prussians might have better mobilization procedures, they also made it evident that Austrian morale was higher. Clermont-Tonnerre observed that the Prussian army envisaged the war "without pleasure, almost without confi-

[126] Vincennes: Clermont-Tonnerre to Randon, January 31, 1866, no. 63 bis.
[127] Vincennes: Clermont-Tonnerre to Randon, May 2, 1866, no. 71.
[128] Loë, p. 128.
[129] Merlin to Randon, May 13, 1866 (Origines, IX, 130).
[130] Merlin to Randon, April 28, 1866 (Origines, VIII, 384).
[131] Merlin to Randon, June 19, 1866 (Origines, X, 226).

dence";[132] and also revealed that the prospect of war was ill-received by the public at large.[133] This information was corroborated by the French ambassador in Frankfurt.[134] Meanwhile Merlin's reports suggested a far more cheerful tone in Vienna. Merlin did criticize the Austrian officers on the grounds that in too many cases they had been selected for social position rather than for military talent;[135] but he also reported that Benedek, the commander in the northern theater, had stipulated upon taking over his commission that promotions would be based on merit;[136] and a recent pamphlet in the possession of the French government indicated that advancement according to talent was increasingly the rule.[137] As for the soldiers, Merlin suspected that they lacked the "sacred fire";[138] but he noted that the prospect of fighting Prussia "continues to be more and more popular." He pointed out that there were large numbers of volunteers,[139] a fact which tended to confirm his earlier report that the war was very popular with the civilian population at least in Vienna,[140] as well as with the army.

One other point of comparison was the financial resources of each country. Figures within the possession of the French government revealed the very heavy military expenditures made by both Austria and Prussia in 1865 and showed a large Austrian deficit.[141] This constituted a real burden and Clermont-Tonnerre reported in 1866 that both Austria and Prussia would find it difficult to continue to finance

---

[132] Clermont-Tonnerre to Randon, May 9, 1866 (*Origines,* IX, 73).

[133] Clermont-Tonnerre to Randon, May 18, 1866 (*Origines,* IX, 176).

[134] Reculot to Drouyn de Lhuys, May 20, 1866 (*Origines,* IX, 198–9).

[135] Vincennes: Merlin to Randon, May 30, 1866, no. 10.

[136] Vincennes: Merlin to Randon, May 27, 1866, no. 7 (misfiled with the Merlin-Colson correspondence).

[137] Vincennes: G. de Milly, "Notice sur le mode d'avancement dans l'armée autrichienne en 1864," February, 1865 (Reconnaissances: 1606).

[138] Merlin to Randon, May 30, 1866 (*Origines,* IX, 327–8).

[139] Vincennes: Merlin to Randon, June 11, 1866, no. 11.

[140] Merlin to Randon, April 25, 1866 (*Origines,* VIII, 335).

[141] For the Prussian figures, see Vincennes: "Bericht . . . über den Etat der Militair-Verwaltung für das Jahr 1865" (Reconnaissances: Plans et Projets 1536); for the Austrian, Vincennes: "Budget . . . d'Autriche pour . . . 1865," extract from *l'Italia militare* (Reconnaissances: 1606).

"the armed peace" for any length of time.[142] It was hard to ascertain how the two governments would fare in case of a shooting war. The more or less chronic Austrian embarrassments which had recently culminated in the Austrian loan suggested that the Hapsburgs would have trouble, but reports varied as to the comparative Prussian position. Reculot from Frankfurt reported that people in general expected fiscal difficulties,[143] although Clermont-Tonnerre was quite optimistic.[144] Since he was closer to the situation, his information seems more credible. The advantage of financial strength may be assigned to the Prussians.

The important consideration, however, was the needle gun.[145] The French were by no means so ill-informed on this subject as has been suggested. One source of information was provided by Frenchmen who had observed the Prussian army, notably Clermont-Tonnerre. Active French concern with the Prussian needle gun goes back at

---

[142] Clermont-Tonnerre to Randon, May 7, 1866 (*Origines*, IX, 41).

[143] Reculot to Drouyn de Lhuys, May 20, 1866 (*Origines*, IX, 199).

[144] Vincennes: Clermont-Tonnerre to Randon, February 23, 1866, no. 65.

[145] A brief description of the weapons hereinafter discussed is appended at this point.

The famous needle gun was so named because of the needle which touched off the explosion. Instead of loading from the muzzle, the needle gun loaded from the breech. This was quicker and safer, for the soldier could remain in hiding while he was loading. The principle was not a Prussian monopoly: a gun of this design was used during the American Civil War, particularly by the Northern armies, and in 1866 guns of the breech-loading type were under consideration by the Austrians and the French. However, there were disadvantages to the early models, and only the Prussians and the Americans had adopted them. The other weapon to be considered here was the canon rayé, a cannon that, in contrast to the old smooth-bored artillery, had a rifled barrel, which spun the shell around and sent it further. The cannons conferred a less significant advantage than the needle guns, for similar cannons had been in the possession of the Austrians since 1863. However, Prussian military thinking emphasized coordination of cannons and guns in order to pepper the enemy advance with a long-range fire novel in intensity. By contrast it was evident at Sadowa that Austrians wasted their cannons by placing the guns badly. See J. C. Fuller, *War and Western Civilization, 1832–1932* (London, 1932), pp. 103–4, 107–9; Cyril Falls, *A Hundred Years of War* (London, 1953), pp. 69–71; Cyril Falls, *The Art of War* (London, 1961), pp. 64–6, 77; James M. Gavin, "Civil War: Great Advances that Changed War," *Life*, 50:66–82 (February 17, 1961), esp. pp. 66–7, 70–1; Theodore Ropp, *War in the Modern World* (New York, 1962), pp. 162–70; H[enri] Bonnal, *Sadowa* (Paris, 1901), pp. 179–87.

least to 1864, the time of the Danish campaign, when Randon authorized Clermont-Tonnerre, at the attaché's own request, to accompany the Prussian army. Randon, in giving his permission, specifically asked for information on the needle gun and on the new breech-loading cannons with rifled barrels.[146] Shortly thereafter, on February 27, 1864, Randon sent Clermont-Tonnerre a detailed questionnaire about the two new weapons, which the attaché was to use as a guide in reporting on their performance during the war.[147] Randon's interest must have been thoroughly aroused, for he also instructed the attaché to procure for him a test model of a gun of the breech-loading type. From later and similar requests this initial effort must have proved unsuccessful. In September, 1864, Randon sent Bourbaki as an observer to the Prussian exercises at Spandau.[148] Bourbaki returned from this visit a convinced believer in Prussian military prowess. Although his views were not widely shared in French military circles, renewed efforts were made during 1865 to acquire models of the Prussian innovations. In April, 1865, there was a hopeful flurry when a German manufacturer volunteered to hand over, for a price, his designs for the needle gun. This occupied the War Ministry for some time, but, in the end, came to nothing. At the same time, Randon ordered a study of the Prussian cannons with a view toward their adoption in France, but a perfectionism determined in part by the difficulty of justifying expensive alterations to parsimonious members of the Corps Législatif slowed down the work seriously.[149]

Clermont-Tonnerre's reports continued to emphasize the impressive performances of the Prussian weapons in practice sessions.[150] Progress was made in December, 1865, when Clermont-Tonnerre

[146] Randon to Clermont-Tonnerre, February 24, 1864 (quoted by Randon, II, 133–5).
[147] Questionnaire quoted by Randon, II, 136–41.
[148] Randon, II, 141.
[149] Randon, II, 142.
[150] Vincennes: Clermont-Tonnerre to Randon, December 10, 1865, no. 61; note also the communication of December 11, 1865, listed in the table "1865. Pièces manquantes . . ."

managed to make and send a series of five diagrams which illus-
trated the construction of the needle gun in detail. At the same time,
he provided the War Ministry with a copy of a book by a M. César
Ruston which dealt with the new guns.[151] Later in the month, the
attaché complemented this most valuable report with five designs of
the canon rayé. These seem to have been devoted to its mounting,
rather than to the construction of the barrel and the loading mech-
anism,[152] but they must nonetheless have been of the highest interest
to the War Ministry. These communications represented an important breakthrough. The French continued their efforts to procure
actual models, concentrating now on the canon rayé. Independently
of each other, Clermont-Tonnerre inquired about the cost of buying
a specimen from Aal, while Randon actually ordered two from
Krupp.[153] No evidence has turned up as to the fate of these orders,
but, from a later letter of Clermont-Tonnerre, it would seem that a
model of the canon rayé was eventually obtained from the firm of
Leue and Timpe in Berlin.[154] In short, the War Ministry was well
informed, not only about the existence of the new weapons but also
about the details of their fabrication. Clermont-Tonnerre's reports
further emphasized the enormous effort which the Prussians were
making to equip the army as completely as possible with the new
inventions: he reported, for example, in November, 1865, that during
the year just past, the Prussians had manufactured 1050 new canons
rayés and he revealed that it was the Prussian intention to arm the
artillery entirely with the improved cannons before the year was
out.[155] This rapid revision was possible because of the speed with
which the arsenal at Spandau could turn out cannons: Clermont-
Tonnerre asserted that the rate of production was eighty-three cannons a month, a very impressive figure.[156]

[151] Vincennes: Clermont-Tonnerre to Randon, December 2, 1865, no. 60; Clermont-Tonnerre to Randon, December 10, 1865, no. 61.

[152] Vincennes: Clermont-Tonnerre to Randon, December 27, 1865, no. 63.

[153] Vincennes: Clermont-Tonnerre to Randon, January 31, 1866, no. 63 bis.

[154] Clermont-Tonnerre to unnamed correspondent, May 11, 1866 (*Papiers famille
impériale*, III, 119).

[155] Vincennes: Clermont-Tonnerre to Randon, November 14, 1865, no. 59.

[156] Vincennes: Clermont-Tonnerre to Randon, December 10, 1865, no. 61.

In addition to these excellent reports from Clermont-Tonnerre, the War Ministry had another source of information which was valuable with regard to the needle gun. There were experiments with a French gun of the needle design. The progress of French research will be discussed at greater length in the Epilogue in relation to the strength of the French army; but it seems relevant to summarize here the principal events. This survey will show how sophisticated the French War Ministry should have been in interpreting information about the Prussian equipment. French concern with the needle gun went back to 1855, when a simple worker at the arsenals of Saint-Thomas d'Aquin, a man named Chassepot, informed Napoleon that he had invented a new gun of the breech-loading variety. Napoleon inspected a model, liked it, and ordered copies made for test purposes. The gun was considered and rejected by an official committee in 1858 and the decision was sustained by Vaillant, then Minister of War. Napoleon disagreed with the committee's conclusion and ordered further studies designed to correct some defects in the model. During the years after 1858, a few samples were around, and it is said that a small number were actually used in the Italian War.[157] Randon, in his memoirs, tells much the same story, although he omits mention of the decision against the guns in 1858 and its reversal by Napoleon. He does agree that copies were being tested on a very small scale between 1858 and 1865 in both France and Algeria. Chassepot was given a prominent place in supervising these experiments.[158] In 1865, the committee, now headed by Leboeuf, considered the guns again and determined to order 1500 models for a more extensive trial. This decision was vetoed by Randon.[159] Randon, who prudently omits this detail, does state that 500 guns were finally ordered for testing during the summer practice session at Châlons in 1866.[160]

The War Ministry, then, had full information about the needle gun. Its existence was no surprise in the 1866 campaign. How did it

[157] Bapst, IV, 47–8.
[158] Randon, II, 234–5.
[159] Bapst, IV, 47–8.
[160] Randon, II, 236.

happen that the French government, possessed of such detailed knowledge of the decisive Prussian advantage, failed to anticipate correctly the results of the war? This question can be answered in part by an examination of the defects of the needle gun as the French understood them. Later, Randon was to produce an exhaustive list of the factors which discouraged the French command from a more rapid development of their model. This discussion merits some skepticism. Randon was naturally anxious to justify himself in the face of suspicions of negligence which sprang up readily after 1871; but some of the major items in Randon's list should be mentioned. They included the very complex loading device, which the French considered difficult to repair in wartime; the need for a special variety of cartridge whose manufacture would require changes both in personnel and in supplies; and the fact that the drain on the reserves of cartridges would be great, since the new guns permitted more rapid firing. Finally, Randon asserted, it was thought that the new invention would have only a limited usefulness, since it was not primarily designed either for offensive strategy or for skirmishing, where the chief requisite was not the rapidity of the shooting but its accuracy.[161]

These criticisms of the efficacy of the needle gun might be discounted were it not for the fact that they were simultaneously voiced by the Prussian experts. Among the papers of the French War Ministry in this period, there is a copy of an article by Moltke, dated July 8, 1865, in which he discusses many of the same problems.[162] Moreover, Moltke described from experience certain tactical difficulties which the French had not as yet faced at first hand. It seems likely from its location in the archives that this document came into the War Ministry's hands before the outbreak of the Austro-Prussian War. It may have directly influenced Randon's opinion as expressed in his memoirs, and it could hardly have failed to

---

[161] Randon, II, 232–3.

[162] Vincennes: Moltke, "De l'influence des armes perfectionnées sur le combat," Supplement to *Militair Wochenblatt*, July 8, 1865 (Reconnaissances: Plans et Projets 1536).

affect the expectations in high French circles as to the results of the campaign.

The problem of the new weapons, as described by Moltke, was the need for greater accuracy. In considering the use of both the needle gun and the canon rayé, Moltke emphasized three vital prerequisites for efficient use of the weapons: first, it must be possible to see the target; second, the distance between the target and the gunner must be known; third, the gunner must be calm. Moltke declared that the canon rayé was extremely useful for shooting at long distances; it would be possible to direct a destructive battery at a large objective 2400 paces away, while within a range of 1600 paces, one could be certain of hitting the target. This was impressive; but there were also certian difficulties. The effectiveness of the cannons was greatly reduced in the following situations: first, if the field consisted of broken ground or if there were much cover, making it difficult to sight the target exactly; second, if for some reason it were hard to judge the distances; third, if the distances changed very rapidly, as would be the case, for example, in a cavalry attack; fourth, if it became necessary to move the cannons, since this process, while simple enough in itself, woud necessitate a pause to recalculate all the distances. In short, as Moltke concluded, "the superiority of the canon rayé . . . shows itself especially on a plain and at great distances."

Moltke's discussion of the needle gun was also rather sobering. He reported excellent test results, which showed that the gun worked well at distances of up to 600 or 800 paces. In addition, the model was noted for the speed and simplicity of the reloading process. Moltke cautioned, however, that conditions were very different in battle from a practice shoot in camp. At long distances, a miscalculation of 30 or 40 paces would cause the gunner to miss the target. In view of the likelihood of misjudging a distance of 600 or 700 paces by 30 or 40 paces, this must have seemed a serious defect. Moltke himself admitted that under such circumstances, the gun worked best if the enemy were lined up "in deep columns," and he was also aware that it would not take an intelligent enemy long to learn to avoid "deep columns" at all costs. In fact, the skill required to use the weapon effectively at long distances was so great that Moltke reported a decision to train certain soldiers specially as "sharpshooters." It might not be possible to provide more than 20 or 30 of these highly trained experts for each battalion; but Moltke believed that even such a small group could inflict "important losses" on the enemy if its shooting was properly supervised. Since Moltke confessed that at that point the Prussians had more guns than they had sharpshooters, it is a question how long this system could last once battle losses began to take a toll of the élite group. Moltke did envision letting all the soldiers use needle guns when the battle had finally been joined and the calculation of distances was no longer important; but he cautioned against allowing the ordinary soldier to shoot during the enemy's approach, for two reasons. The difficulty of hitting the target would demoralize the soldiers by destroying their faith in their guns; and the consumption of cartridges, with each soldier able to shoot off three per minute, would be enormous. Moltke admitted: *"In effect that ease of loading and of shooting which is such a powerful means of success in the hand of the expert who knows how to turn it to profit at the appropriate moment, constitutes a danger if the men are not submitted to sufficient control."*

Moltke added some conclusions on the tactics of battle to be followed by a commander whose army was equipped with needle guns and canons rayés. He advised that the force take up a position where the enemy's approach would be across ground favorable for the action of the new weapons. The army should stay there, on the defensive, until the last possible moment. Moltke noted: "An infantry force which would charge with bayonets, from a great distance, *across a plain,* would be overwhelmed by the fire of the adversary, especially if the latter stayed in position." Moltke observed that the effects of such tactics against a cavalry charge would be far less impressive, for the cavalry could move quickly enough to upset the calculations of distance. It was the infantry and the artillery, not the cavalry, that were most heavily influenced by the new weapons. There was an important difficulty to the plan of battle outlined above. It emphasized, in accordance with the requirements of the new inventions, a defensive line of action. But Moltke noted that an offensive course was usually more apt to be successful and was nearly always essential for "a decisive result." Consequently, he suggested that the commander of the force armed with the new guns hold his men on the defensive as long as he could in order to benefit from the full impact of the new inventions; then, at the final moment before contact of the two armies, the commander should change abruptly to offensive techniques and launch a bayonet charge.[163] From this point, the battle would continue according to the traditional pattern.

Moltke's resumé of the potentialities of the new weapons was certainly far from enthusiastic and it probably does much to explain the French miscalculation of the odds in the war. There was also some reason to believe that the Austrians too possessed the needle gun. A report from the usually well-informed Clermont-Tonnerre indicated that the Austrians were working with a breech-loading model called after its inventor the Lindner gun.[164] Merlin's reports confirmed the existence of the Lindner gun, although only by hearsay, for the attaché never actually saw one.[165] After the disaster of Sadowa, he found out why: although a contract had been drawn up for the production of the Lindner gun, it remained unsigned at the end of July, 1866, because Franz Joseph and the Minister of War could not agree on the model.[166] Only two guns were in existence, constructed as samples.[167] But even discounting these misleading rumors, there was reason enough in Moltke's article to doubt that the Prussians had acquired an overwhelming advantage through

---

[163] This discussion of the needle gun and the canon rayé has been taken from Moltke, "De l'influence des armes perfectionnées," pp. 1–14.

[164] Vincennes: Clermont-Tonnerre to Randon, January 31, 1866, no. 63 bis.

[165] Vincennes: Merlin to Randon, May 1, 1866, no. 5.

[166] Vincennes: Merlin to Randon, July 17, 1866, no. 20.

[167] Vincennes: Merlin to Randon, July 21, 1866, no. 21.

their technological gains. While Moltke emphasized the impressive results obtained under test conditions, his report made clear that special circumstances were necessary for effective use of the weapons in battle. It does not seem too much to assume that the French experts concluded that the Prussian command might manage to create these conditions once or twice in a campaign, with disastrous results. But surely it would be impossible for the Prussians to "rig" the setting of every battle, especially in a war fought in the mountainous defiles of Bohemia, where the ground was broken, there was plenty of cover, and skirmishes and sneak offensives were the order of the day. Ultimately, then, the decision would seem to rest on the question of Austrian manpower. The Prussians might inflict one defeat; the problem was whether the Austrians had the human resources to equip another army to carry on the campaign, win battles when the Prussians had been unable to select advantageous terrain, and eventually conquer when their enemy collapsed through a failure of soldiery, morale, or money.

The statistics available, undependable and ever-changing though they were, suggest that the French War Ministry answered this question in the affirmative. At the beginning of May, 1866, Clermont-Tonnerre estimated that the Prussians had mobilized about 380,000 men.[168] By the end of May, he numbered the Prussian army at 523,400 men, but he emphasized that to attain this figure the Prussians had taken many undesirables: there were soldiers in the artillery, for instance, who were thirty-nine years old.[169] Similar shortages of men had forced the command to reduce the number of men in each battalion of the Landwehr from 1002 to 586.[170] The Austrian situation compared rather favorably with these reports. The actual number of men under arms was no greater: figures published in 1865 placed the Austrian army at that period at 416,311 men at its height;[171] information in late May, 1866, stated that the

---

[168] Clermont-Tonnerre to Randon, May 4, 1866 (Origines, IX, 5).

[169] Vincennes: Clermont-Tonnerre to Randon, May 21, 1866, no. 80.

[170] Vincennes: Clermont-Tonnerre to Randon, May 11, 1866, no. 78.

[171] Vincennes: "Effectif de l'armée autrichienne (Année 1865)," from La Gazette militaire de Vienne (Reconnaissances: 1606).

Austrians had 500,000 soldiers, 150,000 on the Italian front and the rest in the north.[172] In addition to this, the Austrians would have the dubious help of many of the small German states. Some observers, Benedetti for example, felt that this might turn the scale.[173] It is true that it would give the Austrians extra soldiers, for the Bavarian army alone numbered 82,900;[174] but it might also create confusion through differences in training. There was a report that "the same military signal that means 'forward' with one means 'retreat' with the others." [175] Even with these reinforcements, however, the Austrians would probably have approximately the same number of men as the Prussians; but the significant point was that in gathering these forces they would have used a far smaller percentage of the available manpower. At the beginning of May, Merlin reported that the Austrians would have sufficient reserves to rebuild their forces after most serious losses; he had even heard that it would be possible to replace the entire army.[176] Shortly thereafter he wrote that the Austrian army could number 800,000 to 850,000 men and emphasized the youth and fine training of the recruits then being called up.[177] Although these figures later proved exaggerated, there was no denying the contrast, pointed out by Merlin, between the Austrian population of thirty million and the Prussian population of seventeen million.[178] It seems likely that French military circles and Napoleon, under their influence, argued that although the Prussians' technical advances might insure them one or two smashing victories when the circumstances were right, the Austrians would be able to produce new recruits and carry on the war until they had worn out the Prussians by attrition.[179]

Events, of course, did not follow this pattern. Moltke had been unduly pessimistic over the worth of the needle gun, for the Austrian

[172] Vincennes: Merlin to Randon, May 26, 1866, no. 9.
[173] Benedetti to Drouyn de Lhuys, May 19, 1866 (*Origines,* IX, 184–5).
[174] Vincennes: Merlin to Randon, May 21, 1866, no. 8.
[175] Reiset to Drouyn de Lhuys, June 9, 1866 (*Origines,* X, 95).
[176] Vincennes: Merlin to Randon, May 1, 1866, no. 5.
[177] Merlin to Randon, May 6, 1866 (*Origines,* IX, 35).
[178] Merlin to Randon, April 25, 1866 (*Origines,* VIII, 336).
[179] Cf. Metternich to Mensdorff, June 29, 1866 (Oncken, I, 285, and n. 4).

losses were enormous in every battle; and even when the Austrians fought on the defensive, as at Sadowa, this circumstance did not destroy the Prussians' advantage.[180] Merlin's estimate of Austrian manpower, like so much of his information, had been too optimistic. The numerical strength of the reserves was not revealed, since they were never called out; but the figures finally given for the army of the north were markedly lower than Merlin's initial reports. Merlin announced at the beginning of June that they numbered 260,000–265,000 men;[181] the information coming from Berlin was even more sobering, for the Austrians were credited with 180,000 against the Prussians' 260,000.[182] Another French mistake, later disclosed by Persigny, was that Napoleon did not allow for the difficulties of reorganizing an army after a defeat as severe as could be inflicted with the needle gun.[183] However, none of these facts were clearly forecast in the spring of 1866.

At that time, Napoleon found himself in a situation where further French action was as unavoidable as it was difficult. The most informed military calculations available to him indicated that the Prusso-Italian combination would be defeated. This might mean the destruction or curtailment of Italian national freedom. A man like Schmitz might say cheerfully: "We made Italy, we will unmake her."[184] For Napoleon, with sentiment and prestige and perhaps even definite support pledged to the Italian cause, such an alternative was impossible to contemplate. However, other courses seemed daily less feasible: the Italians and the Austrians were growing increasingly irreconcilable, while Napoleon's attempt to abet the Prusso-Italian side through an agreement with Bismarck had failed because

---

[180] Fuller, pp. 107–9.

[181] Vincennes: Merlin to Randon, June 4, 1866, no. 10.

[182] Benedetti to Drouyn de Lhuys, June 12, 1866 (*Origines*, X, 138–9).

[183] Persigny, *Mémoires*, p. 367. In a work available to me only recently, Gordon Craig, *The Battle of Königgrätz* (Philadelphia and New York, 1964), confirms my belief that there was a general expectation that Austria would win the war and in his explanation of the upset emphasizes the superiority of Prussian strategy, a factor widely underestimated.

[184] Vincennes: Schmitz to Colson, July 19 [1866], no. 8.

of Bismarck's unwillingness to offer acceptable compensations and because of the opposition to Prussia in the Corps Législatif. The problems which had beset Napoleon's attempts to formulate a policy in the winter of 1865–66 were still prominent in the early spring; and Napoleon's maneuvers in February and March had accomplished little or nothing toward a solution. The major change was that, with the Italians closely implicated in the German crisis, the situation in Central Europe had become even more significant for French interests. Before the signing of the Prusso-Italian alliance, Napoleon might have evaded the problem by following his oft-repeated protestations and staying out of the German settlement altogether. Once the future of the Italians was engaged, this course was untenable. Some solution of the obstacles to French action had to be found.

IV

THE FINAL
DECISIONS

EVENTS DURING THE SPRING of 1866 had created a difficult dilemma for Napoleon III. The problem turned on the Prusso-Italian treaty, signed on April 8. Although the treaty in no way implicated the French, its effect, given Napoleon's well-known predispositions, was greatly to narrow his freedom of action. Napoleon's foreign policy during at least the preceding ten years had had a strongly pro-Italian slant; if Cavour was the father of Italian independence, it would be no more than just to term Napoleon the godfather. This commitment, originally made on sentimental and philosophical grounds, had been reinforced by the engagement of French prestige. Now the Italians were determined to join the Prussians in a campaign which, they hoped, would complete the liberation of the peninsula by giving them the Austrian province of Venetia. Napoleon's misgivings had been overridden by Italian enthusiasm and demonstrable Austrian stubbornness; as things had worked out, Napoleon could not have prevented the Prusso-Italian treaty although he may have tried. His involvement in the question seemed certain to prove highly embarrassing. The best estimates of the experts at the War Ministry confirmed the popular impression that, in case of war, the Austrians would defeat the Prussians and Italians. Should this happen, there was no telling the consequences for the new Italian nation, for there were many indications that the Austrian government had not yet accepted the concept of Italian unity as a permanent arrangement. But Napoleon, although he was not entirely pleased with the strength and centralization of the Italian state as it existed, could hardly tolerate a return, partial or complete, to the old system of Hapsburg rule. His interest demanded that he find some course of action that would serve to strengthen, or at least to rescue, the Prusso-Italian side. It was far from evident how he could accomplish this goal. The obvious solution, an arrangement with either Vienna or Berlin, had been tried with most discouraging results: the Austrians were unyielding, while the Prussians had been unwilling to make concessions great enough to surmount the certain French resistance to an alliance with them. It was time for a new plan. At the end of April, Napoleon seemed to have found one: renewal of his often proposed project of a European congress.[1]

This idea, which Napoleon mentioned to Goltz and to Metternich around the middle of April,[2] seemed to promise success. In the first place, it seemed possible that the European powers might solve the crisis by working out a comprehensive settlement of Central European problems. The initial reaction to the plan in the capitals of the great powers was not exactly enthusiastic, but it was far from hostile. London and St. Petersburg both testified qualified approval of the proposal, although both governments considered independent action by the neutral states a more fruitful approach. Gortchakov discussed with the French ambassador the current Russian efforts at good offices between the two German powers, while Clarendon suggested a joint démarche to be made by England, France, and Russia.[3] The two German great powers also indicated moderate willingness to consider Napoleon's proposition, although both divulged a desire to reach agreement with the French Emperor before the meeting.[4] As for the Italians, they were more or less forced to agree to a congress if the Austrians, Prussians, and English, as

[1] Gramont to Drouyn de Lhuys, May 8, 1866 (*Les Origines diplomatiques de la guerre de 1870–71*, IX, 66).

[2] Goltz to Bismarck, April 25, 1866 (Oncken, I, 140); HHSA: Metternich to Mensdorff, April 28, 1866, no. 60; Bush, "Napoleon III and the Redeeming of Venetia," p. 85. These authorities are not in agreement as to the precise date of Napoleon's initial démarches, but all place the development around the middle of the month.

[3] Clarendon to Cowley, May 2, 1866 (*Origines*, VIII, 440–2); Talleyrand to Drouyn de Lhuys, May 3, 1866 (*Origines*, VIII, 458–9).

[4] Benedetti to Drouyn de Lhuys, May 3, 1866 (*Origines*, VIII, 447–8); Gramont to Drouyn de Lhuys, May 3, 1866 (*Origines*, VIII, 461).

well as the French, favored it.[5] All this did not exactly constitute an eager reception, but at least there seemed to be no insuperable obstacles.

However, the plan for a congress was double-barreled. If the sessions failed to resolve the problems outstanding, there was still the possibility that before or during a meeting Napoleon might be able to force either Austria or Prussia into the kind of arrangement which had, up to that time, proved so elusive. Shortly after the idea of a congress was broached, there were signs that this calculation was justified. Metternich began to make new overtures, as yet ill-defined, while Napoleon seized the occasion of a court ball to hint informally to Goltz that he was ready to consider new proposals from Prussia.[6]

What were the possibilities for an agreement at that time? This question involves not only the diplomatic situation, but also the state of opinion within France. Events early in May pushed the alternative of an arrangement with Austria to the forefront, both through the tenor of statements in the Corps Législatif and through diplomatic movements. On April 27, Emile Ollivier, a prominent opposition member of the Assembly, announced his intention of making a speech on foreign policy during the session of May 3.[7] The prospect filled the government with consternation; no less than three meetings of the Council of Ministers were held before May 3 in an attempt to work out strategy. The plan eventually adopted was presentation of a prepared statement of official policy. It was hoped, not altogether

[5] Malaret to Drouyn de Lhuys, May 3, 1866 (*Origines*, VIII, 453).

[6] Goltz to Bismarck, May 1, 1866 (Oncken, I, 146–7). The importance of the motive of possible compensations is well discussed by Adolf Kulessa in *Die Kongressidee Napoleons III. im Mai 1866* (Giessen, 1927), pp. 57–8, in opposition to the contention of Ollivier (*L'Empire libéral*, VIII, 144–8) that Napoleon was sincere in desiring a congress as a means of preserving the peace. The present author, as should become apparent in the narrative below, believes that both factors were significant and that the predominance of one over the other varied almost from day to day.

[7] *Origines*, VIII, 403, n. 1.

confidently, that this declaration would ward off, or at least modify, the inevitable debate.[8] Accordingly, on May 3, Rouher called for peace, the avoidance of entanglements, and the maintenance of "entire liberty of action." A more specific comment was offered with regard to the Italian situation. Rouher said that France would "disapprove highly" of an Austrian attack on Italy, and he reiterated that the Italians would attack Austria "à ses risques et périls." These remarks made, Rouher endeavored to prevent a debate.[9] He was not to escape so easily. Ollivier had arrived with the text of a speech in his pocket. His colleague, Thiers, had begged permission to take his place. Ollivier was rather annoyed, but he decided that there was nothing to do but agree;[10] as result, the government was faced with an even more hostile and eloquent adversary.

Thiers' speech has been described by his mother-in-law in her diary for May 5:

He began in a voice at first a little weak, but soon recovering its strength, the most admirable discourse which he had ever delivered. Friends, enemies, confirmed him in his thinking by noisy approbation. Admiration seized them. All surrendered to the wise, firm, patriotic arguments which he alleged. Many had tears in their eyes . . .

After two hours of stirring improvisation, M. Thiers, having finished, was surrounded by his colleagues who shook his hands with enthusiasm. M. Péreire, the famous speculator, transported with admiration, came to shake his hand while shedding tears. At that moment, the entire Chamber was on his side, senators, tribunes, even some ministers, for M. Fould didn't stop repeating:—"He is right! He is right." . . . One of the academicians . . . said:—"Do you think that Cicero and Demosthenes were more eloquent than M. Thiers?" . . .

. . . .

In the clubs, in the cafés, on the boulevards, the impression continued. Jules Simon, deputy of the left, was one of the first to announce this success to the family of M. Thiers. From that evening, the visits began.

[8] AN: Rouher's notes on the meetings of the Council of Ministers, April 28, April 30, and May 2, 1866 (45 AP1, cahier 1).
[9] *Annales (1866)*, V, 68–9.
[10] Ollivier, VIII, 111.

The next day, "there was a real reception of men and women distinguished by intelligence and birth." The day after that, the iron gate still opened every minute. People entered their names, people sent letters of congratulations.[11]

The speech and its message were a sensation. Thiers urged, in the strongest terms, the adoption of an anti-Prussian and hence pro-Austrian line. He admitted that he was not opposed to reform of the German Confederation, but he warned that that reform, as envisaged by the Prussian government, amounted to a revision of the balance of power. It went far beyond the requirements of increased rationality or effectiveness in constitutional forms to create an entirely new entity. Thiers charged that the Prussians intended to bring about a war as the prelude to their own aggrandizement through the annexation of certain North German states. The Confederation would then be changed in such a way as to make Prussia the predominant power; and this new grouping would receive its final infusion of strength through a loose tie with Austria. Thiers called on France to oppose these ambitions "in the name of the independence of the German states, in the name of her own independence, in the name, finally, of the European balance." But Thiers did not wish the French to take up arms in defense of these goals. He advised, rather, that the French government use diplomatic channels to convince Bismarck that France would not condone the unification of Germany under Prussian auspices. He added that Napoleon's policy of aid to Italy in support of Italian unity might have confused Bismarck by leading to illusions of eventual French support for a similar policy in Germany. The French government should state conclusively that these hopes were without foundation. Thiers noted the possibility that Bismarck might try to tempt the French with compensations; he termed the acceptance of such a bribe "shameful." In conclusion, Thiers recommended a firmer line toward Italy designed to restrain that nation from action. Florence should be told

[11] Eurydice Sophie Dosne, *Mémoires,* ed. Henri Malo, 2 vols. (Paris, 1928), I, 276–8.

that French aid was out of the question even in the event of an
Austrian offensive.[12]

This speech marked the most complete opposition to Napoleon's
policies. It was anti-Prussian; through arguments based on the
balance of power it opposed the principle of nationalities; and, in the
contemporary constitutional setting, it advanced the cause of the
liberal opposition by effectively casting doubt on the government's
wisdom.[13] The Council of Ministers immediately decided to combat
Thiers' proposals in the official press.[14] In addition to these journals,
a group of nonofficial newspapers which had recently adopted a pro-
Prussian position joined in violent denunciations of Thiers' speech.[15]
They included the *Journal des Débats,* the *Opinion Nationale,* and
the *Siècle.*[16] This chorus was opposed with extreme enthusiasm by
the rest of the papers, reflecting massive support in the country at
large, particularly among the middle and upper classes.[17] The
extraordinarily warm reception of the speech in the Corps Législatif
was reinforced as prominent individuals came forward to attest their

[12] *Annales (1866),* V, 69–81; extracts printed in Oncken, I, 154–9.

[13] At the time, it was believed in some circles that the speech was entirely motivated by the desire to discredit Napoleon's régime. (Cf. Joseph Maria von Radowitz' Diary, May 3, 1866, as quoted by Oncken, I, 159, n. 1.) There has also been
some controversy over the charge that since Thiers knew of the Prusso-Italian alliance, his suggestions were impracticable and were designed merely as rabble-rousing. See André Armengaud, "L'Opinion publique en France et la crise nationale
allemande en 1866," unpubl. thèse complémentaire, Faculté des Lettres de Paris
(Paris, 1958), p. 71, n. 7. The present author agrees with those who feel that this
accusation is too harsh, for, as will be shown below, an arrangement which would
have implemented Thiers' proposals was still theoretically possible. Nevertheless,
the vital importance of constitutional motives in the entire legislative opposition to
Napoleon's German policies must not be understimated.

[14] AN: Rouher's notes on the meetings of the Council of Ministers, May 5, 1866 (45
API, cahier 1).

[15] Armengaud, pp. 72–3.

[16] Armengaud, pp. 12–3. The pro-Prussian forces had not yet reached their full
strength; later recruits were to include *La Liberté* and *L'Avenir National* (Armengaud, pp. 12–3). Despite contemporaries' immediate suspicions, there is no evidence
that this stand was determined by bribery, although considering the venality of the
French press at this time, the possibility cannot be excluded (Armengaud, pp.
174–7).

[17] Armengaud, pp. 73–5.

support. Walewski, the President of the Corps Législatif and Napoleon's relative, actually entertained Thiers at dinner on the evening after the speech and helped Thiers proofread the version sent to the *Moniteur*.[18] It is to be expected that a court functionary like Mérimée might remark that the speech was "the most anti-patriotic thing possible." [19] It is undoubtedly more significant that Guizot wrote from his retirement: "You have saved the honor of the political spirit in France." [20]

How practicable were Thiers' suggestions? There is evidence to show that they were feasible, although not in the simple form he advocated. The time had passed when a mere warning would have sufficed to stop Bismarck. By May, 1866, the only means certain to restrain Bismarck would have been to detach Italy from the alliance. This in turn could only have been managed through a promise of Venetia; and this presupposed an arrangement with Austria, which the French alone could bring about. However, at the time of Thiers' speech, it seemed as though the Austrian position might be thawing. The Austrian government had known of the Prusso-Italian treaty negotiations since early March.[21] In mid-April, the English government, joined by Gramont, had begun a campaign directed at persuading the Ballplatz to cede Venetia. A third threat to the Austrian position was posed by the possibility of a congress.

The Austrian response was formulated on April 18 in a letter so secret that it has never been found.[22] Fortunately, its contents can be reconstructed from the summary given in Metternich's reply of April 21. Mensdorff suggested a far-reaching reorganization of the map of Europe to be carried out through Napoleon's mediation in the event of war. Austria would give Venetia to France (for re-ceding to

---

[18] Philippe Poirson, *Walewski, fils de Napoléon* (Paris [1943]), p. 300.

[19] Mérimée, *Panizzi*, II, 189.

[20] BN: Guizot to Thiers, May 24, 1866 (Nouvelles acquisitions françaises XIX, 20619).

[21] HHSA: Mensdorff to Metternich, March 1, 1866, no. 1, and March 8, 1866; cf. Heinrich Ritter von Srbik, *Deutsche Einheit*, 4 vols. (Munich, 1935–42), IV, 330.

[22] Clark, *Franz Joseph and Bismarck*, pp. 408–10.

Italy) once she had won compensations in Silesia. In receiving Venetia, the Italian government would make a financial payment for the Austrian fortresses which would enable the Austrian government to establish the defenses of the new frontier. The dispossessed rulers of Modena and Tuscany would receive compensations, in return for which they would renounce their rights. The temporal power of the Pope would be guaranteed. All these provisions would have served to check the tide of Italian nationalism. In Mensdorff's proposals regarding Germany, a similar ambivalence toward nationalism was apparent. The Austrian minister, as already mentioned, expected to force the Prussians to give up Silesia; but they would be allowed to annex territories in North Germany so that they would end up as strong or even stronger than before the war. As a counterweight, however, some of the more important small states, such as Saxony and Bavaria, would also receive increases of territory. Such was the comprehensive program which Mensdorff outlined for his ambassador's comment. Metternich's assessment was by and large favorable, but he pointed out that Napoleon would require compensations as payment for his efforts as mediator. Metternich guessed that the Emperor would not bring up the question of the Rhine provinces. He thought Belgium might be a possibility and suggested that the Austrians facilitate French control in that area by offering a newly created kingdom on the Rhine to the Belgian monarch after his overthrow. In general, Metternich's forecast as to French reception of the plan was cautious. He reported that Drouyn would favor it, but said he doubted Drouyn's importance. He did not know how Napoleon would react. The ambassador described the success of his first tentative démarches, directed at ascertaining whether the French were free from other commitments. He declared that he would await definite word from Mensdorff before revealing the plan.[23]

This authorization was transmitted in a letter of April 30. At the same time, the terms dealing with Italy were made far harsher:

[23] *Quellen zur deutschen Politik Österreichs 1859–66,* ed. Oskar Schmid and Heinrich Ritter von Srbik, 5 vols. (Berlin, 1934–38), vol. V, pt. 1, pp. 527–9.

Mensdorff declared that the Ballplatz wished to turn Italy into a federation through restoration to the Pope of the old papal domains and reinstatement of the rulers of Modena and Tuscany either in their old territories or in new ones carved out of the province of Venetia. Should this latter condition prove impossible, Mensdorff stated that he would be willing to consider instead the return of the King of Naples. The cession of Venetia was hedged about with new provisions: the Italian government was to assume the Venetian share of the Austrian national debt and to promise that the port of Venice would never be used as a naval base.[24] This represents substantial tightening of the plans, possibly on the initiative of Franz Joseph, since he did see the April 30 letter.[25]

Metternich now had to present this plan to Napoleon. This was rather ticklish, since the cession of Venetia was promised only on a contingent basis, and the plans for reorganizing Italy were highly controversial. The ambassador did not trust his own persuasive skills entirely. He wanted to enlist the aid of some Frenchman whom Napoleon trusted and he chose the ex-minister and ardent Bonapartist Persigny. Meeting him at a race track, Metternich revealed the new scheme, to Persigny's great excitement.[26] Persigny immediately told Napoleon, whose reaction was chilly.[27] Metternich approached the Emperor at about the same time, for on May 4 he cabled Mensdorff: "I believe that I shall have results tomorrow . . . The Emperor asked me for several days for reflection." [28] This was a significant moment. Napoleon was subjected to the opinions of everyone in his entourage: Eugénie and Walewski, who did not favor Italian nationalism, agreed with Persigny in seeing the proposition as a great advance. Drouyn de Lhuys also favored the plan,

[24] Quellen, vol. V, pt. 1, pp. 549–50.
[25] Quellen, vol. V, pt. 1, p. 551. Clark (p. 411) suggests that the changes reflected Mensdorff's chagrin at Napoleon's congress plan; but Bush (p. 85) shows that the congress proposal antedated and presumably caused the initiation of the new Austrian line.
[26] Ollivier, VIII, 138.
[27] Honoré Farat, Persigny [Paris, 1957], p. 290.
[28] HHSA: Metternich to Mensdorff, May 4, 1866, no. 68.

although more cautiously. A middle ground was adopted by Plon-plon: he thought the Austrian plan deserved consideration, but he believed that it needed modification in view of Italian involvement with Prussia.[29] On the other hand, Rouher and Fould were firmly opposed on the grounds that French interests necessitated the maintenance of peace and that any involvement in the quarrel tended to hinder that goal.[30] On May 4, Rouher and La Valette spent several hours with Napoleon and Eugénie arguing this thesis, but they walked out unsure of their success.[31]

Napoleon's thought at this point is as obscure to historians as it was to his ministers. The position he eventually adopted was closest to that of Plon-plon, but it does not necessarily follow that the Emperor was influenced by his relative, for his counterproject was largely determined by the Italian interests which had throughout been closest to his heart. In a talk with Metternich on May 5, Napoleon demanded that the Austrian government promise to cede Venetia as soon as the first shot was fired in Germany, instead of waiting until after compensations had been won from Prussia. In return, Napoleon pledged himself not to ask for compensations. He also promised to keep the Italians neutral and, although he emphasized his own desire to remain at peace, he declared that he would be willing to take minatory steps against the Italians, should they attack despite an agreement on Venetia. Metternich was disappointed by these modifications of the plan. He agreed to report them to the Ballplatz, but he warned that Franz Joseph would probably not accept such an agreement unless he had received very stringent assurances as to Italian neutrality and as to French willingness to give moral support in case the German campaign was less successful than anticipated.[32]

Napoleon's counterproposals were at best harshly realistic. This in itself, however, would not indicate that Napoleon opposed an

[29] Ollivier, VIII, 139–40.
[30] Ollivier, VIII, 140–1.
[31] PRO: Cowley to Clarendon, May 4, 1866 (F. O. 519/232).
[32] *Quellen*, vol. V, pt. 1, pp. 598–9.

agreement with Austria. It was more significant that even before the results of his suggestions had been learned, Napoleon made his most forceful attempt to lead the French into a pro-Prussian commitment. Actually, the Austrian plan was destined to fail at this time. Napoleon had communicated the plan to the Italian government. On May 5, La Marmora replied in a most discouraging tone. He considered that acceptance of the Austrian scheme would force the Italians into betrayal of the Prussians and therefore termed it inadmissible. He pointed out that the treaty would expire in July and suggested that it might be possible to arrange matters through a congress.[33] Meanwhile, the Austrian reaction to the counterproject had been even more unfavorable. On May 8, Mensdorff cabled Metternich that the Ballplatz could not promise to cede Venetia unless the campaign in Germany had brought compensations and would not make commitments as to the postwar status of Italy.[34] Negotiations had been rejected in both Vienna and Florence; but the conversations held later in the month between Metternich and Drouyn show that further maneuvering was not impossible. Even before the consequences of the démarches at Vienna and Florence were known, however, Napoleon had dropped this project and initiated a new effort to explore the possibilities of an arrangement with Prussia.

Undoubtedly Napoleon had hoped from the start that the threat of European intervention through a congress might impel Bismarck to make new offers to the French. Thiers' anti-Prussian speech forced the Emperor's hand. If he were ever going to lead France in a pro-Prussian policy, he needed to answer Thiers' challenge, clarify the impression of French opinion abroad, and rally the public to his own views. His thinking, as well as his timing, shows that events in

[33] Ollivier, VIII, 141–2; La Marmora, Un peu plus de lumière, pp. 215–26. Heinrich Ritter von Srbik, "Der Geheimvertrag Österreichs und Frankreichs vom 12. Juni 1866," Historisches Jahrbuch, 58:454–507 (1937), esp. pp. 482–3, believes that Napoleon was angry with the Italians for their refusal of the Austrian overtures; he points out, however, the seemingly contradictory fact that Napoleon wanted an unconditional promise of Venetia and so was dissatisfied with the Austrian offers as they stood.
[34] Mensdorff to Metternich, May 8, 1866 (Oncken, I, 178).

the Corps Législatif had had their influence. Simply stated, Napoleon's offer to the French people ran as follows: if they would aid him in supporting Bismarck's unification policy, he would procure for them ample compensations such as the much coveted banks of the Rhine.[35] Even before May 3, the Emperor had been throwing out such hints to the deputies.[36] But his real opportunity came on May 6, when he was scheduled to make an address at Auxerre in the farming district of the Yonne. Napoleon used this occasion to express his views on the international situation. From the notoriety of this Auxerre speech, one might expect a rabble-rousing harangue, couched in terms the masses could understand. Nothing could be further from the truth.

According to eyewitnesses, the famous portion of the speech, the words that had "the effect of a cannonshot in the middle of a concert," [37] were never actually pronounced. Instead, Napoleon added a highly charged paragraph to the version of the talk published the next morning in the *Moniteur*. This step was taken without anyone's knowledge, even the ministers.[38] The crucial paragraph was unusually enigmatic even for Napoleon. Speaking of the metaphorically personified Department of the Yonne, the Emperor said: "It knew, like the great majority of the French people, that its interests were mine and that I detested as it did those treaties of 1815 which one wishes to make nowadays the sole base of our policy." [39]

Historians have been as confused as were contemporaries by these cryptic phrases. Consensus has favored an interpretation along these lines: Napoleon favored nationalism, especially as it worked against the Vienna settlement, rather than the balance-of-power theory in the form in which it had been construed as the foundation of that

[35] Lynn M. Case, *French Opinion on War and Diplomacy during the Second Empire* (Philadelphia, 1954), p. 200.
[36] Goltz to Bismarck, May 2, 1866 (Oncken, I, 153).
[37] Mérimée, *Panizzi*, II, 191.
[38] Oncken, I, 165, n. 1.
[39] Extract from the published text of the Auxerre speech, *Moniteur*, May 7, 1866 (Oncken, I, 165).

settlement and in which it was now advocated by Thiers. He hoped for redress of the curtailment of French territories decreed by the First and Second Peace of Paris. Specifically, in the present situation, he favored a war in the belief that it would further nationalist goals and might enable him to acquire new territories for France. He probably did not consider the latter indispensable; but it was an important point in his attempt to gain French support.[40] The implication of the speech was thoroughly pro-Prussian, since it was Prussia which was the revisionist power and the self-appointed champion of the cause of German nationalism.

Napoleon's motives in this declaration might be open to doubt, were it not for his simultaneous backstage maneuvers. If the speech was considered alone, it would be possible to argue that the Emperor had intended it as a threat to Austria calculated to increase the willingness of the ministry in Vienna to pursue the negotiations already in process. However, the seriousness of Napoleon's statement is shown by the fact that on or before May 5, immediately before the speech, Loë, the Prussian military attaché, received secret overtures in the same vein. The choice of the attaché, rather than the ambassador, was explained plausibly by the fact that Goltz had displayed consistent hostility to any arrangements involving the cession of German territory.[41] It is impossible to prove Napoleon's direct connection with these overtures, but a brief review of the evidence suggests that he sponsored them as the implementation of the policy expressed in the Auxerre speech.

In the first place, the choice of a messenger is completely compatible with Napoleon's complicity. Loë was approached by Vimercati, a rather unsavory and comparatively insignificant diplomat who had patched together a spotty career through influence in high places. He had served under Canrobert in the Italian campaign of 1859[42] and had been for a time a civil servant in the French government,

---

[40] Case, *French Opinion on War and Diplomacy,* p. 200.
[41] Radowitz' Diary, May 5, 1866, as quoted by Oncken, I, 184, n. 1.
[42] Bapst, *Le Maréchal Canrobert,* IV, 28–9.

thanks to Rouher's influence. More recently, he had held a minor post at the Italian embassy in Paris. He had had a quarrel with Nigra, with whom he disagreed profoundly on matters of policy, and had been recalled to Italy at the ambassador's wish. His enforced exile had been brief, however, for his favor with Victor Emmanuel, for whom he frequently performed unspecified errands, insured his reappointment.[43] Vimercati's roster of distinguished friends also included Plon-plon, as well as Victor Emmanuel's fiancée, and General Fleury,[44] who from the time of the coup d'état in 1851 had been frequently entrusted by Napoleon with confidential undertakings.[45] It would be natural for Napoleon, eager to make private propositions to the Prussians but unwilling to appear in the matter directly, to approach Fleury with the request that the general find and instruct a messenger who could carry these ideas to receptive ears in the Prussian embassy; and it is clear that Vimercati was acting on behalf of Fleury in this instance.[46]

But it is not enough to know that, if Napoleon had sought a go-between, Vimercati would have been a logical choice. In order to prove Napoleon's involvement, more direct evidence is needed. There is further, rather negative corroboration in the fact that there seems to be no one else who might have taken the responsibility of suggesting Vimercati's overtures. Prince Napoleon was certainly capable of vigorous independent action when he felt that it was dictated by the best interests of France—and Italy—but at this juncture he was not even in France. He was traveling in Italy and did not return until the middle of the month.[47] This provides an alibi. Another possibility is the Minister of State, Rouher, but he seems in general to have followed Napoleon's directions and, although he

[43] Goltz to William, May 10, 1866 (Oncken, I, 181–2); Loë, *Erinnerungen aus meinem Berufsleben 1849–67,* p. 86.

[44] Loë, pp. 86–7; Bapst, IV, 28.

[45] [Emile Félix] Comte Fleury, *Souvenirs,* 2 vols. (Paris, 1897–98), *passim.*

[46] Oncken, I, 186, n. 1.

[47] Dieudé Defly to Drouyn de Lhuys, May 11, 1866 (*Origines,* IX, 102); PRO: Cowley to Clarendon, May 16, 1866 (F. O. 519/232).

frequently urged his opinions with decision, it is unlikely that he would have gone so far as to initiate these negotiations. The same objections apply to General Fleury, who was undoubtedly involved in the discussions. In fact, Oncken, on the basis of later Prussian belief that Fleury was Napoleon's spokesman, sees in Fleury's agency an important proof that Napoleon ultimately sponsored the démarche.[48]

Finally, there is the suggestive coincidence that Vimercati's proposals embodied the program set forth in the Auxerre speech. After the initial contact with Loë around May 5, the day before the speech, conversations were delayed until May 7. On that date, Vimercati assured the Prussian attaché that France could not stand by while Prussia acquired new territories. The French government could only condone her neighbor's aggrandizement if compensations were assured. Vimercati proposed specifically that the Prussian government offer the Rhine provinces to France. This promise would become the basis for an arrangement between Paris and Berlin designed to insure Prussian victory. The agreement should be worked out by some competent Prussian representative and General Fleury, whom Vimercati designated as the immediate instigator of his mission. The next day, a second talk took place, in which Vimercati urged the same proposals, but with even more emphasis.[49] After that, the talks tapered off. On May 11, another discussion was held but Vimercati now urged a general trading of territories similar to Metternich's suggestions.[50] However, this conversation occurred after abundant opposition to the program of the Auxerre speech had become evident, and the change to a more popular plan can probably be traced to this source.

The Prussians were not seriously impressed by Vimercati's mission. Loë, who must have been a legalist, was embarrassed by Vimercati's attempt to evade Goltz. He immediately safeguarded himself by

---

[48] Oncken, I, 186, and n. 1.
[49] Loë to Goltz, May 10, 1866 (Oncken, I, 185–7).
[50] Goltz to William, May 11, 1866 (Oncken, I, 192).

telling Goltz about the overtures. Goltz, although he disapproved ultimately of Vimercati's plan, felt that it was important to explore every avenue; he therefore encouraged Loë to talk to him.[51] Bismarck took the attitude that Vimercati was an untrustworthy adventurer.[52] His suspicion was doubtless reinforced by the fact that he had never trusted Plon-plon, with whom Vimercati had been closely associated.[53] As result Vimercati's overtures were abortive; but the failure of Napoleon's plan was not entirely due to Bismarck's unwillingness to negotiate.

A mission such as Vimercati's depended for its success on two factors: not only its favorable reception by the Prussians, but also the depth and breadth of its backing in France. The Prussian diplomats were, without exception, highly skeptical as to the genuineness of the proposals. Another problem was the French reaction to the Auxerre speech which was one of universal hostility. The prefectural reports, despite inevitable slanting to support the government's hopes, indicate considerable coolness.[54] As random instances here are two samples from the sensitive eastern area of France. From Metz:

> ... the Auxerre speech has been received as the vigorous expression of national aspirations . . . People desire ardently the continuation of the peace, provided that it is compatible with the honor and security of the country, and people have faith in the wise capacity of the Emperor to reconcile and safeguard these great interests.[55]

At about the same time, the Procureur Général at Colmar, in Alsace, reported:

> The possibility of an increase in territory is not regarded with indifference by anybody, and Alsace has too patriotic a spirit to deny herself, in

[51] Goltz to William, May 10, 1866 (Oncken, I, 181).

[52] Oncken, I, 182, n. 1.

[53] Bismarck to Usedom, February 25, 1866 (APP, VI, 600, n. 2). Later on, when official communications from Nigra seemed to support some of Vimercati's remarks, Goltz changed his mind and decided that Vimercati's claims to inspiration from high places were genuine. (Goltz to William, May 22, 1866 [Oncken, I, 225–6].)

[54] Case, French Opinion on War and Diplomacy, p. 201.

[55] AN: Metz, Report of July 7, 1866 (BB^{30}380: Metz 1865–68).

that respect, a noble and legitimate ambition. But this preoccupation is only secondary in this country where the spirit of the masses is generally directed by the industrial aristocracy which prefers peace and the revival of business to all the glorious advantages which war might procure.[56]

These statements could not be considered wholehearted endorsements of the activist policy of the Auxerre speech, and the survey of the reports of the prefects and procureurs généraux carried out by André Armengaud extends this impression. Armengaud concludes that the speech was greeted with opposition all over France. As one would expect, the hostility was strongest in bourgeois circles, for business interests expected that war would harm prosperity and economic stability. But among the lower classes too the response was far from favorable. In the cities, the latter were favorably influenced to some degree, but in the countryside, anxiety about the effect of the war upon the harvesting tempered considerations of national and Bonapartist pride.[57] This is interesting, for it has been suggested that Napoleon chose the occasion of a speech in the rural Department of the Yonne as an auspicious opportunity for his statement because he believed that he could rally the support of the agricultural lower classes against the program of the urban bourgeoisie as expounded by Thiers.[58] Apparently, however, he did not deliver the crucial words at Auxerre, and even if he had, such a maneuver would have been unsuccessful. Most Frenchmen, regardless of class, were anti-Prussian, for they blamed the Prussians both for the present crisis and for the rigors inflicted on France in the invasion of 1814, and pacifist,[59] with much support for suggestions, such as that of a congress, which seemed to safeguard peace.[60]

These reactions were also reflected in the press, which, owing to the heavy imperial censorship, was a less accurate index of public opinion than the reports of the prefects and the procureurs généraux.

---

[56] AN: Colmar, Special Report of July 5, 1866 (BB30376: Colmar 1865–66).
[57] Armengaud, pp. 81–3.
[58] Armengaud, p. 77.
[59] Armengaud, p. 45.
[60] Armengaud, pp. 85–6.

Lynn Case found that about half the newspapers that he selected for use in his excellent study, *French Opinion on War and Diplomacy during the Second Empire,* opposed the speech. In view of the degree of governmental control, he considers this percentage significantly high.[61] The few pro-Prussian papers such as the *Siècle* and the *Opinion Nationale* did approve Napoleon's position.[62] In contrast, one may cite the fulminations of Thiers' friend, Prévost-Paradol, in the *Courrier du dimanche.* Prévost-Paradol admitted that Napoleon's line was "intelligible," but called it a "trap" for "naïve patriotism" which might indeed seduce the lower classes but could only be viewed with "disgust" by intellectuals. Prévost-Paradol revealed the overmastering concern of his group when he went on to say that if peace continued, the Liberal cause would unquestionably win, whereas a war would strengthen the reigning imperial system. He accused the advocates of war of disguising authoritarianism as love of country.[63]

The opposition to the policy of the Auxerre speech reached its height in business circles, where opinion, whether dictated by estimates of the requirements of the economy or by private concerns, was strongly pacifist and anti-Prussian. These trends were already evident before the beginning of May. Armengaud cites impressive figures both from the stock market and from the gold reserves of the Bank of France to show that the period of the spring and early summer was a time of economic stagnation and even decline.[64] The anxiety about the future which had, in part, caused the downturn was, of course, reinforced by evidence of the apparent justice of such anxiety and the situation deteriorated further. As early as the middle of April, Rothschild had estimated the damages at eight hundred million francs.[65] In an attempt to stem the losses, such arch-

[61] Case, *French Opinion on War and Diplomacy,* p. 200.
[62] Armengaud, p. 76.
[63] *Courrier du dimanche,* May 13, 1866 (Prévost-Paradol, *Quelques Pages d'histoire contemporaine: Lettres politiques,* IV, 85–91). The government condemned this article. (Prévost-Paradol, IV, 94–6.)
[64] Armengaud, p. 58, n. 61.
[65] PRO: Cowley to Clarendon, April 13, 1866 (F. O. 519/232).

enemies as Rothschild and Péreire[66] united to urge a policy of peace upon the Emperor but it seems unlikely that their representations had any specific results. Napoleon's reply to the financiers was discouraging,[67] although he was distressed and bewildered by the conflict between their excellent arguments and his own analyses.[68]

In such a moment of economic uneasiness, the Auxerre speech came as a rude shock. The stock market, already highly sensitive, reacted immediately. In the day or so following the speech, the losses totaled at least eighteen hundred million.[69] Emile Péreire, even more pessimistic, set the figure of the losses at two milliards.[70] These effects were not permanent. Within a short time, the market began to rise gently. By the end of May, the news of progress toward a congress had strengthened the rally.[71] Directly after the speech, however, important financiers such as James Rothschild, the Paris

---

[66] Egon Caesar, Count Corti, *The Reign of the House of Rothschild 1830–71*, p. 378.

[67] Wächter to Varnbüler, April 11, 1866 (Oncken, I, 132).

[68] PRO: Cowley to Clarendon, April 17, 1866 (F. O. 519/232). In point of fact, both the Rothschilds and the Péreires would lose considerable sums in the event of belligerent or pro-Prussian policy. The Rothschilds were heavily involved in the finances of both Austria and Italy and tended to favor plans involving the transfer of Venetia to Italy in return for a money payment—the money, naturally, to be furnished by a loan from the Rothschilds (Corti, pp. 370–1). At all times, the Rothschilds urged peace on the Austrian government as they had on the French. The Péreires, through the ill-fated Crédit Mobilier, were even more interested in the outcome of the German crisis. By 1866, the Crédit Mobilier was in serious difficulties, with dividends standing at zero. See Johann Plenge, *Gründung und Geschichte des Crédit Mobilier* (Tübingen, 1903), pp. 115–20. Like the Rothschilds, the Crédit Mobilier had large investments in Austria and Italy (Corti. p. 363), although its heaviest and, ultimately, more disastrous commitments were in Spain (Plenge, pp. 115–8). Of course, it was directly and adversely affected by the slump on the stock market in the spring of 1866 (Plenge, p. 115). It had had connections with the Finance Minister, Achille Fould, who had been involved indirectly in the founding of the Crédit Mobilier. See AN: "Observations pour les administrateurs du Crédit Mobilier," p. 8 (25 AQ1), but Fould had turned against the organization (Plenge, p. 114). It seems probable that neither the plight of the Rothschilds nor the catastrophe of the Crédit Mobilier influenced the government except in the most general way.

[69] Radowitz' Diary, May 8, 1866, as quoted by Oncken, I, 170, n. 2.

[70] Armengaud, pp. 80–1.

[71] Armengaud, pp. 84–5.

brother, suffered heavy losses and the latter, at least, did not hesitate to make his views clear. A number of people noticed Rothschild's gloom at a ball at the Tuileries on May 7;[72] he is said to have declared: "The Empire means slump."[73] Naturally, the disaster for Rothschild was only relative; Mérimée wrote sarcastically:

Nothing was more curious than the Empress' ball, Monday evening. The mien of the ambassadors was so long, that one would have taken them for people condemned to death. But the longest of all was that of Rothschild. They say that he lost ten millions the evening before; but he still has a lot more than you and me.[74]

However, Rothschild's chagrin was a source of concern to Napoleon, for he made a point of telling the banker of his hopes for the solution of the German question through a congress.[75]

Meanwhile, the ministers were even more concerned than Napoleon by the opposition to the Auxerre speech, a reaction with which many of them sympathized. Both Rouher and Randon begged the Emperor to adopt a pacifist policy;[76] while, as one would expect from the outcry in business circles, the Finance Minister, Fould, was particularly upset and expressed vigorously this general distrust of the imperial policy. Cowley relates:

To return to the Emperor's speech, Fould saw H.M. this morning and if his account of the conversation is correct, he told his master some home truths. Indeed he represents himself as having said that H.M. was marching to his own ruin and to that of France, that his encouragement of an alliance between Italy and Prussia was madness, that the confidence of the country was gone—and that his speech at Auxerre was an insult to his Ministers and to the Chambers—that he had demeaned himself by replying to Thiers, etc., etc.[77]

To add to Napoleon's misfortunes, the speech did not make a favorable impression on even the Prussians, whom he had hoped to

---

[72] PRO: Cowley to Clarendon, May 8, 1866 (F. O. 519/232).
[73] Radowitz' Diary, May 7, 1866, as quoted by Oncken, I, 165, n. 1.
[74] Mérimée, *Panizzi*, II, 192.
[75] PRO: Cowley to Clarendon, May 8, 1866 (F. O. 519/232).
[76] Radowitz' Diary, May 8, 1866, as quoted by Oncken, I, 170, n. 2.
[77] PRO: Cowley to Clarendon, May 8, 1866 (F. O. 519/232).

conciliate. In Berlin, Bismarck was thoroughly upset by the hints about the Rhine provinces, whose cession he opposed, both on the grounds of German national feeling and of a belated concern for the European balance of power. Bismarck went so far as to wonder whether Napoleon was trying to discourage the Prussians from a decisive policy by making war unattractive. Whatever Napoleon's intentions, this was the result of the speech, for his remarks were an important factor in Bismarck's determination to try for a last-minute reconciliation with Austria through the Gablenz Mission.[78]

The impact of this general opposition to the speech caused an important shift in Napoleon's policy which we can pinpoint from Goltz's dispatches. The ambassador saw Napoleon immediately after Fould's fulminations. Goltz found Napoleon in a mood which must have been entirely unexpected, and which the ambassador attributed, probably quite justly, to Fould's remarks.[79] Napoleon pronounced himself in favor of peace and declared that he believed this goal could be attained through a congress which would consider the three major problems of the day: the Venetian question, the Schleswig-Holstein question, and the German question. Napoleon evidently conceived of himself as an "honest broker," for he announced that he did not wish to gain territory for France.[80] France's reward would be the maintenance of peace. Despite the apparent suddenness of this return to the idea of a congress, the move was, to judge by later events, perfectly sincere and it seemed to offer a solution to all the problems raised by the events of early May. A congress was reconcilable with Thiers' emphasis on pacifism. Napoleon's secret discussions with the Italians and the Austrians on the Venetian

---

[78] Bismarck to Goltz, May 5, 1866 (Oncken, I, 161–2); for a full discussion, see Sybel, *The Founding of the German Empire*, IV, 425–45.

[79] Goltz to William, May 10, 1866 (Oncken, I, 182). Goltz points out that Napoleon's emphasis on the congress in the ensuing conference would have been perfectly reconcilable with Vimercati's pleas for an arrangement, made to Loë on the same day, for if. as Goltz quite reasonably believed, it was Fould's representations which had tipped the scale in the Emperor's mind, there would not have been time to reach Vimercati and change his instructions.

[80] Goltz to Bismarck, May 8, 1866 (Oncken, I, 172).

question indicated that it might be the inescapable prerequisite for an arrangement in that quarter, since the Italians believed that they had lost their freedom of action until the treaty with Prussia ran out in July.[81] The hostility to the Auxerre speech had incidentally revealed considerable support for a congress. The reports of the prefects and the procureurs généraux indicated some eagerness for the congress as a pacifist measure, while a businessman such as James Rothschild viewed it as an eleventh-hour chance for salvation.[82] Finally, the policy was favored by a number of ministers. In short, the Emperor's renewed interest in the congress, although sudden, was based on many considerations and on seemingly solid expectations, for Napoleon believed that, now that Franz Joseph had mentioned the possible cession of Venetia in Metternich's secret overtures, he might be brought, through skillful diplomacy and group pressure, to agree to a generally acceptable solution of the problem.[83]

Once Napoleon had returned to support of a congress, it was possible to arrange the preliminaries, which were already under consideration, with great rapidity. On May 8, Drouyn wrote the ambassadors at London and St. Petersburg suggesting that the French, English, and Russian governments, as the neutral powers, issue invitations to a congress. He ruled out the possibility of a previous agreement. The congress was to be a working session.[84] Difficulties immediately arose. The English were afraid that Drouyn hoped to pledge the neutrals to the imposition of a solution by armed force should negotiations fail,[85] and it was necessary to reassure them that no such joint measures were contemplated.[86] Furthermore, both the English and the Russians would have preferred a vaguer description of the problems to be considered by the congress than

---

[81] Oncken, *Napoleon III and the Rhine*, p. 49.

[82] Corti, p. 374.

[83] Ollivier, VIII, 147–8.

[84] Drouyn de Lhuys to La Tour d'Auvergne and Talleyrand, May 8, 1866 (*Origines*, IX, 53–4).

[85] La Tour d'Auvergne to Drouyn de Lhuys, May 9, 1866 (*Origines*, IX, 77–8).

[86] Drouyn de Lhuys to La Tour d'Auvergne, May 10, 1866 (*Origines*, IX, 85).

that favored by the French.[87] Finally, however, on May 15, it was possible to hold a preliminary meeting of the English and Russian ambassadors in Paris with Drouyn de Lhuys. According to rumors in diplomatic circles, this talk broke down on the question of the feasibility of finding compensations to offer the Austrians for the cession of Venetia.[88] However, this contretemps did not delay the group for long, for on May 16, a draft invitation was ready for approval by the English and Russian governments.[89] Clarendon agreed to the text at once;[90] Gortchakov insisted on a less explicit wording[91] and was able to carry his point.[92] With this concession made, the Russian acceptance was forthcoming immediately,[93] and it was possible to send out the formal invitations on May 24, 1866.[94]

Meanwhile, behind the scenes in the Quai d'Orsay, much thought had been devoted to the organization of a congress, both as to practical arrangements and to suggestions for solutions. Cowley reports a low moment in the planning: "There have been all sorts of wild projects on foot. Among them that the Conference sh. meet at Vichy while H.M. cleansed his stomach and the P.P. did, I suppose, as much into the bargain. A water drinking Congress wd have been something new." [95]

On a more serious level, however, there was much discussion of French recommendations for solutions of the problems to be considered. The results closely parallel, although they slightly modify, Napoleon's own views as delivered to Goltz in the conversation which had taken place immediately after Napoleon's talk with

[87] Goltz to Bismarck, May 21, 1866 (Oncken, I, 223); Talleyrand to Drouyn de Lhuys, May 9, 1866 (*Origines*, IX, 82).

[88] Wendland to von der Pfordten, May 16, 1866 (Oncken, I, 201, n. 1).

[89] Drouyn de Lhuys to Talleyrand and La Tour d'Auvergne, and Annexe, May 16, 1866 (*Origines*, IX, 145–7).

[90] Clarendon to Cowley, May 17, 1866 (*Origines*, IX, 162–3).

[91] Talleyrand to Drouyn de Lhuys, May 21, 1866 (*Origines*, IX, 210).

[92] Drouyn de Lhuys to Talleyrand, May 22, 1866 (*Origines*, IX, 219).

[93] Talleyrand to Drouyn de Lhuys, May 24, 1866 (*Origines*, IX, 246).

[94] Drouyn de Lhuys's circular to the French representatives to Prussia, Austria, Italy, and the German Confederation, May 24, 1866 (*Origines*, IX, 248–9).

[95] PRO: Cowley to Clarendon, May 31, 1866 (F. O. 519/232).

Fould. It seems likely that the official program was directly inspired by the Emperor while the Quai d'Orsay merely polished the program. Napoleon had suggested that Venetia be ceded to Italy. The official version elaborated this proposal by suggesting that Italy and Prussia give the Austrians monetary compensations for the lost province which the Austrians could use to buy equivalent territories from the Ottoman Empire. Both Napoleon's comments and the official program indicated that the Schleswig-Holstein question should be solved by annexation of the two provinces by Prussia, although the Foreign Office draft stated this goal in more obscure language. But the most interesting question for present purposes was the future of the German Confederation. Napoleon had proposed rather bluntly that Prussia be given a predominant position in the north while the southern states be free to form their own union. The Quai d'Orsay suggestions reaffirmed that the powers were interested in the constitution of the Confederation only in so far as it affected the balance of power. The draft then went on to note that the small states of the north tended to gravitate toward Prussia while those of the south were more apt to work with Austria. It was accordingly proposed that the Confederation be reformed on this basis.[96] This program, inexplicitly stated though it is, implies an arrangement similar to that envisaged by Napoleon, except that the Austrians are given a more important role by the Foreign Office. On the surface, this might seem important; but in view of the problems raised by any union of the multinational Hapsburg Empire with the South German states it is doubtful that this combination would have been a real threat to the Prussian-dominated group in the north.

Even before these plans had been completed, indications from Vienna opened the future of the congress to serious question. Gramont reported on May 22 that Mensdorff seemed to be taking the attitude that "there is no Venetian question." Although Mens-

[96] Goltz to Bismarck, May 8, 1866 (Oncken, I, 172); "Projet d'allocution pour l'ouverture du Congrès," May 29, 1866 (*Origines,* IX, 298–303).

dorff reasserted his secret offers to Napoleon of early May, he declared that he doubted the feasibility of finding practicable compensations for Venetia. He was already murmuring his eventual suggestion that all the powers bind themselves to seek no additional territory.[97] Mensdorff expressed these views in more stringent form in a dispatch of May 25 to Metternich.[98]

Gradually increasing doubts as to Austrian willingness to participate constructively in a congress were one factor which led Napoleon, despite his new conviction that this plan represented the best hope for a solution, to continue to explore possibilities for a bilateral agreement with either Austria or Prussia. It seems probable that the Emperor was skeptical about the results of such overtures. His recent experience made it seem unlikely that either side would offer desirable concessions until the situation had become even more threatening. Still, it was at least useful to keep communications open. Since the conclusion of the Prusso-Italian alliance, with its probable corollary of a severe Italian defeat, he was forced at the very least to insure himself a voice in the final settlement. Another motive for action was his continued predilection for the Prussian cause. Finally, there were at least two reasons for continued negotiations with Austria: any abrupt cessation of talks upon French initiative would have convinced the Austrians that they had lost their only friend and would have greatly heightened their suspicions of a congress; and secondly, in view of the widespread support for Thiers' speech, Napoleon was in no position to block prematurely any avenue which might lead, in case of ultimate necessity, to a realization of his opponent's pacifist and anti-Prussian program.

A combination of these motives inspired Napoleon's response to a démarche by his ex-minister, Persigny. As we have seen, Persigny had become involved in the German question through Metternich's desire to use him as a channel to present his overtures

<hr/>

[97] Gramont to Drouyn de Lhuys, May 22, 1866 (*Origines*, IX, 233–4).
[98] Mensdorff to Metternich, May 25, 1866 (*Origines*, IX, 267–8).

of early May. The démarche had collapsed with the revelation of opposition in Florence and Vienna, but Persigny, who was nothing if not persistent, had continued to urge this arrangement upon Napoleon. The Emperor, who now favored a congress, evidently desired to get rid of his old friend tactfully and had referred him to Eugénie. She in turn had sent him back to Napoleon, so that poor Persigny had become a shuttle.[99] Eugénie had disliked him for years,[100] but she approved of the Austrian program and threw her weight behind him in this instance, in opposition to the ministers Rouher and La Valette, who favored a congress as a pacifist gesture.[101] Persigny had been quite excited by this show of favor and had told Metternich of his success. Since he had seemed quite certain that he had converted Napoleon, Metternich was momentarily elated. Later, in talking to Eugénie, he realized that Persigny had exaggerated, and that, although Eugénie approved the plan, Napoleon's assent was far from certain.[102] It was at about this time that the Austrian ambassador remarked, with even more truth than he knew: "I have the feeling . . . of a man who, involved by duty and by patriotism in the events of the day, understands nothing, but nothing at all, of the situation." [103] Meanwhile, it was essential from Napoleon's point of view to do something to quiet Persigny's ardor without fatally alienating the Austrians at a moment when it was vital to keep communications open. Napoleon's solution was to invite Persigny to present his ideas at a joint meeting of the Council of Ministers and the Privy Council, to be held on May 18.[104] This

[99] Metternich to Mensdorff, May 16, 1866 (Oncken, I, 205–6); Radowitz' Diary, no date, as quoted by Oncken, I, 206, n. 1.

[100] Elizabet Esslinger, *Kaiserin Eugenie und die Politik des zweiten Kaiserreiches* (Stuttgart, 1932), p. 118.

[101] Metternich to Mensdorff, May 16, 1866 (Oncken, I, 203). Metternich believed that Drouyn de Lhuys also favored a congress, but, as will be shown below, it seems unlikely that Drouyn did more than go through the motions of supporting a congress, in deference to Napoleon.

[102] HHSA: Metternich to Mensdorff, May 16, 1866, no. 25D.

[103] Metternich to Mensdorff, May 16, 1866 (Oncken, I, 204).

[104] The date of this meeting has been the subject of considerable controversy. Ollivier (VIII, 177–9) assigns it to mid-June and Robert Schnerb *(Rouher et le*

was a masterly way of coping with the difficulty, for Persigny would hardly be able to say that his offers had been slighted, while Napoleon would have valuable allies among the ministers, who could be made to carry the opposition.

Persigny has left us a description of the crucial meeting which gives us an unusually colorful picture of the atmosphere of the government and of the personalities involved. He wrote:

As always, M. Drouyn de Lhuys explained to the council, with perfect clarity, the history and the present state of recent diplomatic relations; but after this beautiful exposition, after having exhibited before the council all his dispatches well ordered and well arranged, the minister, enchanted with himself, had nothing more to say and especially nothing to propose.

On his side, M. Rouher, the light of the council in the discussions of public affairs and especially in the expedients of parliamentary tactics or *rouhereries,* as the Emperor used to say, of the political kitchen, M. Rouher disguised the emptiness of his ideas and his lack of resolution under the glitter of his habitual loquacity. He lectured about the chances of Austria or of Prussia, of tumults in the opposite direction of public opinion in Germany, of the diversion which Italy was going to provide, etc. In the role of a very shrewd man, and to the great displeasure of M. Drouyn de Lhuys, he showed his portfolio, his file, full, so he said, of important documents. He had received such a piece of information from Frankfurt, such another from Vienna, such another from Silesia; and spreading before us a whole mound of letters pulled from I do not know where, as if he were, at least, as well informed by his private correspondence, as the minister of foreign affairs by all our diplomacy, he profited by the incidents of this setting to heave the lead here and there, in search of the undecided or unknown thinking of the Emperor. But as for the question itself, one felt clearly that he was swimming in a sea of obscurities. Like M. Drouyn de Lhuys, and with the exception only of his very decided opinion that it was necessary that nothing be asked of the Chambers in order not to frighten the country, he concluded nothing and proposed nothing.[105]

Second Empire [Paris, 1949], p. 185) has followed this chronology. It seems to the present author, however, that the fact that Rouher's notes on the session are dated May 18 is decisive (AN: Rouher's notes on the meetings of the Council of Ministers, May 18, 1866 [45 AP1, cahier 1]). For a similar view, see Oncken, I, 211, n. 1.

[105] Persigny, *Mémoires,* pp. 325–6.

After this beginning, Persigny, very sure that he was about to set forth the definitive solution, exposed the plan which had originated in Metternich's overtures. Although the derivation of Persigny's suggestions is clear, it is evident that he arranged his emphasis in order to play up the more attractive proposals and minimize the objectionable. Rather than lingering on the controversial Italian settlement, he underlined the importance of the principle of nationalities which Napoleon favored and the necessity of allowing the Prussians a measured success in this direction by condoning their assumption of hegemony in North Germany. He added that this would be a limited fulfillment of German nationalist ambitions. But most of his talk concerned the Rhineland. He painted a glowing picture of the advantages to France of stripping the Rhine provinces from Prussia and establishing them under independent princes. Persigny maintained that it would be feasible, over the years, for the French to achieve the annexation of these provinces through the multiplication of economic and cultural ties; but this gradual method would carry the inestimable benefit of avoiding outrage to German national feeling.

Naturally, there was some debate on these proposals, for their extraordinary clearsightedness did not seem as apparent to the ministers as it had to Persigny. Drouyn de Lhuys declared that the plan was impracticable. Persigny retorted that the great obstacle to French intervention in German affairs was the general suspicion of French ambitions. If the French proclaimed at the start that they did not wish to acquire new territories, it would be possible to cooperate with the German authorities. Eugénie came to Persigny's support by pointing out the danger to France of a completely united and greatly strengthened Germany and the implications for French power of the principle of nationalities. Another view hostile to Persigny was added by Walewski, who remarked that in view of the moral commitment to Italy and the impossibility, at this point, of restraining her belligerence, the hands of the French government were essentially tied. The reception given Persigny's plan was cold, and it was finally repudiated, for the ultimate decision of the Council determined that French efforts should be concentrated on the congress.[106] To be sure, Napoleon did summon Persigny next morning and reiterated his interest in the plan.[107] This may be regarded as soothing syrup, administered because of Persigny's connections with Metternich. In its current form, the plan was dead.

These events did not mean that the conclusion of an agreement with Austria dropped from view. Discussion of the situation continued, but through ordinary diplomatic channels rather than the special missions envisaged by Persigny. In the talks, the plan sponsored by Metternich and Persigny inevitably formed the starting point, but attention was concentrated on modifying or changing the Austrian proposals in order to make them acceptable to the French. There was, as usual, a difference between the positions of Napoleon and his Foreign Minister. Drouyn was quite eager to promote an arrangement with the Ballplatz. He feared that Persigny might be superseding him in the Emperor's favor and would have preferred a congress to a decision which would have marked imperial concurrence in Persigny's schemes;[108] but in ordinary circumstances, he opposed the congress privately[109] and worked against Napoleon's pacifist policies where he dared.[110] Meanwhile, his attitude toward Metternich was reassuring. On May 19, for example, he declared that he believed that France and Austria would conclude an alliance if war broke out or if the congress proved a failure.[111] But Drouyn's greatest effort, which occupied him throughout the latter part of May, was an attempt to hammer out a position on the Italian question more acceptable to the French. Metternich's proposals of early May had included the intention to

---

[106] Protocol of the session of the Council of Ministers and the Privy Council, May 18, 1866 (Oncken, I, 209–10).

[107] Persigny, pp. 326–39.

[108] HHSA: Metternich to Mensdorff, May 16, 1866, no. 25E.

[109] PRO: Cowley to Clarendon, May 13, 1866 (F. O. 519/232).

[110] PRO: Cowley to Clarendon, May 15, 1866 (F. O. 519/232).

[111] HHSA: Metternich to Mensdorff, May 19, 1866, no. 80.

modify or destroy Italian unity and independence. It was this aspect of the overtures which chiefly occupied Drouyn. He suggested that the Austrians restrain themselves from overt steps designed to break up the Italian nation and content themselves with waiting for the new nation to crumble of its own weight.[112] These suggestions stood in reasonable harmony with Napoleon's views, which, according to Metternich, involved acquiescence in or even pleasure at the prospect of Austrian victory, but opposition to unilateral Austrian gains.[113] Metternich objected to either Napoleon's or Drouyn's line of thought, for, as he pointed out to Drouyn with some justice, it was unreasonable to expect the Austrians, in case of success, to refrain from profit. Drouyn fell back on the old proposal that the Austrians await the expiration of the Prusso-Italian treaty, when new combinations might be possible.[114]

In contrast to the Foreign Minister, Napoleon evidently regarded negotiations with Austria at this time as out of the question. Metternich gives us considerable insight into the Emperor's views through his report of a conversation which took place at a court ball on May 21.[115] Napoleon sought out the ambassador in a side room and they discussed Franco-Austrian relations for nearly an hour. Metternich expressed great disgust at Napoleon's hopes for a congress based on the cession of Venetia. He remarked to the sovereign: "Your Majesty has just thrown on the gaming-table a card which we had furtively passed You," [116] and he declared that "the congress ... is ... the first act of hostility undertaken against Austria ..." [117] In response to these accusations, Napoleon explained his reasoning at length. He claimed that the German situation did not worry him, while the Italian question was a matter of deep concern. He was certain that the Austrians would win and he did not wish to

[112] HHSA: Metternich to Mensdorff, May 29, 1866, no. 29B.
[113] HHSA: Metternich to Mensdorff, May 20, 1866, no. 81.
[114] HHSA: Metternich to Mensdorff, May 29, 1866, no. 29B.
[115] HHSA: Metternich to Mensdorff, May 22, 1866, no. 84.
[116] HHSA: Metternich to Mensdorff, May 23, 1866, no. 28B.
[117] HHSA: Metternich to Mensdorff, May 23, 1866, no. 28B.

see Italian unity destroyed nor did he wish to go to war to save it. He had hoped that it might be possible to make a three-way agreement with Austria before the war, but this had proved impossible because the Italians were unwilling to remain neutral. To dramatize the hopelessness of an arrangement in the present situation, Napoleon asked Metternich if the Ballplatz would be willing to negotiate from the premise that Venetia would be given up, even if the Austrians won in Italy. This was indeed the only condition on which an agreement with Austria would be acceptable to the Emperor, now that an Austro-Italian war and its corollary, an Italian defeat, seemed inevitable to him. Metternich was horrified, and Napoleon, who had been carefully leading him to this point, explained that this was the reason for his belief that there could be no Franco-Austrian agreement now, except through a congress or a war.[118]

Meanwhile, the alternative of an agreement with Prussia was still in the air, but it seems doubtful that Napoleon regarded it as any more feasible than an arrangement with Austria. The non-success of the Vimercati overtures, added to the violently hostile reception accorded the Auxerre speech, combined to make Napoleon's hopes look illusory. But, ironically enough, it was just at this moment, according to the most logical construction of the evidence, that Bismarck made a new démarche, the famous Kiss Mission. Historians have usually assigned this mission to French initiative, but there are substantial reasons for assuming that its original instigator was Bismarck. A thaw had been discernible in the Prussian attitude toward France for some weeks before the overtures. In the middle of May, Bismarck had sent a special messenger to Napoleon in the person of Major von der Burg, who brought a private letter from King William to Napoleon. The mission was motivated, at least in part, by Bismarck's desire to circumvent Goltz, whose reports seemed to him contradictory and perplexing. Unfortunately, Goltz realized that the sending of a special emissary reflected no

[118] HHSA: Metternich to Mensdorff, May 23, 1866, no. 28B.

credit upon his conduct of affairs and further feared that through Burg, the Prussians might be brought to agreement upon Goltz's nightmare, the cession of German soil. Accordingly, he sabotaged the démarche with a series of untenable reasons, including the arguments that the letter was not .couched in the best terms, that no letter at all should have been sent, that Napoleon, who had had slight connections with Burg in the past, would not remember him, that it was impossible to arrange a time for the interview. The result of the incident was greatly to embitter the already strained relations between Bismarck and his ambassador.[119] While the episode testifies to Bismarck's eagerness to establish new and more flexible contacts with Napoleon, its aftermath must have created an even greater need for them. Another factor which might have contributed to Bismarck's willingness to work through special missions, was that, about this time or a little later, the Prussians began to believe that Napoleon had been behind the Vimercati overtures. This belief would make the attempt to establish extraofficial contacts seem more promising.

These incidents form the immediate background of the Kiss Mission. The events surrounding its origins offer further evidence that the new attempt at negotiation sprang from Bismarck's initiative. Kiss de Nemeskér was a Hungarian expatriate resettled in Paris who, like Vimercati, boasted connections with a roster of men of far greater importance than he. Early in May, 1866, upon the advice of the great Hungarian leader, Kossuth, he had gone to Berlin to discuss the possibilities of joint action between the Prussians and the oppressed and restive Hungarians. He arrived in Berlin on May 7[120] and in his first letter, written the next day, urged Bismarck to grant him an interview.[121] The talk took place

---

[119] Goltz to William, May 11, 1866 (Oncken, I, 190–1, and n. 1, 190); Benedetti to Drouyn de Lhuys, May 15, 1866 (*Origines*, IX, 136–7).

[120] Oncken, I, 241, n. 1.

[121] Merseburg: Kiss to Bismarck [May 8, 1866] (AAZB no. 86). My dating of this and the May 14 letter is confirmed by the researches of Dr. Welsch, of the archives at Merseburg.

on May 12,[122] but evidently Kiss was unsatisfied, for he wrote again on May 14 and once more on May 17 begging for further conversation.[123] He had originally planned to leave Berlin on May 20,[124] but he found himself detained by Pentecost, and spent his enforced holiday drawing up, in rough form, a small blueprint for a Hungarian revolution, to be run as a diversionary campaign in an Austro-Prussian war. From comments within the sketch, we can gather that Bismarck distrusted such suggestions, partly because he feared possible Russian intervention, but partly because, as he admitted to his ambassador in Italy, he doubted Kiss's authority and accuracy and believed that an unsuccessful revolt in Hungary would merely strengthen the Austrians.[125] Apparently, however, Kiss's fully elaborated scheme impressed Bismarck for he saw Kiss again and used him to further his own plans; this must be the logical interpretation of Kiss's next letter, written on May 25 after his return to Paris. Kiss wrote mysteriously:

> While traveling I reflected on the urgency of the *wines* and *linens* and while waiting until the French furniture can arrive, a matter which always requires 4 to 5 days, I allow myself to call to Your attention a personage that you have right at hand in Berlin.[126]

Apparently Bismarck was eager for support of some kind from France ("*wines* and *linens*"). Kiss had to wait until conversations with his contacts in Paris had produced definite offers ("furniture") but he was afraid that Bismarck might grow impatient in the meantime and so put him in touch with a second conspirator in Berlin who could answer questions and keep Bismarck interested.

[122] Merseburg: Kiss to Bismarck, May 17, 1866 (AAZB no. 85).

[123] Merseburg: Kiss to Bismarck [May 14, 1866] (AAZB no. 86); Kiss to Bismarck, May 17, 1866 (AAZB no. 85).

[124] Merseburg: Kiss to Bismarck, May 17, 1866 (AAZB no. 85).

[125] Merseburg: Kiss to Bismarck, May 21, 1866 (AAZB no. 86); Bismarck to Usedom, May 21, 1866 (Rep. 81 Italien I no. 8).

[126] Kiss to Bismarck, May 25, 1866 (Oncken, I, 242–3). Oncken assumes that this letter refers to a projected Prusso-French alliance and suggests that the plan may have originated either with Bismarck or in French circles. In view of the background given above, the former seems to the present author the more likely hypothesis.

Kiss's principal connection in France was Prince Napoleon, and it was presumably he whom the Hungarian approached upon his return from Berlin.[127] He could not have found anyone more inclined to be favorable. Prince Napoleon had originally been pro-Italian rather than pro-Prussian, but the exigencies of the Prusso-Italian treaty had convinced him by mid-May that an active policy had to be undertaken which would help both powers. He had played for a time with the plan put forward by Persigny,[128] but he soon returned to the idea of a triple alliance between Italy, France, and Prussia.[129] Thus the overtures brought by Kiss were most likely to please the prince. It is not surprising that he assumed a role in the negotiations. Probably, however, he did not act upon his own initiative. There are several reasons to believe that he must have consulted the Emperor and have been assured of his approval, tacit or otherwise. First of all, Plon-plon's exalted birth did not entirely excuse him from conformity; as recently as the summer of 1865, he had been forced to retire from an active position in the imperial regime because of some ill-considered remarks made in a speech at Ajaccio.[130] To circumvent the Quai d'Orsay and carry on private diplomatic negotiations in the name of France would scarcely merit any milder correction. In point of fact, however, the prince, far from being disgraced, was officially reinstated in favor in June, 1866.[131] Another argument in favor of Napoleon's complicity is the fact that Bismarck had always distrusted Plon-plon, whose influence he considered greatly overrated.[132] It seems doubtful, if the Prussian minister did initiate the negotiations, that he would have chosen this channel unless he had been assured that it would lead to the Emperor. Finally, it is noteworthy that Prince Napoleon

[127] Oncken, I, 242, n. 2.

[128] Oncken, I, 231, n. 1.

[129] Radowitz' Diary, May 23, 1866, as quoted by Oncken, I, 232, n. 1.

[130] Ernest d'Hauterive, ed., *Napoléon III et le Prince Napoléon: Correspondance inédite* (Paris, 1925), pp. 265-6.

[131] Napoleon to Prince Napoleon, June 21, 1866 (d'Hauterive, pp. 272-3).

[132] Otto von Bismarck, *GW*, V, 518.

learned about the ultimately successful negotiations with Austria early in June, and his source was possibly Napoleon himself.[133] If this is the case, it looks suspiciously like concerted action. For these reasons it seems logical to conclude that Napoleon favored the Kiss Mission.

There were many aspects of the mission that were calculated to appeal to the Emperor. First, it held out a last hope for the policy of accord with Bismarck. It could be argued, too, that this démarche had a far better chance of success than other recent attempts, for Kiss was actually in touch with Bismarck, whereas efforts earlier in May had collapsed before contact had been made between the top figures on either side. Secondly, the Kiss Mission offered one means of solving the Venetian problem and rescuing the Italians, a concern which lay close to Napoleon's heart.[134] Finally, the timing of this mission was particularly propitious. Previous efforts to reach an agreement with the Prussians had been hampered in part by the bitter unpopularity of such diplomacy within France. Now when early indications suggested that the Austrians might sabotage the popularly favored expedient of a congress, it might be a good moment for the French government to spark an anti-Austrian reaction within France which would greatly aid the Emperor's plan.[135] If this were to be done, however, it was important to start conversations before the plan for a congress faded, for the French would benefit from the pressure on Bismarck created by the threat of a congressional solution. Thus the last days of May represented an excellent moment for a resumption of the effort to reach agreement with Berlin.

The mission itself can be described simply. The crux of the

[133] Metternich strongly suspected that Napoleon had informed Plon-plon about the negotiations (HHSA: Metternich to Mensdorff, June 12, 1866, no. 31A); Drouyn de Lhuys later denied that Napoleon had communicated "the text of the convention" to Plon-plon (HHSA: Metternich to Mensdorff, June 17, 1866, no. 32A), but this rather curiously phrased comment permits the historian to wonder whether he may not have communicated the substance.

[134] PRO: Cowley to Clarendon, May 27, 1866 (F. O. 519/232).

[135] PRO: Cowley to Bloomfield, May 26, 1866 (F. O. 519/232).

matter has been preserved in a draft treaty which, according to the present interpretation, we may assume Kiss carried back to Berlin after consultation with Prince Napoleon in Paris. The document provided for all possible contingencies. If a congress were held, France and Prussia were to unite their efforts to assign Venetia to Italy and Schleswig-Holstein to Prussia. If the congress failed, or if it were never held, the two powers were to conclude a triple alliance with Italy designed for the prosecution of war against Austria. The war aims were specified as follows: Italy would get Venetia; Prussia would be allowed to reform the Confederation and would also annex territories in Germany to the number of seven or eight million inhabitants; France would get the Rhine provinces.[136]

These terms have a familiar ring and are almost a summary of Napoleon's proposals of the preceding eight months. The history of these previous negotiations suggests that any difficulty would lie in the demand for the Rhine provinces. Probably Napoleon realized fully his indiscretion; but from the emphasis on the Rhineland in the Auxerre speech it is patent that he had decided even then that nothing less would convince the French public that a pro-Prussian policy was worthwhile. After the disastrous failure of the speech, there could be no question of lessening the booty. In any event, the Prussian minister apparently refused even to consider the compensations for France which were the basis of the draft treaty brought by Kiss.[137] As result, by June 1 it was recognized by everyone concerned in Paris and Berlin that the Kiss Mission had failed.[138] Although, early in June, Bismarck sent an emissary named Türr to France to offer Belgium, Luxemburg, and portions of the Rhineland to Napoleon in return for French aid,[139] these suggestions were too little and too late. By June 1, the last feasible opportunity for

[136] French Draft Treaty from the secret mission of Prince Napoleon and Kiss, May 30, 1866 (Oncken, I, 243–4).
[137] See Appendix B.
[138] Kiss to Bismarck, June 1, 1866 (Oncken, I, 245–6).
[139] Bush, p. 108.

agreement between Prussia and France, Bismarck and Napoleon, had come to an end.

For a moment it looked as though the plan for a congress, which Napoleon had already accepted as the more practicable alternative, was still tenable. It was quickly ascertained that both the Prussians and the Italians would participate.[140] That left only the Austrian answer in doubt. The first indications after the presentation of the invitation were encouraging;[141] but soon the possibility of a demand for a ban on annexations appeared again.[142] The crucial decision was Franz Joseph's and he made it alone on May 30 or May 31, presumably after talking with one or two of his trusted advisers.[143] The results were embodied in a dispatch of June 1 to the Austrian ambassadors at Paris, London, and St. Petersburg. The essential stipulation was that Austria would take part in a congress only after the conferring powers had agreed to renounce all territorial aggrandizement. In explaining their reasons for this requirement, with its concomitant rejection of the cession of Venetia, the Austrians pointed out that the loss of this province would mark the end of Austria's importance among the European nations. They declared that they could not discover any valid compensation which would repair the damage, for money would be dishonorable, and land grants, with the exception of Silesia, did not seem adequate. They concluded that they could consent to rearrangements of the status quo only after a victorious campaign.[144]

As soon as this dispatch had reached Metternich, he communicated with the French government. Since Drouyn was out of Paris directing an agricultural meeting, he decided to go to Napoleon. The Emperor, doubtless quite as anxious as the ambassador, received

---

[140] Benedetti to Drouyn de Lhuys, May 29, 1866 (*Origines,* IX, 304); Malaret to Drouyn, May 29, 1866 (*Origines,* IX, 312).

[141] Mosbourg to Drouyn, May 29, 1866 (*Origines,* IX, 314).

[142] Mosbourg to Drouyn, May 31, 1866 (*Origines,* IX, 336); HHSA: Mensdorff to Metternich, May 23, 1866, and May 25, 1866, no. 2.

[143] Clark, p. 428, n. 204.

[144] Austrian Foreign Office to the Ambassadors at Paris, London, and St. Petersburg, June 1, 1866 (Oncken, I, 251, n. 2).

him in his study at the Tuileries. His first words were: "You're bringing me bad news, aren't you?" Metternich diplomatically replied that he brought "what he had foreseen." He then gave Napoleon the Austrian answer. Napoleon, after reading it, said that the ban on territorial annexations was, from his point of view, equivalent to rejection of the congress. Metternich began a speech of justification, which was brushed aside by the Emperor; Napoleon declared that the Venetian question was for him the "pivot of the deliberations" and refused to be distracted by the other papers which Metternich waved before him. Instead, "opening a drawer of his desk, the Emperor said . . . : 'Here is a very short and very simple little project which I submit to you.'" The document, which Metternich read with some astonishment, was the basis of the subsequent French treaty proposals. A long discussion followed, in which Metternich expressed suspicion and disgust. Napoleon admitted frankly his flirtations with Berlin, which he attributed, rather speciously, to his friendship for King William and his hope for "a bridge of gold" in the form of the Rhine provinces. He asserted, however, that he had abandoned these hopes and was sincere in wishing for an Austrian alliance. He restated the position on Italy which had been thrashed out in the May conversations between Metternich and Drouyn: he could not, as a matter of prestige, permit the Austrians to reverse Italian unification, but he would not intervene if it collapsed of its own weight. Finally, while reiterating his desire to reach an agreement which would permit the maintenance of French neutrality, Napoleon added a threat. He warned that if the Austrians refused his proposals: "I would be *forced to arm in my turn and to intervene eventually*." [145]

Napoleon's overtures to the Austrians were sudden and dramatic, but they sprang logically from the course of his policy during the spring. Some kind of an agreement which would guarantee Napo-

---

[145] HHSA: Metternich to Mensdorff, June 6, 1866, no. 30B. Cf. Oncken, I, 254, n. 3, as to that authority's belief in the decisiveness of this threat in bringing eventual Austrian compliance.

leon a voice in the final settlement had become a sine qua non once the Prusso-Italian treaty of alliance had exposed Napoleon's protégés to the supposedly superior Austrian might. The attempt to reach an agreement with Bismarck had not been successful. This fact could hardly be questioned after the failure, revealed just a day or two before, of the Kiss Mission. Austria's reply to the invitation to join in a congress sabotaged that solution. As result, the only remaining hope for Napoleon was a treaty with Austria.

Once Napoleon had made up his mind, he acted quickly. He had told Metternich that he intended to send Gramont back from Paris to Vienna to negotiate on the basis of his draft.[146] After his conversation with Metternich, Napoleon outlined his plan to Drouyn de Lhuys. A program was drawn up which was put into Gramont's hands an hour before his departure.[147] The plan was remarkably simple, containing merely three articles. The first stated that in the event of war in Germany France would preserve "absolute neutrality" and would try to influence the Italians to adopt the same position. The second pledged the Austrians to hand over Venetia to France upon the conclusion of the peace treaty, whatever the results of the war. The third provided that if the war brought about changes in Germany which would affect the European balance of power, Austria would consult France.[148]

The Austrians reacted violently to these proposals. Metternich wrote that he was "half crazy over the situation." He wavered between faith in Austrian victory, which made him furious at "Shylock-Napoleon" and certainty of Austrian defeat, which made Napoleon's terms absolutely inescapable. He concluded with a suspicion of wishful thinking: "Yet will crucified Austria rise again, for God is just." [149] Meanwhile in Vienna, according to Gramont's reports, each article raised difficulties. The first article was opposed

[146] HHSA: Metternich to Mensdorff, June 6, 1866, no. 30B.
[147] Drouyn de Lhuys to Gramont, June 4, 1866 (Origines, X, 26–7, and p. 26 n. 3).
[148] "Project de Convention secrète entre la France et l'Autriche" (Origines, X, 27).
[149] Metternich to Mensdorff, June 6, 1866 (Quellen, vol. V, pt. 2, pp. 839–40).

because the Austrians wished an absolute promise that the Italians would remain neutral. Gramont disposed of this demand by pointing out that it was impossible.[150] The second offended susceptible Austrian pride: the government preferred a formula for the cession of Venetia which would stipulate its transference to French hands only in the event of victory in Germany. The Austrians pointed out that this change in wording would make no practical difference, for they were well aware that Venetia was forfeit in case of defeat. They seemed to derive a great comfort, however, from the prospect of avoiding the signing of a document which envisaged the possibility of catastrophe before the war had even begun. Gramont argued strongly in favor of allowing this salve to national honor.[151] The last article, which involved French sanction of changes in Germany, also provoked patriotic objections; the Austrians were loath to give France the right to intervene in a matter which should be considered a German domestic concern. Here Gramont stood firm and won agreement.[152]

The French reaction to Gramont's efforts was quite favorable. Napoleon pronounced himself willing to accept the Austrian version of the second article,[153] but Drouyn cautioned the French ambassador to discourage the Austrians from further postponements by making it clear that this was the limit of French concessions.[154] Gramont evidently followed instructions, for Mensdorff complained: "Gramont seems to want to present his proposition as a compelling ultimatum." [155] Despite this pressure, the Austrians did, after a day's delay,[156] present a new version of Article II in which Venetia was to be ceded only in return for "equivalent compensation." [157] The Quai d'Orsay regarded this modification with suspicion; Drouyn

[150] Gramont to Drouyn de Lhuys, June 10, 1866 (*Origines*, X, 110).
[151] Gramont to Drouyn, June 7, 1866 (*Origines*, X, 66).
[152] Gramont to Drouyn, June 10, 1866 (*Origines*, X, 113).
[153] Metternich to Mensdorff, June 7, 1866 (Oncken, I, 259).
[154] Drouyn de Lhuys to Gramont, June 7, 1866 (*Origines*, X, 60).
[155] Mensdorff to Franz Joseph, June 8, 1866 (Oncken, I, 259).
[156] Mensdorff to Gramont, June 8, 1866 (*Origines*, X, 86).
[157] Gramont to Drouyn, June 9, 1866 (*Origines*, X, 96-7).

replied that the word "equivalent" seemed to him fertile source for future disagreements. He accordingly refused to sanction the change[158] and again urged speed on his emissary.[159] Faced with firm resistance, the Austrians finally yielded.[160]

The treaty was signed on June 12. In its final form, the first article stipulated French neutrality with the hope that the Italians would follow the same policy. The second declared that the Austrians would cede Venetia to France if they were victorious in Germany and would consult France before changing the Italian status quo if they were victorious in Italy. The third stated that the Austrians would confer with the French before making changes, now specifically described as territorial changes, in Germany which would affect the European balance.[161] The treaty was provided with an "Additional Note" which defined more exactly the realignment of territory considered possible. The May discussions of the Italian situation bore fruit in the specification that in the event the war caused a spontaneous reaction against Italian unity among the Italian people the French would not intervene to champion the cause of nationalism. As to Germany, the French agreed to allow the Austrians to keep any conquests they might make as long as they did not upset the balance of power by unifying Germany as a whole under their rule.[162] In his report, Gramont explained that the provision with regard to Germany had been necessary in order to get the Austrians to accept Article II; when faced with the French refusal to allow the stipulation of "equivalent territorial compensation" as the prerequisite for the cession of Venetia, the Austrians wanted to be certain that the French were not planning to strip from them any and all advantages they might win by victory in Germany. However, the paragraph was also important for the French, for in discussing it, the Austrians had thrown a sop to Napoleon's ambitions

[158] Drouyn de Lhuys to Gramont, June 10, 1866 (*Origines,* X, 97).

[159] Drouyn de Lhuys to Gramont, June 11, 1866 (*Origines,* X, 119).

[160] Gramont to Drouyn, June 11, 1866 (*Origines,* X, 119).

[161] Franco-Austrian Treaty of June 12, 1866 (Oncken, I, 266).

[162] Franco-Austrian Treaty of June 12, 1866, note additionnelle (Oncken, I, 267).

by agreeing verbally that if the war resulted in gains for the pro-
Austrian small states, Saxony, Württemberg, and Bavaria, they
would allow the creation of "a new independent German state" in
the Rhine provinces.[163] As Persigny had already pointed out, this
might prove the prelude to eventual French annexation of the
Rhineland.

The signing of the treaty must have come as a relief to Napoleon.
Metternich relates that the Emperor, upon learning the news, came
up to him at a party at the Elysée Palace and said: "All is arranged . . . I am very glad about it, because now I will be able to
calm people down and catch my breath." [164] The concern for popular susceptibilities was a real one. At about the same time, Drouyn
mentioned the Corps Législatif's renewed interest in foreign affairs
as a reason for hurrying the conclusion of the agreement.[165] In fact,
he and Napoleon were preparing to present the government's position to the country.[166] The resulting document, cast in the form of a
letter from Napoleon to the Foreign Minister, was communicated
to the Council of Ministers and the Privy Council at a joint meeting
on June 12. After a lively debate, it was accepted in substance for
announcement in the Corps Législatif.[167] The letter, which Rouher
read to the Assembly on June 13, was a brief, comprehensive, and,
as usual, unintelligible statement of official French policy. However,
against the background of diplomatic maneuvering, it is possible
to establish from the document where Napoleon stood on the eve of
the war. In the first place, he implied his disillusionment with the
hope of an arrangement similar to the Plombières agreement. He
declared that he was not interested in the annexation of territory
and would not consider this alternative unless some other European
power gained so much land as to necessitate a revision of the balance,

---

[163] Gramont to Drouyn de Lhuys, June 12, 1866 (Oncken, I, 268).
[164] Metternich to Mensdorff, June 12, 1866 (Oncken. I, 264).
[165] Drouyn de Lhuys to Gramont, June 11, 1866 (*Origines,* X, 119).
[166] Eugénie, *Memoirs,* II, 151.
[167] AN: Rouher's notes on the meetings of the Council of Ministers, joint meeting
of the Council of Ministers and the Privy Council, June 12, 1866 (45 AP1, cahier 1).

or unless a spontaneous desire for union with France arose in the areas concerned. Secondly, he expressed a continuing preference for solutions which would be consonant with his principle of nationalities. He offered as his private solution to the questions agitating Europe the following plan: the small German states should be organized as a "Third Germany"; Prussia should be allowed to build up her power by gaining control of land in North Germany; Austria's role should be maintained unchanged. Napoleon asserted that he had intended to work for this program through a congress. Now that the congress had been aborted, the program could be realized only through war. The Emperor outlined in some detail the French attitude toward this war: briefly summarized, France's sole definite requirements were the maintenance of the balance of power and the continuation of an independent Italy. Finally, Napoleon reasserted the pacifist position strongly desired by French public opinion. He reassured his people that, safe in the pledges of the belligerents to consult France in questions affecting her interests, the nation could stand by in an attitude of "attentive neutrality." [168]

This document did have some effect in calming popular agitation. A desperate effort by the opponents of the government to force a debate on the letter was defeated.[169] The newspaper press greeted the declaration with reactions varying from strong approval in the *Siècle,* the *Opinion Nationale,* and the *Presse* to charges of impracticability in the *Liberté* and the *Avenir National.* Most people, however, were pleased by the reference to neutrality; and when the letter was criticized, it was usually because it was considered not pacifist enough.[170] In point of fact, the epistle was open to varying interpretations: as Cowley wrote, "it appears . . . that it may mean anything or nothing." [171]

The war, widely expected, began immediately. On June 10, Bismarck had presented a new plan for reform of the Confederation

[168] Napoleon III to Drouyn de Lhuys, June 11, 1866 *(Origines,* X, 120–2).
[169] *Annales (1866),* VIII, 25–8.
[170] Armengaud, pp. 89–92.
[171] PRO: Cowley to Clarendon, June 15, 1866 (F. O. 519/232).

to the Federal Diet at Frankfurt. Austria had responded on June 11 with condemnation of Prussia's activities in Holstein and a call for federal mobilization against Prussia. The passage of this measure on June 14 marked the outbreak of the war[172] and the end of the long weeks of confused and indecisive maneuvering. The diplomacy of this period just before the war is probably the most complex and the most difficult to disentangle with any degree of certainty. Yet, from the conflicting missions and countermissions, projects and counter-projects, group meetings and individual initiatives, a certain basic pattern governing the Emperor's own policy does emerge. His methods may appear contradictory and perplexing, but his ends varied surprisingly little. Throughout the crisis, Napoleon favored the nationalist cause, as represented by the Italians and the Prussians. He tried to adjust the changes which nationalist ambitions would entail to the framework of a balance-of-power system, and he hoped for, although he did not insist on, territorial compensation for France, preferably the Rhineland. In his attempts to implement these goals, he had to contend with the pressures of French opinions, from his foreign minister down to the peasants, and with the policies of the countries most deeply concerned in the crisis, that is, Prussia, Austria, and Italy. It is hardly astonishing, given these opposing pressures, that the means he used to reach his ends differed greatly, even from week to week.

At the end of April, he had been faced with the problem created by the Italians' attachment to the Prussian cause through the treaty of April 8 and by the certainty in France that these two powers would be defeated. Napoleon's long-term commitment to Italian nationalism and his weaker pro-Prussian sympathies demanded that he rescue the Prusso-Italian side. At the end of April, he had hoped to do this in collaboration with either Austria or Prussia and to achieve that collaboration through the threat of a solution imposed by a congress. However, this strategy failed. While agreement between the Austrians and the Italians on Venetia seemed almost as

[172] Clark, pp. 466–9.

unlikely as ever, the Prussians refused to take the Vimercati overtures seriously, and the response in France to the dramatic debate
between Napoleon and Thiers reaffirmed the Emperor's isolation.
He was forced by pressure of circumstances to turn seriously to his
plan for a congress. It became increasingly apparent, however, that
the Austrians were not prepared to discuss the international situation, especially the Italian problem, in a constructive way. Bismarck's
overtures through the Kiss Mission offered momentary hope of an
arrangement with the Prussians; but Bismarck remained unwilling
to grant concessions on a scale sufficient to win over the French. As
result, once the hope for a congress had faded, Napoleon had only
one alternative: an agreement with Vienna. But the Franco-Austrian
treaty was not the climax of Napoleon's German policy. The agreement assured Napoleon of a voice in the peace settlement. It was still
far from certain what Napoleon would say.

V

THE DIPLOMACY
OF THE WAR

NAPOLEON III's SHADOW boxing with Bismarck was now entering the final round. It is this aspect of the story which has received the greatest attention; but concentration has clouded rather than clarified the subject. The blame cannot be laid entirely at the door of scholarship. Many complex factors had influenced Napoleon's thinking during the preceding eleven months—nationalism, especially as used by Bismarck and the Italians, the treaties of 1815, the traditionalist foreign policy of the Tiers Parti, the pacifism of business magnates, the massive and often mysterious temper of the public at large—and, in effect, these variables had operated principally to neutralize each other. After all the discussion and all the maneuvering, the result as measured by diplomatic action was surprisingly slight. Furthermore, the activity that had taken place had not forced definite choices between alternatives and final commitment to a single line of policy. On the eve of the war, France was allied with Austria and Napoleon had obtained a guarantee that the Italians would receive Venetia through the peace settlement. But the Austrian treaty had been a last resort for Napoleon, and its conclusion had not resulted from nor had it led to the defeat of any of the conflicting pressure groups within France. Napoleon himself still favored the nationalist and hence, by implication, the Prusso-Italian cause. Among his entourage, sympathizers with Austria or Italy or Prussia could be found. The hope of compensations, specifically denied in Napoleon's June 11 letter to the Corps Législatif, still stirred some French statesmen, notably Drouyn de Lhuys. And, at a moment when French military involvement seemed increasingly certain, French public opinion remained rootedly pacifist. The

French position was full of anomalies and contradictions, which could now be worked out only in the course of the war. This method of resolving the problems added still further complications. First, there were the universal difficulties of wartime diplomacy, for instance, the necessity of adjusting to a rapidly fluctuating military position and to the obstacles raised by uncertain communications. Second, in the present instance circumstances soon presented the diplomats with a wholly unforeseen situation: against all calculations and expectations, Prussia was victorious in the field. This startling fact jolted all Napoleon's preconceptions and forced him, along with everyone else, to re-examine French policy. The story of the seven weeks of the war is largely the story of the Emperor's efforts to further the nationalist cause without overlooking his commitments to Austria, the wishes of his public, and the well-founded doubts raised in his own mind by the specter of Prussian power.

The fateful month of July, 1866, opened in Paris with a spell of damp, changeable weather. Mérimée wrote: "Humid heat, rain and cold succeed each other ten times in a day, which makes me very ill." [1] The first news from the battle grounds was indecisive, but by and large, it was soon evident that the Prussians were somewhat stronger.[2] Then, on July 2, Mensdorff telegraphed Metternich instructions to ask the Emperor to effect an armistice on the southern front, between Austria and Italy. Mensdorff declared that the Austrian government would be willing immediately thereafter to arrange to cede Venetia. These steps would free the Austrians for full concentration in the northern theater, where Prussian opposition had proved unexpectedly and alarmingly tough.[3]

Metternich was quite ready to act upon these orders, for they would bring closer the expedient he had always cherished, a Franco-Austrian military alliance. He proceeded to the Tuileries at once and

[1] Mérimée, *Panizzi*, II, 217.
[2] Case, *French Opinion on War and Diplomacy*, pp. 205–6.
[3] Mensdorff to Metternich, July 2, 1866 (Oncken, I, 297, and see n. 2).

asked for Napoleon's active support. Napoleon demanded a day's grace to consider the proposition;[4] but Metternich was much encouraged, for he telegraphed the Ballplatz, saying that Napoleon "refuses nothing" and added:

Prepare people for French intervention in the event that Prussia should menace all Germany. I will be grateful to You if You would send me Baron Oldenburg with the résumé of what You would demand in the case of active alliance with France. I have demanded Glatz and the portion of Upper Silesia before Cracow, Sassau and Ratisbon if Bavaria doesn't move.[5]

Perhaps Napoleon was thinking in terms of a military campaign with the Austrians, but in view of his request for a day to think things over, it is more plausible that any questions he may have posed along these lines were purely exploratory and that the imminence of armed support, in the seemingly specific terms of Metternich's telegram, existed only in the ambassador's mind. At any rate, Napoleon's answer, delivered the next day, was discouraging. Napoleon expressed himself willing to mediate between Austria and Italy, but he also stipulated that the mediation be extended to Austria and Prussia. He declared that as mediator, he would work from the bases of his June 11 letter. If Italy should refuse the armistice, he would aid the Austrians.[6] Since there would have been little logical reason to suppose that the Italians would oppose an armistice[7] now that they had gained their prime objective, Venetia, the significant aspect of Napoleon's acceptance is the extension of the mediation to Germany. This was a notable alteration of Mensdorff's original proposal, for in asking Napoleon's intervention, the Austrians had hoped to free themselves in the south for a full-scale campaign in the north. Contemporaries explained this move on the basis of the Prusso-Italian Treaty. Since the two powers had pledged themselves to conclude no separate peace, it would, strictly speaking,

---

[4] HHSA: Metternich to Esterhazy, July 7, 1866 no. 36A.
[5] HHSA: Metternich to Foreign Office, July 2, 1866, no. 119.
[6] Metternich to Mensdorff, July 3, 1866 (Oncken, I, 298-9).
[7] The Italians, however, were not logical.

have constituted a breach of faith for the Italians to accept the Austrian propositions as they stood.[8] This is a perfectly good reason; but it is a question whether Napoleon would have been so tender of Italian honor if it had not suited his convenience. In point of fact, the Prussians by July 3 were in a very favorable position: they controlled the entire area north of the Main River.[9] In view of his long-held skepticism as to Prussia's military prowess, one might expect Napoleon to hope that the Prussians would stop while their luck held, would, as he advised Goltz on July 3, turn to the "consolidation" of their victories.[10] These goals could be facilitated by the prompt conclusion of an armistice, followed by shrewd mediation on the part of the wily Emperor.

So things stood on July 4, the "day of patriotic agonies." [11] Napoleon was getting ready to leave for Vichy, where he planned to spend some weeks taking the cure.[12] He suffered from a chronic ailment, variously attributed to kidney stones or prostate trouble; the condition was bound to have some effect upon his decisiveness in 1866 although it was probably not as drastic as some scholars would have us believe.[13] At any rate, however necessary a rest at Vichy might be for Napoleon's health, he was not destined to enjoy it. As he was making his preparations, word came of the overwhelming Prussian victory at Sadowa. The Emperor's initial reaction to this most unexpected news is hard to determine. Ollivier tells us that "he pinched the tip of his moustache, his habitual gesture of satisfaction." [14] Ollivier does not tell us the source of this tidbit. Most of the evidence suggests opposite feelings: Goltz reported that Napo-

---

[8] Ollivier, *L'Empire libéral*, VIII, 411; PRO: Cowley to Foreign Office, July 5, 1866 (F. O. 519/14).

[9] Reculot to Drouyn de Lhuys, July 3, 1866 (*Les Origines diplomatiques de la guerre de 1870–71*, X, 309).

[10] Goltz to William, July 4, 1866 (Oncken, I, 301).

[11] Schnerb, *Rouher et le Second Empire*, p. 186. The phrase is Rouher's own.

[12] Ollivier, VIII, 410; Vincennes: Randon to unknown marshal, June 9, 1866 (Correspondance Générale G8116, dossier 9–12 Juin, 1866).

[13] See Epilogue.

[14] Ollivier, VIII, 410.

leon was greatly surprised;[15] Canrobert found him greatly upset;[16] while Oncken repeats the story that the Emperor remarked to a companion: "We have won Venice for others and lost the Rhine for ourselves." [17] A certain distress on the Emperor's part is understandable. True, he had favored the Prussian cause wherever feasible throughout the crisis. But he had believed Prussia to be something other than she now demonstrably was. He had thought that the Prussian state, even in alliance with Italy, was too weak to defeat the Hapsburgs decisively. He had supported German nationalistic aims, as represented by Prussia, but he had believed that the result wanted was a small unified state comprising the area north of the Main River. Such a state, while it might not, any more than Italy, turn out to be a satellite, could at least pose no important threat. Now, however, the unexpected Prussian victory seemed to open all sorts of undefined and alarming potentialities. Cowley had probably been right when he had observed even before the war: "The Emperor is getting alarmed at his Frankenstein." [18]

The new circumstances required a good deal of deliberation. The Emperor received and weighed the advice of all the important figures of the French government, as well as his own opinions. At this point the story becomes confused, and it is difficult to establish the course of events with finality. It seems quite clear that on the evening of July 4, the day the news of Sadowa had arrived, Metternich finally received from Mensdorff the acceptance of the terms for mediation laid down by Napoleon the day before. He at once hurried to the Tuileries to inform Napoleon. The Emperor, according to Metternich, was much relieved to find that the Austrians had accepted his plan for mediation and, with Metternich beside him, he drew up the documents necessary to implement the project, backed by the force of French arms. Telegrams were sent to William and Victor Emmanuel calling for an armistice as the preliminary

[15] Goltz to Bismarck, July 8, 1866 (Oncken, I, 321).
[16] Bapst, Le Maréchal Canrobert, IV, 43.
[17] Oncken, Napoleon III and the Rhine, p. 60.
[18] PRO: Cowley to Clarendon, July 3, 1866 (F. O. 519/233).

to mediation;[19] a communication went to Gramont explaining his intention of intervening militarily on Austria's behalf if the mediation were refused; and an announcement was drawn up for the *Moniteur*, telling of the invitation to mediate.[20] At about the time that Napoleon had finished drafting these documents, Drouyn de Lhuys appeared and the three men speculated, a bit sadly, a bit reflectively, about the chances, military and otherwise, of the days ahead.[21] The events of the evening of July 4 give the inescapable impression that Napoleon had decided on armed mediation, with the threat of intervention in case of refusal. He was, presumably, very much worried by the possibilities opened to the Prussians through the crumpling, if only temporary, of Austrian resistance; he felt it essential to stop the Prussian advance at once. After that, mediation could be effectuated. It is impossible to say what terms Napoleon would have offered; but in view of his attitude throughout the crisis, it is by no means a foregone conclusion that he would have been zealous for Austrian interests.

The next practical step in a policy of armed mediation was to secure the agreement of the Council of Ministers. This group was called together the next morning, July 5,[22] at Saint-Cloud, and a

[19] Napoleon to William, July 4, 1866 (Oncken, I, 302); Napoleon to Victor Emmanuel, July 4, 1866 (*Origines*, X, 315).

[20] Metternich to Mensdorff, July 5, 1866 (Oncken, I, 302).

[21] This account has been drawn from HHSA: Metternich to Esterhazy, July 7, 1866, no. 36A. Other sources, including G[ustave] Rothan, *La Politique française en 1866* (Paris, 1879), p. 189, and Ollivier (VIII, 415) say that Drouyn talked to Napoleon on the morning of July 5, before the meeting of the Council of Ministers, rather than on the preceding evening; but there seems no reason to suppose that Metternich would be mistaken on such a simple point.

[22] There has been disagreement as to whether this meeting occurred on July 4 or July 5. It is assigned to July 5 by Schnerb (p. 186); Jules Bertaut (*L'Impératrice Eugénie et son temps* [Paris, 1956], p. 234); Albertini ("Frankreichs Stellungnahme zur Deutschen Einigung," p. 336); Oncken (*Napoleon III and the Rhine*, p. 61); Ollivier (VIII, 415); Sybel (*The Founding of the German Empire*, V, 248); G[ustave] Rothan (*L'Affaire du Luxembourg* [n.p., 1883] p. 44); Case (*French Opinion on War and Diplomacy*, p. 207); and Bernard d'Harcourt (*Les Quatre Ministères de M. Drouyn de Lhuys* [Paris, 1882], p. 259). Unfortunately, most of these authors do not cite their sources but the story is supported both by material in the Prussian diplomatic correspondence and by the testimony of La Valette. The editors of the *Origines* (X, 329, n. 4) oppose to such accounts the testimony of

lively debate ensued. The meeting was a confused one, but it is possible to reconstruct the stands taken by the principal figures. Eugénie, Drouyn de Lhuys, and Randon favored the idea of an active military policy.[23] The plan was to back up the proposed mediation by sending an observation corps to the Rhine border. The Prussians would be given firm warning that France must sanction any territorial changes in Germany. To implement this scheme, the order for the meeting of the Chambers, who would have to vote the requisite funds, was to go out on July 6. Randon assured the Council that it would be possible to send a group of eighty thousand soldiers to the Rhine at once, while two hundred and fifty thousand could be mobilized within three weeks.[24] This plan was opposed by Rouher, La Valette, and Baroche.[25] Their motives differed: Rouher, always interested in France's material prosperity, feared the effects of war upon the economy;[26] La Valette, Minister of the Interior, was concerned about the impact on French public opinion;[27] Baroche apparently failed to realize the seriousness of the situation.[28] Some of the arguments advanced can be deduced from these positions. In addition, La Valette evidently maintained

---

Rothan in his first account (*La Politique française en 1866*, pp. 187–9) and of Jules Hansen (*Les Coulisses de la diplomatie* [Paris, 1880], pp. 97–8). However, neither author really refutes the case for the July 5th date. The supposedly differing evidence offered by Rothan's *Politique française* seems to be based on a misreading of the text, for Rothan says that the news of Sadowa reached Goltz on July 3 but was not known to the Emperor until "the next day" (July 4); at once a meeting of the Council of Ministers was called, but apparently did not take place until the following day (July 5), for Rothan continues: "The next morning, before its meeting . . ." Hansen's description is equally inconclusive, for as the editors note he does not mention the session of the Council at all, but merely relates the conversation of Drouyn with Napoleon, which almost certainly did take place on July 4. Hansen does, however, assign the conversations of Rouher and La Valette with the Emperor to a later hour on the evening of July 4, rather than to July 5, after the meeting of the Council (see p. 160 below). At this rate, Napoleon's evening was becoming rather crowded, and it seems safe to follow the weight of numbers in assigning the ministerial debate and the talks with Rouher and La Valette to July 5.

[23] Case, *French Opinion on War and Diplomacy*, p. 208; Bertaut, p. 235.
[24] Ollivier, VIII, 415–7; Oncken, I, 303, n. 1.
[25] Albertini, p. 336.
[26] Schnerb, p. 179.
[27] Case, *French Opinion on War and Diplomacy*, p. 208.
[28] Maurain, *Un Bourgeois français au XIXᵉ siècle: Baroche*, p. 311.

that the army was unfit for the demands that would be made on it.[29] Napoleon already favored the plan for armed mediation put forward by Eugénie, Drouyn, and Randon; despite the comments of Rouher, La Valette, and Baroche, he concurred in the more active scheme. He solemnized his agreement by putting his signature to a decree for the convocation of the Chambers and by preparing an article for the *Moniteur* of July 6 describing his policy. It is noteworthy, however, that he postponed the signature of the order for mobilization. Still, he did intend to do this the next day,[30] so that when the meeting broke up, there was every reason to believe that the policy of armed mediation was established.

The events of the day had barely begun, however. Some time after the meeting, the Emperor talked to Plon-plon. Napoleon's influential cousin had been watching the course of French policy with the greatest misgivings. It was presumably through his inspiration that Kiss had attempted to revive the negotiations of the end of May in a letter to Bismarck of June 22.[31] During the early days of the war, his anti-Austrian statements reached a new pitch of bitterness. There was a story, later contradicted, that in an after-dinner speech he had called for an alliance with Prussia and Italy with a ringing, autocratic demand to crush Austria.[32] It was further reported that he had said to the Emperor: "I know that you are counting on the promises of Austria—but You will certainly be forced to intervene and then, instead of two fresh and vital allies, You will have beside You two ruins." [33] Naturally, the Prince looked with deep suspicion on the design for mediation, which seemed to fulfill his worst forebodings. When he learned of the plan on July 5, his reaction was violent; he remarked: "Let no one come to congratulate me on what is happening! Were it my best friend, I would throw

---

[29] Rothan, *L'Affaire du Luxembourg*, pp. 44–7; Ollivier, VIII, 417–9.
[30] Oncken, I, 303, n. 1.
[31] Merseburg: Kiss to Bismarck, June 22, 1866 (AAZB no. 86).
[32] Armengaud, "L'Opinion publique en France et la crise nationale allemande en 1866," pp. 171–2.
[33] HHSA: Metternich to Mensdorff, June 29, 1866, no. 35A.

him out the window!" He then marched off to the Tuileries to talk things over with the Emperor.[34] History does not record what occurred, but Plon-plon's intransigeance can be gathered from several new steps. On July 5, he telegraphed Victor Emmanuel urging him to reject the armistice proposal. He assured Goltz that France did not constitute a threat to Prussia.[35] And at about the same time he sent an emissary to reassure Bismarck as to French intentions.[36] Doubtless, his remarks to Napoleon embodied a heartfelt plea in favor of the Italo-Prussian cause. Some idea of the arguments he used may perhaps be gathered from a later letter, in which the Prince revived the nightmare of a German nationalist crusade against French intervention. He also pointed out that in allying with Austria against Prussia and Italy, Napoleon would be turning against the causes of nationalism and liberalism.[37]

This appeal undoubtedly made an impression upon the Emperor, whose pro-Prussian sentiments had by no means disappeared. Plon-plon's reassurances to Victor Emmanuel, Goltz, and Bismarck probably reflect some encouragement in the attitude of his imperial cousin for, as has been noted, Napoleon did not allow Plon-plon much independence. At about the same time another event occurred which tended to influence Napoleon in the same direction. Telegrams arrived from William and from Victor Emmanuel answering Napoleon's message of July 4. William's reply seemed to be a simple agreement to the proposals for mediation and armistice.[38] Victor Emmanuel's was less straightforward, for he declared that he must discuss the matter with his ministers and with the Prussians.[39] Already there were indications that the Italians considered the acquisition of Venetia through peaceful means an affront to their

[34] Ollivier, VIII, 413–4.
[35] Goltz to Bismarck, July 5, 1866 (Oncken, I, 304).
[36] Ollivier, VIII, 446. The emissary, the Hungarian Count Seher-Thoss, arrived on July 8, but his protestations did not dispel Bismarck's alarms.
[37] Prince Napoleon to Napoleon, July 14, 1866 (Papiers et correspondance de la famille impériale, III, 111–2).
[38] William to Napoleon [July 5, 1866], quoted by Sybel, V, 255–6.
[39] Victor Emmanuel to Napoleon, July 5, 1866, quoted by Ollivier, VIII, 424.

national reputation.[40] However, it was easy for Napoleon, far removed from his adversaries, to conclude that their telegrams constituted genuine adhesion to his suggestions.[41] This belief further weakened his readiness for armed mediation, since in making that decision, the Emperor had been influenced primarily by fear lest the Prussians take advantage of their striking victory to expand drastically their plans for aggrandizement. If, however, the Prussians were ready to halt their advance and accept a settlement along the lines laid down by Napoleon, there might seem less reason for the outfitting of an observation corps, an expedient already questioned by Prince Napoleon.

One more conversation influenced Napoleon in his gradual reconsideration of the decision on armed mediation. During the evening of July 5, the ministers Rouher and La Valette returned to make a new entreaty for the avoidance of military steps.[42] Both men had firmly opposed any kind of intervention by force. Both had reason to be upset by the outcome of the ministerial Council meeting. In addition, the evidence suggests that La Valette had not been present during much of the discussion;[43] he might have felt entitled to seek an interview with the Emperor to express his views. In their evening interview, the two statesmen reiterated the argument that the posting of an observation corps would bring serious military involvement.[44] Besides this, there is the almost inescapable conclusion that La Valette, as Minister of the Interior, developed another theme: the claim that the French people were so profoundly devoted to peace that it would be impolitic to try to push them into military intervention, especially given the risk that the venture might end in full-scale war.[45] This deterrent from an active policy was reinforced by the contentions raised in Napoleon's early conversations. There

---

[40] Malaret to Drouyn de Lhuys, July 5, 1866 (Origines, X, 323).
[41] Ollivier, VIII, 425.
[42] Oncken, I, 303, n. 1.
[43] Sybel, V, 248–50; Rothan, L'Affaire du Luxembourg, pp. 44–7; Case, French Opinion on War and Diplomacy, p. 208.
[44] D'Harcourt, pp. 340–1; Oncken, Napoleon III and the Rhine, pp. 61–2.
[45] Cf. Case, French Opinion on War and Diplomacy, pp. 208–11.

was, as Prince Napoleon had pointed out, the embarrassment of getting into a false ideological position by seeming to come to Austria's aid against the nationalistic powers, Prussia and Italy. There was the danger, which was probably not taken very seriously, that in case of a general war, France's military preparation might prove inadequate. But the simplest and probably most conclusive argument was the fact that both Prussia and Italy, so Napoleon believed, had accepted mediation. Since Napoleon's use of arms had been intended to halt a further Prussian advance, the motive had vanished once the Prussians had agreed to an armistice, and the additional reasons in favor of a peaceful intervention simply became so many reasons for dropping the idea of an observation corps with an alacrity which, as it turned out, was decidedly premature.

As early as July 6, it began to be evident that the policy of simple mediation would be fraught with difficulties. Napoleon and Drouyn de Lhuys spent considerable time on July 6 and 7 trying to concert with Metternich definite terms for the transfer of Venetia. The discussions were heated. Metternich's lively temper apparently flashed several times.[46] Drouyn, who saw his pro-Austrian sympathies denied by events, commented: "I am profoundly saddened by what is happening." [47] Napoleon, according to Metternich, was "in a state of prostration." [48] Meanwhile, during July 6 a telegraphic correspondence was carried on with Victor Emmanuel in an effort to make the Italians accept conditions of transfer. The chief effect of this attempt was to bring to light a series of Italian requirements touching such matters as the handing over of certain fortresses in Venetia and the arrangement of the Roman question.[49]

The rapid establishment of an armistice on the southern front seemed particularly pressing because it was clear that in its absence, the Italians were continuing military operations as vigorously as possible. On July 7, there was news that the Italian fleet had set sail.[50]

[46] HHSA: Metternich to Esterhazy, July 7, 1866, no. 36A.
[47] HHSA: Drouyn de Lhuys to Metternich, July 6, 1866, no. 36C.
[48] Metternich to Mensdorff, July 7, 1866 (Oncken, I, 319).
[49] Ollivier, VIII, 438–9.
[50] Castellane to Drouyn, July 7, 1866 (*Origines*, X, 349).

On July 8, it was reported that Italian troops had crossed the Po.[51] Meanwhile, it was said that Garibaldi was trying to start revolutions in Trentino and Friuli. This rumor was especially ominous because these areas were not included in the boundaries of Venetia as envisaged by the Austrians.[52]

These obstacles to the plan of armistice and mediation had their effect upon French policy. Two possible lines of conduct were actively considered. The first was a return to the plan of reinforcing mediation with the threat of armed intervention. This alternative was discussed at a meeting of the Council of Ministers on July 7. The results were somewhat vague, since the group recognized that the situation might change. However, the choice of using force against the Italians was definitely ruled out. Incidentally, the option of using force in the German question was expressly held open.[53] Despite this decision, which seems conclusive, there were rumors during the next few days, eagerly culled by Metternich, that military action in regard to Venetia was still a possibility. On July 8, Metternich telegraphed the Ballplatz that Napoleon was thinking of sending the French fleet to the Adriatic.[54] The next day, Metternich received telegraphed instructions to make sure the fleet was sent.[55] He wrongly reported to Vienna that the fleet was already on its way and that Napoleon was saying that his mediation would "probably be armed." [56] There is a curious report to the effect that French vessels were seen off the Italian coast,[57] but the only basis that can be found for this tale is that on July 10, the Naval Minister did order one frigate to go to Venice and await further commands.[58]

The other alternative for dealing with the Italian situation was

---

[51] Gramont to Drouyn, July 8, 1866 (*Origines*, X, 363).

[52] Dieudé Defly to Drouyn, July 8, 1866 (*Origines*, X, 367).

[53] AN: Rouher's notes on the meetings of the Council of Ministers, July 7, 1866 (45 AP1, cahier 1).

[54] HHSA: Metternich to Foreign Office, July 8, 1866, no. 129.

[55] HHSA: Esterhazy to Metternich, July 9, 1866.

[56] HHSA: Metternich to Foreign Office, July 9, 1866, no. 133.

[57] Bush, "Napoleon III and the Redeeming of Venetia," p. 137, n. 3.

[58] Chasseloup-Laubat to Captain de Surville, July 10, 1866 (*Origines*, X, 378).

the sending of a special mission. Although Napoleon may have thought of a reversion to armed mediation in a moment of temporary irritation,[59] it is probable that the possibility of negotiations was always favored. Napoleon's choice of an emissary comes as somewhat of a surprise, for it was none other than the hitherto intractable Prince Napoleon, who was in that very period encouraging Italian resistance. However, Prince Napoleon's Italian connections and the high respect in which he was held in that country were powerful arguments in his favor; and, in point of fact, when he did eventually undertake the mission, he fulfilled the Emperor's intentions scrupulously, whatever their divergence from his private convictions.[60] The plan for the mission was launched on July 8.[61] By the next day, Drouyn was able to define the plan fairly precisely. Plon-plon was to arrange an armistice with the Italians in return for which they would be given Verona immediately as a token of the future cession of the entire province.[62] Napoleon's instructions, which were drawn up on the same day, authorized the Prince to use veiled threats of force in case of rejection of his offers.[63] At the same time, Benedetti was to be sent to the Prussian headquarters on a parallel mission.[64]

This plan seems promising, for it offered a concession to Italian national vanity at the same time that it put pressure on Italian military weakness. Plon-plon was provided with both the carrot and the whip. However, on July 10, the project was suddenly postponed.[65] The only reasonable explanation lies in the arrival in Paris of Prince Reuss on a special mission from Prussia.[66] As Drouyn de Lhuys put

[59] Cf. Ollivier, VIII, 441–2, and Bush, p. 137.

[60] Ernest d'Hauterive, "La Mission du Prince Napoléon en Italie (1866)—Lettres inédites," *Revue des deux mondes,* 27:88–9 (May 1925).

[61] Napoleon to Prince Napoleon, July 8, 1866, quoted by d'Hauterive, "La Mission du Prince Napoléon," p. 90.

[62] Drouyn de Lhuys to Malaret, July 9, 1866 (*Origines,* X, 369).

[63] Napoleon's Instructions for Prince Napoleon, July 9, 1866 (*Origines,* X, 372).

[64] Eugénie to Metternich, July 9, 1866 (Oncken, I, 326).

[65] Drouyn de Lhuys to the French representatives to Prussia, Italy, and Austria, July 10, 1866 (*Origines,* X, 377).

[66] Gramont to Drouyn de Lhuys, July 12, 1866 (*Origines,* XI, 21–2).

it, since the Italians claimed that their acceptance of the armistice depended on a prior acceptance by Prussia, it seemed more sensible to start by discussing the Prussian conditions, which was now possible through Reuss's presence in Paris, before putting pressure on the Italians.[67] In point of fact, the Italians and the Prussians had put the French in an awkward position. While the Italians were maintaining that they could not agree to an armistice until Prussia had done so,[68] the Prussians declared that they would accept the armistice only on the condition of Italian concurrence.[69] Evidently, this move was concerted between the two powers. There is some evidence that the Italians were secretly urging the Prussians to refuse the armistice.[70] They were presumably motivated in part by the desire to make good the claim to Trentino which they had put forward more or less in the middle of the campaign.[71] Meanwhile, the Prussians also saw many advantages to continuing the war. Moltke had been questioning Loë as to his opinion of French military strength. Loë declared that he still considered the French army inadequate, since his belief in its defectiveness was based on long-term conditions, rather than on temporary situations.[72] This was encouraging; for a certain amount of military mopping-up was desirable both in Bohemia and in the small states.[73] Moltke had even more ambitious projects. He wanted the army to follow up Sadowa by a march on Vienna.[74] Meanwhile, from the diplomatic viewpoint, Bismarck was unwilling to tie his hands by agreeing to an armistice until he had made certain that Napoleon would sanction peace terms commensurate with his ambitions; and so, with this ulterior motive, he told the Italians to reject the armistice.[75] Napoleon's plans for mediation

[67] Drouyn de Lhuys to Benedetti, July 13, 1866 (Origines, XI, 22–3).

[68] Malaret to Drouyn, July 7, 1866 (Origines, X, 340).

[69] Drouyn de Lhuys to Metternich, July 7, 1866 (Oncken, I, 314).

[70] Malaret to Drouyn, July 9, 1866 (Origines, X, 374); Benedetti to Drouyn, July 9, 1866 (Origines, X, 372, and n. 3).

[71] Malaret to Drouyn de Lhuys, July 10, 1866 (Origines, X, 382).

[72] Loë, Erinnerungen aus meinem Berufsleben 1849–67, pp. 111–2.

[73] Benedetti to Drouyn de Lhuys, July 7, 1866 (Origines, X, 351).

[74] Loë, p. 112.

[75] Benedetti to Drouyn, July 7, 1866 (Origines, X, 351); Benedetti to Drouyn, July 28, 1866 (Origines, XI, 264).

were caught in a vicious circle, and the Reuss Mission offered the best chance of breaking the chain.

When Reuss arrived in Paris, the Emperor had become very discouraged about the success of his projected mediation and apparently expected that he might yet be forced to arms in support of his proposals.[76] Reuss talked to Napoleon and Eugénie immediately upon his arrival on June 10. Evidently in anticipation of French distrust, he had been instructed to commence with a vague approach. Rather than presenting the Emperor with a detailed list of conditions, the emissary had been ordered to discover Napoleon's requirements, with due respect to his assumed position of mediator.[77] Reuss's own report of the conversations indicates the wisdom of this method, for he found Napoleon very much worried about the scope of Bismarck's unification plans. Eugénie, who was even more anxious, predicted: "I shall go to bed French and I shall wake up Prussian." [78] The Prussians found themselves exposed to a fairly representative cross-section of the conflicting opinions in high governmental circles. Napoleon was ready to discuss peace terms with Reuss as a condition of the armistice, but he was upset by the Prussian desire to exclude Austria from a remodeled German grouping[79] and he still hoped for the possible restoration of the 1814 boundary to France, although he showed no inclination to insist in the face of Goltz's rather evasive reply.[80] This relatively cooperative attitude was not universally shared by his entourage, for both Eugénie and Prince Napoleon were urging a Rhenish buffer state.[81] Meanwhile, although comprehensive later studies have indicated that public opinion was strongly pacifist,[82] there was sufficient evidence of anti-Prussian sentiments to worry Prussian envoys. Reuss reported that the army felt that it

---

[76] PRO: Cowley to Stanley, July 10, 1866 (F. O. 519/233); Goltz to Bismarck, July 14, 1866 (Oncken, I, 354).

[77] Sybel, V, 270–2.

[78] Reuss to William, July 10, 1866 (Oncken, I, 328–30).

[79] Goltz to Bismarck, July 11, 1866 (Oncken, I, 337).

[80] Goltz to Bismarck, July 11, 1866 (Oncken, I, 341–2).

[81] Reuss to William, July 10, 1866 (Oncken, I, 331); Goltz to Bismarck, July 11, 1866 (Oncken, I, 340).

[82] See Epilogue.

had suffered an indirect humiliation through Sadowa and was eager to come to grips with the Prussians. The urban population in general was troubled by the evidence of Prussian power and the consequences implicit for France. This fear was eagerly fanned by Thiers and other opposition figures. The wealthy were in many cases distressed by losses on investments in Austria. Reuss could hardly help wondering what influence these opinions might eventually have upon the thinking of Napoleon.[83]

These varying cross-currents, at least as represented or reflected by the upper echelons of the government, must have been apparent in the meeting of the Council of Ministers held on July 11. Unfortunately, Rouher's notes give no exchange of views, but since it is evident that the group talked all around the subject,[84] it is hard to believe that the members did not indicate their positions pretty clearly. This is presumably the meeting which Sybel attributes to the evening of July 10. His description of the proceedings is interesting and plausible. He relates that Drouyn de Lhuys suggested that the French present the Prussians with a clearly formulated choice: if they did not agree to Napoleon's proposals, France would give her active support to the Austrians. This plan was strongly opposed by Rouher and Plon-plon. They maintained that such a policy would be untenable since it would represent a complete *volte-face*. Napoleon's attitude, in contrast to these two extremes, was relatively moderate. He admitted that his hopes for the success of mediation had been frustrated, but he felt that the wisest course was to concert peace terms with the Prussians through Prince Reuss. The result of the conference, according to Metternich, was a reaffirmation of the rejection of armed intervention, coupled with the decision to negotiate, rather than impose, an armistice settlement.[85] In accept-

---

[83] Reuss to Bismarck, July 12, 1866 (Oncken, I, 343–4).

[84] AN: Rouher's notes on the meetings of the Council of Ministers, July 11, 1866 (45 AP1, cahier 1).

[85] Sybel, V, 272–3; HHSA: Metternich to Mensdorff, July 18, 1866, no. 39A. Prince Napoleon was pressing his opinions with urgency. (Cf. Prince Napoleon to Napoleon, July 14, 1866, *Papiers famille impériale*, III, 111–2.)

ing the situation, Napoleon must have been aided by his feelings of sympathy for the Prussians. His announcement of mediation had at least sufficed to prevent the continuation of a military campaign on the scale of Sadowa. Beyond that, he was not very upset by Prussian acivities: he was delighted at the end of the old German Confederation, which had been set up by the Congress of Vienna as part of the containment of France;[86] and he was also, as we have seen, prepared to have Prussia gain territory in the northern part of Germany.[87] A few of the proposals, such as the exclusion of Austria from the new federal arrangement, or the acquisition by Prussia of Saxony, could stir him to protest;[88] but by and large, the changes in Germany seemed quite compatible with his belief in the principle of nationalities, his hatred of the treaties of 1815, and his rather optimistic calculation of French interests.

Meanwhile, the Prussians were not alone in their anxiety about French policy. The Austrians on July 9 sent the Saxon Beust on a mission to Paris.[89] His instructions were to find out, once and for all, whether Napoleon intended to provide the Austrians with any tangible military assistance.[90] Since Reuss was already in Paris, the visit was ludicrously ill-timed. Buest first saw Drouyn de Lhuys on July 11. The French had already been reassured about the delays in the armistice by Reuss on July 10. Drouyn declared, in accordance with the decisions of the Council of Ministers, that French military intervention was impossible. He excused the failure to come to Austria's aid by pointing to the military commitments in Mexico, Algeria, and Rome.[91] In so doing, Drouyn was speaking against his own wishes and convictions. Cowley reports that on the afternoon of July 11, Drouyn was referring to the Prussian plans for a settle-

---

[86] PRO: Cowley to Bloomfield, July 25, 1866 (F. O. 519/233).

[87] PRO: Cowley to Stanley, July 13, 1866 (F. O. 519/233).

[88] Goltz to Bismarck, July 14, 1866 (Oncken, I, 352–3).

[89] Gramont to Drouyn de Lhuys, July 9, 1866 (*Origines,* X, 373).

[90] Gramont to Drouyn de Lhuys, July 10, 1866 (*Origines,* X, 391); Lawrence D. Steefel, "A Letter of Franz Joseph," *Journal of Modern History,* 2:70–1 (March 1930).

[91] Beust to Mensdorff, July 11, 1866 (Oncken, I, 334–5).

ment with the gravest distrust. Drouyn remarked that he felt sure that the terms would be so severe that Napoleon would find it impossible to sanction them.[92] In this frame of mind, Drouyn was deeply impressed by Beust's arguments. He accordingly drew up a memorandum for the Emperor[93] in which he restated his suspicions of the extent of Prussian ambitions and suggested once more that the diplomatic steps in progress be reinforced by arms.[94] Meanwhile, Metternich had talked directly with Napoleon that morning, but he had accomplished even less than did his Saxon colleague, for he received the impression that Napoleon had more or less made up his mind.[95] The Austrian ambassador proceeded to appeal to Eugénie.[96] This tactic was hardly more successful. Eugénie assured him that she was doing all she could to push the Austrian cause but was achieving little. She wrote in incoherent desperation:

> They answer me with the immense responsiblity which weighs on him who must decide, we are not ready, and they don't want to plunge into the ventures without having the wherewithal to back up a demonstration, my word no longer has any weight I am almost alone in my opinion, they are exaggerating the danger of today in order to hide better that of tomorrow, who knows, the match is pushed aside, until later.[97]

Metternich himself would attempt to resign on July 18,[98] while poor Eugénie had had to find satisfaction in practical measures of little meaning. She sent Franz Joseph a good-luck piece in the form of a small medallion of the Blessed Virgin. Franz Joseph, who wrote his thanks on July 21, must have considered this an ironical gift.[99]

Meanwhile, on July 11, Goltz had informed Napoleon that definite Prussian proposals would be forthcoming in a day or two. The

[92] PRO: Cowley to Foreign Office, July 11, 1866 (F. O. 519/14).
[93] Oncken, I, 335, n. 2.
[94] Randon, *Mémoires,* II, 146.
[95] HHSA: Metternich to Esterhazy, July 11, 1866, no. 37B.
[96] Metternich to Eugénie, July 10, 1866 (Oncken, I, 332); Metternich to Eugénie July 11, 1866 (Oncken, I, 333).
[97] Eugénie to Metternich, July 11, 1866 (Oncken, I, 333-4).
[98] Cf. HHSA: Mensdorff to Metternich, July 30, 1866.
[99] Franz Joseph to Eugénie, July 21, 1866 (Oncken, I, 334, n. 1).

courier to whom they had been entrusted was scheduled to reach Paris on July 12. He implied strongly that the Prussians would be willing to accept the armistice which Napoleon had proposed if the Emperor in turn would recommend these proposals to the Austrians. At the same time, Goltz made it clear that the Prussian government intended to use these terms as a basis for negotiation with France rather than a unilateral fiat.[100] Napoleon hastened to fulfill his part of the program by writing Metternich on July 12: "I believe I can declare to you frankly that it is impossible for Me to aid you by force of arms. My efforts for the armistice will only succeed if you accept preliminaries of peace." [101] Drouyn de Lhuys wrote, also on July 12, to the same purpose. He pointed out to the Austrians that their choice lay between a graceful compliance with the terms and a last stand alone.[102]

The Prussian courier arrived in Paris late in the evening of July 12. Goltz was able to talk to Napoleon more precisely on July 13. The discussion was apparently a stormy one, for several of the Prussian suggestions were repugnant to the Emperor. He objected, for example, to the Prussians' desire to annex Saxony, and suggested that the Saxons be allowed to join with the South German states. He upheld the freedom of the latter group to create some sort of a loose union which would act as a unit in foreign affairs and military actions. He was evasive, despite Goltz's best efforts, on the subject of French territorial expectations, but brought up again the idea of a buffer state in the Rhine area. He proposed that the Saxon royal house, if dispossessed by the Prussians, might be compensated with the rule of this region. However, Napoleon's failure to press firmly for specific, direct compensations at this decisive moment would seem to indicate that the issue held low priority for him. Finally he insisted that Austria must be exempt from any demands for cessions of German land. With these comments and reservations,

---

[100] Sybel, V, 273–6.
[101] HHSA: Metternich to Foreign Office, July 12, 1866, no. 137.
[102] Drouyn de Lhuys to Metternich, July 12, 1866 (Oncken, I, 346).

Napoleon expressed himself willing to recommend the terms to Vienna with the understanding that he would not aid the Austrians should they refuse them. In order to facilitate the démarche, Napoleon demanded of Goltz a written draft of the peace proposals, which Goltz agreed to draw up that evening.[103]

Napoleon could now be somewhat more specific in his conversation with Beust, who also came to see him on July 13, the day of his departure from Paris.[104] Napoleon tried to reassure the Austrian emissary by emphasizing the positive side of the negotiations with Prussia. He admitted that he had agreed to the Prussian plan excluding Austria from any remodeled version of the old German Confederation, but he pointed out that he had managed to prevent any Prussian demands for Austrian soil. He assured Beust that the Prussian schemes for reorganizing Germany seemed "rather reassuring," a judgment presumably based on the apparent success of his attempts to keep South Germany independent. Finally, he excused his willingness to cooperate with many of the Prussians' desires by declaring that he did not think that France was prepared for military involvement.[105]

The next step in the complex discussions was a conference between Napoleon and Goltz based on the latter's written version of the Prussian requirements. By this time, Goltz's eagerness to reach a definitive solution had been stimulated by conversations the previous day with Rouher and Prince Napoleon. Both men pressed the advisability of a quick armistice settlement. Rouher spiced his words with confidences about Drouyn's continued efforts to turn the Emperor against the Prussians.[106] The terms which Goltz produced were on the whole acceptable to Napoleon, for they followed the direction of the nationalist thinking which had largely motivated

---

[103] Sybel, V, 292–5.

[104] HHSA: Metternich to Foreign Office, July 12, 1866, no. 136, and July 13, 1866, no. 141.

[105] HHSA: Metternich to Foreign Office, July 13, 1866, no. 141. For a further discussion of the French military situation, see Epilogue.

[106] Sybel, V, 295–6.

him throughout the crisis, with the addition of specific commitments which he had already been brought to accept during the preceding few days. In the first article, it was decreed that Austria would be asked to cede no territory except the province of Venetia. In the second, Austria was required to recognize the extinction of the old German Confederation and her exclusion from the new order in the area which it had comprised. The third provided for the organization under Prussia of a North German union in the area north of the Main River. This grouping would have a joint army which would be placed under Prussian leadership. The fourth article concerned the states south of the Main: it laid down that these states could if they so desired set up a South German union which would be "independent." In this case, according to the fifth article, there would be an "entente commune" between the two groupings. Prussia's outright territorial gains were regulated by the sixth paragraph and were almost negligible: only Schleswig-Holstein, with the further limitation that the famous northern strip of Schleswig should be returned to Denmark if the inhabitants, who were largely Danish in nationality, so chose. Finally, in the last article, the Prussian ambassador stipulated that the entire expense of the recent conflict was to be paid as indemnity by the Austrians and the small states which had joined with her.

These terms seemed adequate to Napoleon, with the exception of the last provision, the requirement that the Austrian side assume the entire military costs of the conflict. At his insistence, Goltz changed the paragraph to stipulate a portion only of the total expense.[107] The other arrangements envisaged were relatively close to the Emperor's personal desires, as expressed throughout the crisis. It was unfortunate that the Saxons were to be forced into the North German union, but as long as they were not directly annexed by the Prussians, Napoleon might have relatively little reason to object seriously. The only striking departure from Napoleon's original

[107] Drouyn de Lhuys to Benedetti and Gramont, July 14, 1866 (*Origines*, XI, 30–2, and n. 1, p. 32).

nationalist projects was the exclusion of the Austrians from any ties with the new unions. This concession might seem small in view of the embarrassment to the Emperor's nationalistic sentiments and previous pronouncements which would have been caused by vigorous action against the Prussians and the Italians. Accordingly, it is not surprising that Napoleon informed King William on July 15 that he was ready to accept the Prussian terms without hesitation.[108]

The next steps were even more complicated and delicate. It was necessary to win the acceptance of the Austrians and of Goltz's home government. The Austrians did not pose much of a problem. Their eventual agreement was clear by July 16.[109] As Mensdorff put it, the Ballplatz really had no choice. It was better to accept the Prussian conditions, though they were harsh, rather than risk still harsher terms by a rash continuation of the compaign.[110] This was especially true as the Italians were continuing the war with enthusiasm on the southern front. The best hope for the Austrians lay in agreeing to the Prussian proposals, while attempting to mitigate them by negotiations on such particularly troublesome matters as the indemnity.

The real difficulty was the attitude of Bismarck and King William to the arrangement which their ambassador had worked out in Paris. Benedetti, as soon as he heard the proposed terms, expressed his skepticism. He felt that the French could have made a much better bargain.[111] His observations of the temper at the Prussian headquarters led him to believe that Bismarck was far more nervous than his emissaries, who saw only a part of the picture, about the damage which French military intervention could do. Benedetti guessed that Bismarck was accordingly eager to reach an agreement with the French even at the price of a modification of Prussian gains. However, the most damaging part of the document drawn up

[108] Napoleon to William, July 15, 1866 (Oncken, I, 358).
[109] Drouyn de Lhuys to Benedetti, July 16, 1866 (Origines, XI, 67).
[110] Mensdorff to Metternich, July 17, 1866 (Oncken, I, 361–2).
[111] Gramont to Drouyn de Lhuys, July 17, 1866 (Origines, XI, 90–1).

by Napoleon and Goltz, according to Benedetti's analysis, was that it conceded not merely too much, but the wrong thing. Benedetti believed that the crucial requirements, from Bismarck's viewpoint, were the demands for a North German union and for annexations of territory in the North German area which, although not necessarily large in themselves, would permit the unification into one contiguous whole of the scattered pieces of the Prussian kingdom as arranged by the Congress of Vienna.[112] Conversations with Bismarck convinced Benedetti that if the Prussians were offered these advantages, they might be willing to drop the requirement of Austrian exclusion from German affairs. Consequently Benedetti suggested the following revisions of the conditions sponsored by Napoleon. Austrian cession of Venetia was to be combined with the indemnity provisions. Austrian consent to the ending of the old Confederation was to be worded more strongly, but the provision for Austrian exclusion was to be omitted. The North German union would be based on the consent of the states involved, a provision obviously directed at the Saxon situation. Nothing was to be said about Prussian military leadership. The article dealing with the South German states was to be modified to allow a link with Austria or omitted entirely. No mention would be made of the entente between the North and South German unions. The authorization of Prussian annexation of Schleswig-Holstein was to be retained, while Prussian aggrandizements designed to reunite the two halves of the present kingdom would be specifically sanctioned. Benedetti recommended that this program, which he considered feasible, be reinforced by the threat of action in case of its rejection.[113] In a later telegram, in which he again emphasized the Prussian desire for geographical unity as a sine qua non, he asked for permission to take an active hand in the negotiation of a settlement along these lines on the basis of the French position as "mediating Power." [114]

[112] Benedetti to Drouyn de Lhuys, July 15, 1866, and postscript July 18 (*Origines,* XI, 51-6).

[113] Gramont to Drouyn, July 16, 1866 (*Origines,* XI, 71-2).

[114] Benedetti to Drouyn, July 17, 1866 (*Origines,* XI, 82).

Benedetti's observations may have been offered an opportunity for rectifying the damage done to the French position by the battle of Sadowa. Unfortunately, they came too late. Benedetti's specific suggestions were telegraphed from Vienna by Gramont on July 16;[115] Bismarck received telegrammed word of the terms concerted between Napoleon and Goltz on July 17.[116] It would have been impossible for the Emperor to go back on his agreement once it had been communicated to the Prussians, and so Drouyn de Lhuys's response on July 19 was discouraging in the extreme. He declared that the French were to act in the deliberations as "friendly inter-mediaries," not as "arbitrators imposing . . . solutions" or "nego-tiators taking a direct part in the arrangements." Within these limits he would allow Gramont and Benedetti to do anything they saw fit, but it was clear that the limits had been so tightly drawn that the opportunity for effective action by the ambassadors in the field was nil. Drouyn's over-all conception of the role of his representatives was "to bring the belligerent Powers to a common ground." [117] This was very different from Benedetti's hopes of influential inter-vention. Almost immediately, it was clear that Benedetti had been right. Terms which omitted a rectification of Prussia's geographical situation were unacceptable, or at least, as William put it, acceptable only "to facilitate the conclusion of an armistice," not, as Napoleon had hoped, for use as the outlines of a peace treaty. Bismarck explained to Benedetti that Goltz had completely misunderstood his instructions. Bismarck had told him to demand sanction for Prussian aggrandizement, subject to negotiation. Goltz was to ask first for a "maximum" increase, which would comprise all the territories which the Prussians currently controlled; if this proved inadmissible, Goltz was to lower his claims gradually, within certain defined limits. However, the terms as they stood were considered impossible;[118] and Bismarck had sent his ambassador a new telegram in which he

---

[115] Gramont to Drouyn, July 16, 1866 (*Origines*, XI, 71–2).
[116] Sybel, V, 316–7.
[117] Drouyn de Lhuys to Benedetti, July 19, 1866 (*Origines*, XI, 107).
[118] Benedetti to Drouyn, July 19, 1866 (*Origines*, XI, 112–5).

had again instructed him to seek the French government's approval of aggrandizement. To soften the blow, he had added that the Prussians might refrain from a march on Vienna, as long as the French took no steps to favor the Austrians.[119]

Meanwhile, in Paris, Goltz received Bismarck's telegram. On July 19, he went to see Drouyn de Lhuys and demanded agreement on Prussia's territorial ambitions. The French situation was highly unfortunate. As Benedetti suggested, earlier in the discussions they might have avoided the sanction of Austrian exclusion from the new arrangements if they had been willing to yield on Prussian annexations. However, once they had submitted proposals to Bismarck which admitted Austrian exclusion, it became difficult or impossible to withdraw this concession, while they were now obliged to agree to Prussian territorial claims in order to get any settlement at all. Drouyn, who did not like this state of affairs, managed to beat down the Prussian pretensions to the "minimum" which Bismarck required. The Prussian ambassador, who knew his adversaries, hastened to the Tuileries and obtained Napoleon's consent to the "maximum." The difference was striking: some 300,000 souls comprised the "minimum," while the "maximum" included three to four million.[120] In giving his agreement, Napoleon was doubtless swayed by Goltz's assurances that in return the Prussians would immediately announce a five-day armistice; but a deeper motive undoubtedly was the readiness he had always felt to see the Prussians unify the territory to the north of the Main River. Since this was an objective close to his heart, the distinction between outright annexation and control through association was relatively indifferent to him. He could say with perfect sincerity that the extent of Prussia's gains was "a matter of detail." [121] Goltz, however, must have considered that he had done a good day's work. He safeguarded it by hastening to send a telegram describing the concessions to Bismarck. This pre-

[119] Sybel, V, 318–9.
[120] Ollivier, VIII, 476–7.
[121] Sybel, V, 331.

caution taken, he informed Drouyn de Lhuys of the latest developments. Drouyn was most disturbed; but there was nothing he could
do at this stage. He did go to the Tuileries in his turn, but he
evidently made no attempt to combat the decision on Prussian increases. Instead, he revived, with some success, the old suggestion
of compensations for France.[122]

By this time, the main outlines of the eventual proposals were
clear. The next few days were passed in discussion of less important
aspects of the terms. Bismarck brought up the requirement that
separate negotiations for peace preliminaries be held between Prussia
and Austria and between Prussia and the small states allied with the
Austrians.[123] This suggestion was a convenient way around the
difference between Napoleon's proposed conditions and the revised
terms. Napoleon's version covered the major points at issue between
the Prussians and the Austrians, while the revised version was more
particularly concerned with the settlement with the small states. The
consequences of this plan, however, in depriving the small states of
their most active champion, were to be quite far-reaching. Another
debate turned on the status of Saxony. As late as July 22, Napoleon
still urged Saxon independence. He also proposed another variation
of the familiar buffer state plan: the Prussians would annex part of
Ober-Hessen and compensate its grand duke with the Bavarian
holdings in the Rhineland.[124] But there was a certain unreality in
all these debates. Neither party was likely to initiate a disagreement
of major proportions at this point. Napoleon's final consent to the
revised terms, including the provisions for a double peace and for
Prussian annexations to the extent of four million souls, was forthcoming on July 22.[125] It was now necessary to secure Austrian
agreement, but as with Napoleon's original proposals, this was almost
the corollary of the French sanction. Drouyn wrote Gramont on

[122] Ollivier, VIII, 477.
[123] *Origines,* XI, 164, n. 2.
[124] Sybel, V, 332–4.
[125] Goltz to Bismarck, July 23, 1866 (Oncken, I, 373).

July 19 instructing him to urge the terms upon the Austrian government. He pointed out the advantage to the Austrians of the "independent international existence" for the South German states and
declared, somewhat speciously from the Austrian viewpoint, that this
provision counterbalanced Austria's exclusion from the reorganized
Germany.[126] But however unconvinced they were by Drouyn's
arguments, there was little the Austrians could do. Gramont reported
next day that the Ballplatz agreed to the terms. This acceptance
was kept on an informal basis for the time being, since the Austrians
hoped to use the negotiations for peace preliminaries, which would
take place during the five-day armistice, to strike a better bargain
with the Prussians over the indemnity.[127]

This left one major aspect of the situation unresolved: the Italians
were still campaigning on the southern front. It was necessary to
bring them into the armistice also. The French government had
been working in this direction for some time, but with very limited
results. By mid-July, the Austrians had promised to hand over immediately all four of the fortresses which comprised the famous Quadrilateral.[128] It might seem that this concession would represent a
substantial step toward agreement, but in the meantime Italian
demands had risen even more rapidly as the activists gained ground
at the expense of the more moderate wing led by La Marmora.
Ricasoli, the activist leader, held the opinion that the Austrians
ought to negotiate with the Italians directly, rather than working
through the French. His territorial demands were also very large,
including, in addition to Venetia, the regions of Trentino, Friuli,
and Istria.[129] The French dealt with this situation by sending Prince
Napoleon on a special mission according to the plan postponed
before the Reuss visit.[130] As the French government was thoroughly
anxious, the Prince's mission was harassed or reinforced by a stream

---

[126] Drouyn de Lhuys to Gramont, July 19, 1866 (*Origines*, XI, 111).
[127] Gramont to Drouyn de Lhuys, July 20, 1866 (*Origines*, XI, 120–1).
[128] Drouyn de Lhuys to Pillet, July 14, 1866 (*Origines*, XI, 34).
[129] Dieudé Defly to Drouyn, July 12, 1866 (*Origines*, XI, 19).
[130] Drouyn de Lhuys to Malaret, July 16, 1866 (*Origines*, XI, 68).

of telegrams from Paris pressing for an armistice. On July 19, Drouyn wrote to say that the Prussians had agreed to a five-day truce. This interpretation of the discussions pending in Paris was so optimistic that it seems clearly designed as a means of putting pressure on the Italians.[131] On the 20th, Rouher intervened through a telegram to Prince Napoleon in which he urged him to arrange the armistice as quickly as possible.[132] On the 21st, Rouher sent another telegram in the same vein.[133] On the same day, Drouyn wrote again with more reliable information than before to the effect that the Austrians had accepted the conditions concerted with the Prussians.[134] Meanwhile, in Paris, the Council of Ministers met on July 21. Once again the alternative of staging a naval demonstration in the Adriatic was brought up by the Emperor, but it was dismissed after brief consideration on the grounds that such action would be premature before the results of Prince Napoleon's mission were known.[135] However, Napoleon was so angry with the Italians that he remarked to Metternich, according to the ambassador's own story: "I would ask nothing better today than that you could beat them again, chase them from the Quadrilateral and keep Venetia."[136] It was not very practicable, however, for the Italians to continue fighting once their ally had stopped the campaign in the north. Even Ricasoli seems to have realized this when he had a chance to think things over.[137] Furthermore, there was the obvious advisability, which weighed heavily with La Marmora, of retaining, insofar as possible, the original sympathy of Napoleon III. Aided no doubt by these considerations of Italian interest, Prince Napoleon did a very fine job as French emissary.[138] But the final and conclusive factor in the

[131] Drouyn de Lhuys to Malaret, July 19, 1866 (*Origines*, XI, 108–9).

[132] D'Hauterive, "La Mission du Prince Napoléon," p. 100.

[133] D'Hauterive, "La Mission du Prince Napoléon," pp. 102–3.

[134] Drouyn de Lhuys to Malaret, July 21, 1866 (*Origines*, XI, 138).

[135] AN: Rouher's notes on the meetings of the Council of Ministers, July 21, 1866 (45 AP1, cahier 1).

[136] HHSA: Metternich to Mensdorff, July 26, 1866, no. 41A.

[137] Malaret to Drouyn de Lhuys, July 21, 1866 (*Origines*, XI, 144).

[138] Malaret to Drouyn, July 24, 1866 (*Origines*, XI, 189).

Italians' decision was the serious naval defeat suffered at Lissa on July 20. Influenced by all these circumstances, the government agreed to the armistice, which was to become effective on July 25.[139]

Meanwhile, the Austrians and the Prussians had been debating the final terms for the preliminaries of peace at the Prussian headquarters at Nikolsburg. The French were almost totally excluded from this process, more or less through their own choice. Their representative on the spot was Benedetti, whose initial concern had been dampened by unequivocal instructions from Drouyn de Lhuys. These were reinforced by a further communication, couched in even more explicit language, on July 23.[140] One explanation of this arrangement is offered by a memorandum produced for Napoleon by the Quai d'Orsay on July 21. Benedetti's role was described as that of "the impartial councilor and the equitable conciliator." His specific functions were to include promotion of agreement, insistence that the ultimate arrangement bear a fairly close relationship to the terms worked out in Paris; and mediation in case of arguments arising from misunderstandings of these terms. Benedetti was not to appear in any way as an architect of the settlement, for his superiors believed, according to the note, that it might yet be necessary for the French, at some future date, to repudiate the arrangements resulting from the final treaty. In this case, it would be better if they had not been identified too closely with the original agreement.[141] This argument seems rather specious. A more plausible explanation can be deduced from the fact that the terms had already been worked out in enough detail, and in a manner sufficiently satisfactory to Napoleon, that intervention on Benedetti's part, unless limited to safeguarding the conditions already arranged, could only provide embarrassment. The fact that Benedetti might have succeeded in making the terms lighter for the Austrians was not an argument calculated to weigh very heavily with the Emperor. Bene-

---

[139] Ollivier, VIII, 499.
[140] Drouyn de Lhuys to Benedetti, July 23, 1866 (*Origines*, XI, 162–3).
[141] "Note envoyée à l'Empereur," July 21, 1866 (*Origines*, XI, 131–3).

detti's reaction to all this was unfortunate, however. Very much annoyed that his well-informed advice had been rejected, he took refuge in an attitude of overscrupulous cooperativeness. On July 23, for example, he wrote that although Bismarck had expected him to sit in on the meetings he had refused the invitation on the grounds that it was outside his instructions.[142] And shortly thereafter, he announced that Bismarck was going well beyond the terms sponsored by France, but added: "having no other instruction, Your Excellence will understand that I am abstaining from expressing, about the plans which M. de Bismarck is on the point of realizing, an opinion which could prove to be in contradiction with the intentions of the Government of the Emperor." [143]

What was going on behind the closed doors? Despite Benedetti's doubtless alarmist communications, the terms as they were finally worked out by July 25 did not depart greatly from the arrangements sanctioned by Napoleon. One subject of discussion was the amount of the Austrian indemnity. This was finally fixed at twenty million thalers.[144] Another even more important question was the fate of Saxony. Napoleon had tried to insist on Saxon rights. This determination was communicated to Benedetti in a telegram of July 23.[145] The result was a compromise. The Prussians proposed to respect Saxony's territorial integrity,[146] but they did intend to include the Saxon state in the North German union. The Saxons were distressed by this arrangement, for they judged correctly that their freedom was illusory as long as they were cut off from strong allies, either within or without the union. At this point, however, the five-day armistice ran out, and the Prussians refused to extend it.[147] This meant that the Austrians were faced with the alternatives of abandoning the Saxons or resuming the war. Franz Joseph left the

---

[142] Benedetti to Drouyn de Lhuys, July 23, 1866 (*Origines*, XI, 170).
[143] Benedetti to Drouyn de Lhuys, July 24, 1866 (*Origines*, XI, 183, 188).
[144] Gramont to Drouyn de Lhuys, July 26, 1866 (*Origines*, XI, 214).
[145] Drouyn de Lhuys to Benedetti, July 23, 1866 (*Origines*, XI, 164–5).
[146] Gramont to Drouyn de Lhuys, July 23, 1866 (*Origines*, XI, 215).
[147] Gramont to Drouyn, July 26, 1866 (*Origines*, XI, 215–6).

decision to the Saxon monarch. It was clear to King John that, whatever the Austrians' compunctions, further resistance was in fact impracticable; and he felt himself forced to tell them to accept the Prussian terms.[148] Franz Joseph consequently decided to agree at five o'clock on July 26. This answer was telegraphed immediately to the emissaries waiting at Nikolsburg.[149] The famous peace preliminaries were signed that very day.[150]

The official settlement can be summarized very briefly, for its major provisions have already been described. Austria was assured that she would be required to cede no territory except Venetia. Austria sanctioned the end of the old German Confederation and her exclusion from the new organization. She agreed to allow the formation of a North German union under Prussia, a South German union, and "an entente commune" between the two. She gave up her claims in Schleswig-Holstein in return for a promise from the Prussians that northern Schleswig would be returned to Denmark if a plebiscite revealed such a desire among the inhabitants. She agreed to an indemnity of twenty million thalers. In exchange for a promise from the Prussians that they would respect the territorial integrity of Saxony, she agreed to the principle of Prussian annexations in North Germany. Finally, a series of technical articles provided for Italy's inclusion in the settlements, the ratification process, the negotiation of the final treaty, and a truce which was to begin on August 2.[151]

So the German crisis, which in its acute form had lasted nearly a year, came to an end. The final phases of French policy had been affected by all the pressures which had influenced the previous stages, plus the incalculable elements added by the general conditions and actual events of the war. Napoleon's predilection in favor of

---

[148] Gramont to Drouyn, July 26, 1866, "Annexe" (Origines, XI, 239).

[149] Gramont to Drouyn de Lhuys, July 27, 1866, transmitting telegram from Benedetti, July 26, 1866 (Origines, XI, 241–2).

[150] Benedetti to Drouyn de Lhuys, July 26, 1866 (Origines, XI, 218).

[151] "Preliminaries of peace between Prussia and Austria," July 26, 1866 (Origines, XI, 409–11).

the principle of nationalities as represented by Prussia had received its supreme test after Sadowa, when it became apparent that the new German nation was going to be an unexpectedly powerful force in international politics. In his first moments of panic, the French emperor had thought of armed intervention, but as soon as it seemed likely that the Prussians would halt or at least subdue their military operations after Sadowa, his alarm subsided. Supported by the many practical military and political arguments urged by his advisers, he decided on simple mediation. Although the possibility of a recourse to arms arose again when the situation looked threatening, after July 5 Napoleon relied principally on negotiations and his decisions evolved from the concerns paramount in his mind throughout the crisis. The old German Confederation set up in 1815 was to be permanently destroyed; the Prussians were to consolidate a united state north of the Main River, while the South German states were to remain independent. As had been already assured by the French treaty with Austria, the Italians were to acquire Venetia. In the details of this program, Napoleon was certainly more generous than was necessary, largely because of the conditions inseparable from wartime. Through problems of communications, the Prussian demands were presented to Napoleon in piecemeal form, and the Emperor assented to provisions such as the exclusion of Austria which he might have refused had he been informed in time of Benedetti's suspicions that they were less important in Bismarck's eyes than outright annexations in northern Germany.

The settlement, from the moment it began to take shape, was unpopular with many Frenchmen, although it only gradually assumed the appearance of a major defeat. However, the very pressures which had hindered Napoleon's policy before Sadowa aided him afterwards: the division of forces and strong pacifist trend which had hampered Napoleon's efforts to ally France to Prussia before the war made it equally difficult for pro-Austrian activists, such as Drouyn de Lhuys, to rally support for the Hapsburgs after Sadowa. The result was that Napoleon's policy won in part by default. And his victory was not unmarred. Those who saw in Prussian success the implication of a defeat for France clutched at the possibility of rectifying the balance by winning compensations. Prominent exponents of this policy were Rouher and Drouyn de Lhuys.[152] The persuasiveness which their arguments carried in many circles can be discerned from moves in this direction which began even before the signature of the preliminary peace. The bulk of this story lies outside the scope of the present study, but as evidence of the intimacy with which the compensations demands were tied to the response to the peace settlement, the first manifestation should be mentioned. Drouyn's immediate impulse, once he heard that Napoleon had conceded the "maximum" of Prussian annexation claims, had been to urge the revival of plans for compensations. Napoleon's consent was presumably based on the notion that compensations would be acceptable if possible, rather than on heartfelt personal conviction. Drouyn suggested on July 23 to Benedetti that he try for the restoration of the boundary of 1814 plus Luxemburg in exchange for sanction of Prussian aggrandizement to the number of four million souls.[153]

[152] Loë, p. 120. The policy of compensations, which has received much attention in its later phases, rested upon a very curious base. As this incident suggests, it was a ministerial rather than a popular policy. There was a certain desire for compensations right after Sadowa (Albertini, pp. 338–9), but soon lack of enthusiasm was noticeable among most of the opposition statesmen and newspaper commentators. Various semisophisticated motives were alleged. Thiers and Prévost-Paradol claimed that since compensations would be granted by the Prussians, the net effect of such a policy would be to tie the French more closely to Berlin, whereas in actuality, France's true interest lay in a closer relationship with Austria and the South German states (Albertini, p. 367). This sounds like rationalization. Not much more impressive is the argument put forth by Nefftzer and the pro-Prussian papers that, since in any case compensations would be insufficient, there was no point trying for any at all. There was, in addition, a current of opinion which admitted frankly that compensations were unobtainable. By and large, however, rather than demanding a solution of the problem, with its attendant risks, people tended to blame Napoleon. The result was to make certain members of the government call for compensations as a sop to the public; this move, however, should not obscure the fact that the disgruntlement in general did not emerge in the form of specific popular requirements for compensations (Albertini, pp. 338–43). French opinion as a whole was only indirectly responsible for the policy.

[153] Drouyn de Lhuys to Benedetti, July 23, 1866 (*Origines*, XI, 164–5). Napoleon's failure to seize the opportunity for compensation demands offered by his own ne-

This proposal, which reached Benedetti most inopportunely on the morning of July 26, was extremely awkward. Benedetti felt forced to abandon the demand when Bismarck threatened to refuse to sign the Nikolsburg agreement.[154] Later attempts were made, however, and the result was to undermine any wisdom that the settlement might have contained from the French viewpoint. Bismarck used the threat of French ambitions in his negotiations with the South German governments to persuade those states to conclude secret treaties of alliance with the Prussian-dominated North German union.[155] These arrangements, in undercutting the independence of South Germany and the limitation of Prussian control to the area north of the Main, foreshadowed the enlarged German Empire of 1871. In Bismarck's skillful hands, Napoleon's partial victory had become a defeat.

---

gotiations with the Prussians seems to suggest that he was not committed to the program. Paul Bernstein, in his interesting article, "The Economic Aspects of Napoleon III's Rhine Policy," *French Historical Studies*, 1:335–47 (1960), has argued that Napoleon *was* interested in Rhenish acquisitions because he recognized the future, crucial importance of their coal resources for France's nascent industries. Unfortunately, Bernstein can show no direct evidence that Napoleon was interested in coal or indeed that the need for coal was a generally recognized problem at the time.

[154] Benedetti to Drouyn de Lhuys, July 26, 1866 *(Origines*, XI, 221–3).

[155] Heinrich Friedjung, *The Struggle for Supremacy in Germany, 1859–66*, trans. A. J. P. Taylor and W. L. McElwee (London, 1935), p. 296.

EPILOGUE

RECONSTRUCTION of the course of French policy toward the German crisis reveals the complexity, not to say confusion, of these months of diplomatic activity. Certain main lines should, however, emerge. The chaotic quality of the French response resulted more from stalemates between conflicting opinions within the government than from a lack of definite attitudes and well-elaborated schemes. It was not that the French government did not know what it was doing; it was, rather, that too many people were sure they knew what ought to be done. If the Prussians and Austrians had clarified the alternatives by making acceptable offers, it is possible that the French, after a greater or lesser amount of argument, might have arrived at a precise position. As it was, the conflict was never resolved and the historian is limited to describing policies rather than policy.

The Convention of Gastein in mid-August, 1865, came as a surprise and a disappointment to the French. Some statesmen, such as Drouyn de Lhuys, reacted violently against it and would have liked to take a harsh line, but Napoleon, holding his subordinates in check most of the time, preferred to follow a hot-and-cold policy, in the hope that Bismarck, if sufficiently bewildered by the indefiniteness and contradictions of French policy, would feel obliged to reach an arrangement with the French. This diplomacy bore fruit in the meeting at Biarritz in October, 1865. In contrast to many accounts, it has been suggested here that Bismarck, after outlining fairly candidly his plans for the unification of at least northern Germany, proposed that Napoleon seize the occasion of a war to compensate himself with French-speaking Belgium. Bismarck had hinted at such a solution in his preliminary conversations with Lefebvre de Béhaine, Rouher, and Drouyn de Lhuys. It seems unlikely that he would have abandoned this position in talking to the Emperor himself. The absence of tangible evidence of such a discussion at Biarritz may be explained by the delicacy of the subject. If, however, the Biarritz conversations were as vague and unspecific as official accounts maintain, then Bismarck's earlier indications remain as the key to Prusso-French negotiations during the autumn. These propositions were unacceptable to Napoleon. He did not object to the idea of limited German unification; he may have hoped that Prussia would form a new German state north of the Main River; and he did not even feel deeply persuaded of the necessity of compensations. He did believe, however, that some territorial gains were needed to reconcile a thoroughly pacifist public opinion with active steps; and Belgium did not meet that requirement. It was already evident that the English government would not watch with equanimity a French extension along the Channel. In consequence, Napoleon was forced to recognize that the Belgian scheme was impracticable and accordingly adopted an attitude of temporizing in his conversations with Bismarck throughout the autumn.

At about the same time, the Emperor encountered a new check. Agitation, particularly in economically depressed rural areas, led to reductions in the budget through the expedient of a cutback in the army. Although the War Ministry showed considerable ingenuity in distributing the cuts, so that the fighting force was only slightly weakened, the fact that a policy of reductions was inescapable had distressing implications for any thoughts of an active role in the German crisis. Consequently, during the winter of 1865, Napoleon turned to support of the Austrians, who, as the group supporting the status quo, were likely to maintain the peace as long as they were able to do so. Napoleon's partisanship was manifested through a loan, small in itself but great in its prestige value, by negotiations for a commercial treaty, and by a wide-ranging discussion of outstanding non-German problems. However, the rapprochement left untouched the real obstacle to a Franco-Austrian alliance, the question of Venetia. It is possible that this issue might have been broached eventually, when the hard feelings created in Vienna by the Malaguzzi mission had cooled; but in its absence, the thaw in Franco-Austrian relations was a false spring.

In point of fact, Napoleon soon took advantage of renewed tension between Austria and Prussia to try once again for a rapprochement with the latter power. At the end of February, he hinted to Goltz that the French were ready to consider new offers. His simultaneous sanction of Italian attempts to negotiate a treaty with Berlin leads us to believe that the Emperor was thinking in terms of a triple alliance, dedicated to the completion of Italian unification through the winning of Venetia and the satisfaction of German nationalism through the organization of a German state north of the Main. However, before Goltz could bring back the latest propositions from Berlin, a stormy pacifist demonstration in the Corps Législatif, and the swell of unrest in the country, had convinced Napoleon that his scheme was unworkable. Accordingly, he turned his attention to the other alternative already suggested by the Italians for the acquisition of Venetia, the much discussed Moldavian-Wallachian exchange plan. The Austrians regarded this idea with rooted hostility, however, and, since it was impossible to contain the Italians' enthusiasm a moment longer, the Prusso-Italian Treaty which Napoleon approved, at least at one point, became inevitable.

This step left the Emperor in a most unenviable, and ultimately untenable, position. He was profoundly committed to the cause of Italian national independence both as a matter of private sentiment and as a question of public diplomatic allegiance. To allow the Italians to be defeated—with its probable corollary of renewed Austrian embroilment in Italian affairs—would have been a setback both in prestige and in power. Yet, according to the best calculations of his military experts, this was precisely what was likely to happen. Napoleon needed to find some means of extricating himself and his solution, as usual, was to propose a congress. At first he presumably did not take this suggestion very seriously: he was more interested in the likelihood that the threat implied in a congress might stimulate offers from the Austrians or the Prussians. The results were disappointing, however. The Austrians' propositions, although they would have satisfied public opinion, to judge by Thiers' speech, were not acceptable to the Italians. Napoleon neglected to pursue them to their conclusion. He preferred his own attempts to get in touch with the Prussians; but the Vimercati overtures went almost unnoticed in Berlin, while his attempt at publicity through the Auxerre speech proved disastrously unpopular. So Napoleon was forced to take his congress seriously. Negotiations in this vein occupied the French government throughout the middle and end of May. A not unfavorable reception in most of the European capitals seemed to augur well for the idea, but at the last moment, the program was sabotaged by the Austrian insistence on a preliminary pledge by all the powers concerned excluding territorial aggrandizement. This would have reduced the sessions to nonsense. The plan for a congress was accordingly abandoned.

Napoleon's dilemma could not be put away so easily. He would probably still have preferred an arrangement with Berlin, but the Kiss Mission in the last days of May had proved conclusively that Bismarck was unwilling to consider compensations extensive enough to make a decisively pro-Prussian policy palatable to French public opinion. The small states were following policies which were in most cases ill-defined and mutually contradictory; there seemed little likelihood of constructive cooperative action. Napoleon's only alternative was an agreement with Austria. The treaty of June 12, 1866, comprised an eminently satisfactory escape from the Emperor's point of view. Venetia was guaranteed to Italy in any event, and the Austrians promised to consult Napoleon about changes in Germany. This commitment seemed to assure the Emperor of an opportunity to supervise the German settlement and he probably expected to use his power to prevent disaster for the nationalist cause as represented by Prussia.

On the eve of the war, then, Napoleon's position seemed favorable. The battle of Sadowa changed his circumstances in an afternoon. Napoleon's first reaction to the Austrian defeat was apparently one of near panic. He envisaged the Prussians, whose strength was so much greater than he had estimated, marching to Vienna and dictating a peace which would radically alter the balance of power in Germany and Europe in their favor. He had already accepted the Austrian plea for mediation. On July 5, he decided to support that mediation with an armed demonstration. But calmer, if not saner, counsels soon prevailed. The plan of posting an observation corps was open to several sound objections, which were forcefully urged by some of his advisers. The difficulties included French military strength, the strongly pacifist tenor of public opinion, and the ideological and political embarrassment of helping the Austrians, particularly against the Italians. These arguments put Napoleon in a state of doubt, in which he was only too happy to clutch at straws. In this mood, seemingly favorable responses to his armistice proposals were interpreted by the Emperor as proof of the imminent end of the campaign and the termination of the need for French intervention.

Although military action was considered again from time to time, the rest of July was occupied principally by negotiations with the belligerents over terms for a peace settlement. Throughout these discussions, Napoleon remained faithful to his radical and nationalist predilections. The German Confederation, as set up by the Congress of Vienna, was to be permanently dissolved, while German nationalist ambitions were to receive modest satisfaction through the establishment of a North German union under Prussia in the area north of the Main River. In working out the details of this plan, Napoleon seems to have been even more beneficent toward Prussian wishes than was necessary to achieve a negotiated peace. In part, this kindliness sprang from lack of information due to chaotic wartime communications, but in part it was undoubtedly the result of sympathy for Prussian requirements provided they did not represent a severe challenge to the balance of power. In carrying out this policy, Napoleon was aided by the conflicts of opinion and general desire for peace which had previously hindered his efforts. It was almost as hard for pro-Austrians such as Drouyn de Lhuys to rouse active support for the Austrians as it had been for Napoleon to rally agreement behind a Franco-Prussian alliance. However, the arrangement which Napoleon worked out with Reuss and Goltz, with its pro-Prussian implications, was unpopular in many circles from the start. The result was the decision, in which Napoleon concurred, to demand compensations. This step marked the end of whatever advantage the French might ultimately have won from the settlement, for Bismarck, in using these compromising requests to force alliances from the South German states, was able to commence the second part of his program, the total unification of non-Austrian Germany.

The interpretation given above differs from that offered by many scholars. At most points in the crisis it is difficult or impossible to establish Napoleon's aims. Only in the hours after Sadowa does the issue become clear-cut. It seems impossible to explain Napoleon's failure to intervene on behalf of the Austrians unless it is assumed that he favored the Prussians and was not sorry to see them maintain, although not drastically extend, the position they had won. Scholars who have denied or minimized Napoleon's pro-Prussian sympathies have urged a variety of reasons for his passivity, all of which spring ultimately from contemporary comments. A brief examination of these arguments should prove that they are all demonstrably insufficient to explain French inaction.

The simplest suggestion, and a very plausible one, has been advanced by authors such as Stern and Friedjung. In their descriptions of the maneuvers after Sadowa, both men lay heavy emphasis on the state of Napoelon's health and contend that the Emperor was so debilitated by disease that he could not choose between the different actions urged by his ministers. As result, Napoleon followed the line of least resistance and accepted the Prussian requirements with little or no attempt at revision.[1] There is some truth in these state-

---

[1] Stern, *Geschichte Europas* [*1815–71*], IX, 528–34; Friedjung, *The Struggle for Supremacy in Germany 1859–66*, pp. 238–46.

ments. Ollivier reports that, although Napoleon had never been free from minor irritating illnesses, after 1865 he was genuinely unwell, to the point that his competence was affected. As Ollivier summarized it, "more and more, what had been prudence became uncertainty; what had been reflection, groping; audacity was decided by whims." His condition was finally diagnosed, when it became acute in 1868, as a combination of anemia, gout, and rheumatism, and the baths at Vichy became the prescribed remedy. Meanwhile, it is said that an army doctor pointed out that the real trouble was a kidney stone, an ailment which the cure at Vichy did not help in the least but actually aggravated. The story continues to relate that nothing was done about this diagnosis and that Napoleon even had the doctor sworn to secrecy.[2] Another account has it that Napoleon was suffering from prostate trouble, which eventually improved.[3]

Many observers testify to the fact that Napoleon was clearly ill and in pain in July, 1866. Canrobert, who saw him at the end of the month, was quite shocked by his appearance and reported that he seemed "barely able to rise from his armchair." [4] At about the same time, Metternich wrote: "He is very pale, very emaciated, and has the air of a man in whom the force of will power has had to yield *before a general exhaustion.*" [5] Metternich even reported late in July that Eugénie was so upset about the situation that she had suggested that Napoleon abdicate in her favor.[6] It is well to remember, however, that Napoleon had just carried through a line of policy which Eugénie strongly opposed. Wifely concern may have been mingled, consciously or unconsciously, with political opposition. By the same token, Metternich, who had always believed himself close to the imperial couple, had been deeply disappointed by the events of July; in blaming Napoleon's failure to adopt an actively pro-Austrian line on the state of his health, the ambassador might have been finding

[2] Ollivier, *L'Empire libéral,* VII, 490–2.
[3] Friedjung, p. 270; Metternich to Mensdorff, July 26, 1866 (Oncken, I, 380).
[4] Bapst, *Le Maréchal Canrobert,* IV, 46.
[5] Metternich to Mensdorff, July 26, 1866 (Oncken, I, 378).
[6] Metternich to Mensdorff, July 26, 1866 (Oncken, I, 380).

a solution which would comfort his feelings as a friend. The fact that the Emperor did continue to reign for another four years and even led his army in the Franco-Prussian War, lends plausibility to Cowley's conclusion: "I do not conceive that there is anything seriously wrong with him. He suffers from Rheumatism & neuralgic pains, and, like all of us, he is growing older. It is the fashion to say that his intellect is not what it was. I should rather say that it is in energy, not in intellect, that he is the worse for wear." [7] While poor health may have contributed to the indecisions and confusions of Napoleon's policy in 1866, it is not likely that it was of sufficient proportions to explain the policy.

A more searching argument is concerned with the adequacy of French military preparedness. Doubts were raised on this score as early as the meeting of the Council of Ministers on July 5. A contemporary such as Rothan viewed it as the only good excuse for inaction.[8] This line of thought has been followed by scholars such as Sybel and Oncken, who attribute Napoleon's decision against armed mediation to anxiety about French strength, particularly since military action by France might have touched off a general European war.[9] What were the prospects of success for a military policy? As a matter of fact, it seems probable that the French military establishment, behind a fairly impressive façade, was quite weak. The Prussians, who had every reason to evaluate the situation coldly, reached this conclusion. A group of artillery officers who visited Paris in the summer of 1865 passed this judgment on the maneuvers at Versailles: "Men, horses, equipment, exercises distinguished; the shooting leaves much to be desired." [10] Another observer, dispatched on the eve of the war, formed the opinion that the French would be unable to muster military opposition in under four months.[11]

[7] PRO: Cowley to Bloomfield, July 31, 1866 (F. O. 519/233).
[8] Rothan, *La Politique française en 1866*, pp. 218–9.
[9] Sybel, *The Founding of the German Empire*, V, 248–51; Oncken, *Napoleon III and the Rhine*, pp. 61–5.
[10] Loë, *Erinnerungen aus meinem Berufsleben 1849–67*, pp. 74–5.
[11] Persigny, *Mémoires*, p. 379.

Meanwhile, the regular reports of Loë, the Prussian military attaché, reinforced this impression. Like the artillery officers, he criticized the French weapons. Although a model breech-loading musket was being manufactured for testing at Châlons, Loë estimated that even if the new guns were definitely adopted as expected in July, a couple of years would be required to effect the change-over.[12] Goltz was more optimistic; he believed that a year would be sufficient.[13] Loë also entertained a low opinion of the French artillery. And he had supported this report of French unpreparedness by specific charges. France did not have enough men under arms to fight a general war. The system of "recruitment and enlistment" had many flaws. There were no detailed plans for "mobilization and concentration." Finally, Loë pointed out that the Mexican campaign, which was still in progress, represented a considerable drain on French power.[14] Loë in person urged these views on William and Moltke at the time of his annual visit to Berlin in March for the King's birthday, and it is likely that his advice[15] had an influence on the ultimate decision to station no troops in the Rhineland. This economy of manpower was not without beneficial effects upon the campaign in Bohemia.[16]

Yet the Prussian view of French military readiness, even if it be true, is not the most relevant factor in a consideration of whether or not the French avoided an active military policy through a con-sciousness of inadequacy. It would be far more interesting to know how the French evaluated their strength. It is impossible to return to the scene and carry out an inquiry on the lines of a Congressional investigation, but the scattered comments that can be gathered sug-gest that the higher levels of the French army expected intervention as a matter of course and were innocent of any abnormal anxiety on the subject. Randon's views can be deduced from his stand at the meeting of the Council of Ministers. However, his position more or

[12] Loë, pp. 85-6.
[13] Goltz to William, July 4, 1866 (Oncken, I, 302).
[14] Loë, pp. 80-1.
[15] Loë, p. 83-5.
[16] Case, *French Opinion on War and Diplomacy during the Second Empire*, p. 206.

less forced him to enunciate an optimistic opinion, and the evidence is more impressive when one turns to figures high in the military hierarchy whose judgment was not affected by political responsibilities. To be sure, General Changarnier wrote Thiers on July 7 in a thoroughly pessimistic vein.[17] He seems to have been alone. Metternich would have us believe that the entire army favored intervention.[18] This is certainly partial testimony, but it is clear that Canrobert, Valazé, Chasseloup-Laubat, Bourbaki, and Vimercati[19] all awaited or actively promoted military steps. The prevailing mood in the upper echelons of the army appears to have been one of readiness and even eagerness. This is borne out by the story which may have some basis in truth, that Randon took active steps to back up the claims that he could mobilize 250,000 men by having full mobilization plans drawn up. An artillery officer named Miribel claimed in 1874 that he had been called in after Sadowa to assist Colson in formulating a blueprint for mobilization.[20] There is nothing to prove or disprove the truth of this story, but since Napoleon seemed to be planning armed mediation after Sadowa, the steps described sound like normal bureaucratic procedure.

The weight of the evidence that high French military circles expected and even welcomed intervention is increased when one examines French views on the two areas considered major weaknesses by the Prussian experts, namely the guns in use and the numbers of men available. As has been noted, the French were well aware, even before the outbreak of the war, of the Prussian experiments and advances in weapons, and they had developed a breech-loading musket of their own, the Chassepot model. A long program of research had culminated in January, 1866, with the perfection of a trial model which was manufactured in quantity for testing at the

[17] BN: Changarnier to Thiers, July 7, 1866 (Nouvelles acquisitions françaises XIX, 20619).
[18] HHSA: Metternich to Mensdorff, July 18, 1866, no. 39B.
[19] Bapst, IV, 28–34.
[20] Randon, Mémoires, II, 148–9.

maneuvers at the camp at Châlons.[21] This step was only a stage in the development of the guns, and only five hundred of the breech-loaders—of two different types—were produced. They were to be ready between the 15th and the 25th of July. At the same time, a "control group" of five hundred, later reduced to one hundred, guns of the old muzzle-loading type was ordered.[22] The shoot for which these models were planned was to be an imposing one, for in addition to the new guns, two new models of rifle-barreled cannons were to be demonstrated.[23] The demonstration was to take place during August,[24] although it was hoped to begin the instruction of the troops selected for the experiments as early as July 21.[25] The trials were to be observed by a distinguished group of military experts, including Bourbaki and Chassepot.[26]

It might be supposed, from this information, that the French had reached the most acute stage of competition with Prussia. They had become convinced that the breech-loading muskets merited careful investigation; yet, even excluding Prussian conclusions that a year or two would be necessary before a change could be completed, it is evident that a considerable period of time must elapse before the "weapons gap" could be closed. However, the French did not attribute the Prussian victory entirely to the needle gun, and consequently, the Prussians' demonstrated superiority in this area was only one factor in military deliberations. In the first panicked

[21] Vincennes: *Guerre* (2ᵉ Epreuve, 22 Janvier 1867), "Artillerie," p. 12 (Mémoires et Reconnaissances: 2139, dossier 1866).

[22] Vincennes: Randon to Régnault de St. Jean d'Angély, July 2, 1866 (Correspondance Générale: G⁸117, dossier 1–3, July 1866); War Ministry to Régnault de St. Jean d'Angély, July 8, 1866 (Correspondance Générale: G⁸117, dossier 7–11, July 1866).

[23] Vincennes: War Ministry to Régnault de St. Jean d'Angély, July 4, 1866 (Correspondance Générale: G⁸117, dossier 4–6, July 1866).

[24] Vincennes: Randon to Régnault de St. Jean d'Angély, July 11, 1866 (Correspondance Générale: G⁸117, dossier 7–11, July 1866).

[25] Vincennes: General Besson to General Bataille, July 20, 1866 (Correspondance Générale: G⁸117, dossier 20–2, July 1866).

[26] Vincennes: Randon to Régnault de St. Jean d'Angély, July 11, 1866 (Correspondance Générale: G⁸117, dossier 7–11, July 1866).

moments after Sadowa, both Merlin and Gramont regarded the gun as the sole explanation of what had happened.[27] As the immediate excitement died down, other considerations re-emerged. Merlin re-emphasized the theme of the ineffectiveness of the privilege-ridden Austrian officer class[28] and pointed out that the Prussian army had other merits besides the possession of the guns.[29] By mid-July he was ready to say that the needle gun was "not at all" responsible for the Austrian defeat;[30] the Austrians would have lost even had they had the gun.[31] Here he shared the opinion of Colson,[32] which probably represented the official attitude of the Ministry. Randon's view is well summarized by a remark written in 1867: "Oh! then let us hasten to remember those military virtues of our fathers: that will be worth more than the needle gun." [33] In another revealing passage from the same essay, he declared: "It is during the moments of crisis that it is necessary to have confidence in one's self . . . that is not the moment to let one's self be swept away by the illusions of changes." [34] This combination of conservatism and patriotic pride might well immunize the War Minister from the shock of the Prussian victory. In general it seems evident that concern over the needle gun alone would not have sufficed to determine French in-action in 1865; and if this statement holds true for a campaign it is still more relevant to the gathering of an observation corps, when there would be good reason to anticipate that battles might be avoided.

The other major criticism of the French army leveled by prewar observers was its lack of numerical strength. As we have seen, after the reforms of November 15, 1865, the army counted a paper strength

---

[27] Vincennes: Merlin to Randon, July 6, 1866, no. 16; Gramont to Drouyn de Lhuys, July 5, 1866 (*Les Origines diplomatiques de la guerre de 1870–71*, X, 327–8).

[28] Vincennes: Merlin to Randon, July 7, 1866, no. 16 bis.

[29] Vincennes: Merlin to Colson, July 10, 1866, no. 9.

[30] Vincennes: Merlin to Colson, July 16, 1866, no. 12.

[31] Merlin to Randon, July 17, 1866 (*Origines*, XI, 94–6).

[32] Vincennes: Merlin to Colson, July 25, 1866, no. 16.

[33] Randon, II, 241.

[34] Randon, II, 239–40.

of 631,305, while the number of soldiers actually on duty comprised 390,771 men. The size of the army fluctuated slightly during the course of the year, under normal administrative changes, but the figure remained relatively stable. On August 22, 1866, Randon reported to Napoleon that the "active army" consisted of 385,571, while the total was placed at 662,517. This latter figure was enlarged by adding 16,191 volunteers in case of war.[35] With the number of volunteers subtracted, the total is 646,326, relatively close to that for the end of 1865. This arithmetic by no means tells the whole story, however. The French had military commitments in Algeria, in Mexico, and in Rome, and the resultant drain has an obvious relevance to any scheme for military action in July, 1866. The number of men stationed overseas changed constantly, and the figures given to the Corps Législatif do not always coincide with the records kept in the War Ministry; but it is possible to ascertain the size of the groups under discussion with a degree of accuracy adequate for the present purposes.

Although Mexico is the most notorious example of the drain on French forces, the biggest overseas contingent was stationed in Algeria. On December 1, 1864, this body was said to include 83,002 soldiers.[36] This unusually large commitment had been necessitated by a revolt which had started during 1864 in the south and had moved northwards to jeopardize Oran and the area of European settlement. The French government had accordingly dispatched 20,000 extra troops to the province, but this was never viewed as more than a temporary expedient.[37] The troubles continued during the following year, but a series of French victories did much to stabilize the situation, as the rebels were forced for the most part to flee to the desert.[38] Meanwhile, Napoleon, as result of his observa-

---

[35] Randon, II, 152–3.

[36] Vincennes: *Guerre,* "Effectif de l'armée," p. 6 (Mémoires et Reconnaissances: 2139, dossier 1864).

[37] Vincennes: *Guerre,* "Opérations militaires: Algérie," pp. 3–4 (Mémoires et Reconnaissances: 2139, dossier 1864).

[38] Vincennes: *Guerre,* "Opérations militaires: Algérie," pp. 4–7 (Mémoires et Reconnaissances: 2139, dossier 1865).

tions during a visit to Algeria, had initiated a policy of organizing native troops, in the hope that these groups could gradually replace the French contingents, so that the province could become increasingly self-sufficient.[39] At the same time, with the disturbances diminishing, it was possible to repatriate a sizable number of soldiers.[40] The actual figure varies: both 21,000 and 15,000 appear in the documents.[41] It seems evident that the conflict in this case arises from a sometimes unexplained difference between the net and gross numbers. Thus a table entitled "Troupes et Détachements de l'Armée d'Afrique" declares that during 1865, 22,701 soldiers returned from Algeria, while 8,541 were sent out.[42] This means that the net decrease in French forces was 14,160, a figure not too far from the 15,000 of the more public report. This statistic also lends plausibility to the figure given elsewhere in the records for the size of the army in Algeria on December 1, 1865: this is cited as 69,677.[43] The process of repatriation continued during 1866, so that by the beginning of November, only 62,462 soldiers were left in Algeria.[44] It has not been possible to break down these totals to a shorter span, but assuming that the number brought back during the first half of the year was roughly equal to the number brought back during the second half, it may be concluded that the force tied up in Algeria at the beginning of July, 1866, comprised about 66,000 men.[45] According to the War Ministry's estimates, this group was larger than the

[39] Vincennes: *Guerre* (1re Epreuve, 16 Janvier 1867), "Organisation et recrutement," pp. 3–4 (Mémoires et Reconnaissances: 2139, dossier 1866).

[40] Vincennes: *Guerre,* "Opérations militaires: Algérie," pp. 4–7 (Mémoires et Reconnaissances: 2139, dossier 1865).

[41] Vincennes: *Guerre* (1re Epreuve, 6 Janvier 1866), "Opérations militaires," p. 3 (Mémoires et Reconnaissances: 2139, dossier 1865).

[42] Vincennes: "Troupes et Détachements de l'Armée d'Afrique" (Mémoires et Reconnaissances: 2139, dossier 1865).

[43] Vincennes: "Armée d'Afrique: Situation au 1er Décembre 1865" (Mémoires et Reconnaissances: 2139, dossier 1865).

[44] Vincennes: *Guerre* (2e Epreuve, 22 Janvier 1867), "Organisation et Recrutement," p. 5 (Mémoires et Reconnaissances: 2139, dossier 1866).

[45] In his report to Napoleon of August 22, 1866 (Randon, II, 153), the War Minister estimated the number in Algeria as 60,000, but from the papers officially preserved this seems too optimistic an estimate.

essential minimum. Randon calculated that in the event of a war in Europe, the forces in Algeria could be reduced to 50,000.[46]

The commitment in Mexico was more flamboyant and far more dangerous, but in actual numerical terms it was less. Here again a program of repatriation was in effect. Drouyn de Lhuys had long advocated complete withdrawal;[47] but the Emperor's consent was slow in coming.[48] Nonetheless, plans for departure were being formulated at the beginning of 1866,[49] and in June, 1866, a definite contract between the government and a shipping company was under consideration by the Council of Ministers.[50] Evacuation could not start, however, before the autumn and hence would not be terminated before the following year.[51] Once again, there is a conflict as to the exact number of men involved. Randon later put the figure at 28,693;[52] Loë early in 1866 gave 30,000;[53] papers preserved by Rouher give 26,530 for January, 1865,[54] but later reinforcements bring the figure up to 34,776 soldiers in June, 1866.[55] Since Randon's memory was frequently optimistic, we may assume, for the sake of argument, that, as a result of the necessity of maintaining the French position, despite the eventual plan of evacuation, the number of troops gradually rose, reaching the figure of about 34,000 by July, 1866.

France's other, and numerically least important commitment, was the occupation of Rome. Here again, plans were evolved to ter-

[46] Randon, II, 170.
[47] PRO: Cowley to Foreign Office, September 22, 1865 (F. O. 519/13).
[48] PRO: Cowley to Clarendon, January 13, 1866 (F. O. 519/232).
[49] Randon, II, 105.
[50] AN: Rouher's notes on the meetings of the Council of Ministers, June 16, 1866 (45 AP1, cahier 1).
[51] Loë, p. 83. According to Randon, evacuation was completed on March 11, 1867 (Randon, II, 105).
[52] Randon, II, 105.
[53] Loë, p. 83.
[54] Quai d'Orsay: Ministère de la Guerre: "L'effectif des troupes françaises au Mexique," March 6, 1865 (Papiers Rouher, IV).
[55] Quai d'Orsay: Ministère de la Guerre: "Mexique" (Papiers Rouher, IV). Although this memorandum is not dated, it has been filed by the archivists with the documents from June, 1866.

minate the arrangement, but in this case implementation was already underway. Drouyn de Lhuys favored a program of progressive withdrawal, with the French forces being replaced by a foreign legion.[56] Although Napoleon apparently opposed the idea at first, he eventually gave it his sanction.[57] Definite plans had been worked out by October, 1865.[58] The first group to return to France came in November, 1865, and numbered 3,500.[59] Here again it is difficult to establish how far the evacuation had proceeded at any given moment, but one can ascertain certain statistics of both before and after July, 1866. On December 1, 1864, the garrison consisted of 13,748 soldiers;[60] on November 1, 1866, there were 7,505 men.[61] It seems probable, then, that in this instance, Randon's estimate in August, 1866, of 8,000 men[62] was substantially correct.

What do these figures mean in terms of French military potential in July, 1866? About 108,000 men were engaged overseas in one way or another, and although plans for repatriation existed in each area, it is doubtful that the process could have been speeded up sufficiently to alter this commitment significantly. The implications vary, depending on the figure adopted for the total strength of the French army. Randon, attempting to justify himself in his *Mémoires,* apparently figured from the paper number of around 600,000 and claimed that within one month he could gather a body of 450,000, less the 108,000 who were overseas.[63] At the time, however, estimates were far less optimistic. Papers produced at the time of the army reform of November, 1866, indicate that the actual number of men

[56] Drouyn de Lhuys to Napoleon, August 15, 1865, quoted by Randon, II, 118–20.
[57] PRO: Cowley to Foreign Office, September 29, 1865 (F. O. 519/13).
[58] AN: Rouher's notes on the meetings of the Council of Ministers, October 1, 1865 (45 AP1, cahier 1).
[59] Vincennes: *Guerre,* "Opérations militaires: Rome," p. 8 (Mémoires et Reconnaissances: 2139, dossier 1865).
[60] Vincennes: *Guerre,* "Effectif de l'armée," p. 6 (Mémoires et Reconnaissances: 2139, dossier 1864).
[61] Vincennes: *Guerre* (2ᵉ Epreuve, 22 Janvier 1867), "Organisation et Recrutement," p. 5 (Mémoires et Reconnaissances: 2139, dossier 1866).
[62] Randon, II, 153.
[63] Randon, II, 146; 240.

who could have been put in the field was far smaller than the statistics suggest. One document declared, for example, that out of 600,000, only 360,000, including those overseas, could ever have been mustered against the enemy,[64] while other figures of the autumn of 1866 suggest that from the active army of about 400,000, only 288,000 would have been available in battle.[65] With the total of 108,000 overseas subtracted from these totals, the result is far less encouraging: 252,000 from the entire force, or 180,000 from the active army.[66] Even so, Randon must have been accurate in saying that in July, 1866, it would have been possible to rush to the eastern frontier a body of 80,000 men gathered from the troops stationed in Paris, Lyons, and Châlons.[67] This would have sufficed for an observation corps, for in this, the principle of an armed demonstration, rather than its size, was important. Drouyn de Lhuys is even credited with the remark: "Forty thousand are enough. Policemen would be enough." [68]

If the posting of an observation corps was a feasible step from the military viewpoint, the next question is whether French involvement could have been stabilized at this point, or whether the bluff would have been called and further steps would have been necessary in which the government would have been embarrassed—perhaps fatally—by the surprisingly small armed force available and also by

---

[64] AN: "1er projet," in documents sent by the Minister of War to the Minister of State in connection with the proposed army reforms, November 6, 1866 (45 AP14, cahier 2).

[65] Randon to Napoleon, October 24, 1866, quoted by Randon, II, 182; Bapst, IV, 52-3.

[66] The statistics are unclear as to the reasons for the divergence between Randon's optimistic total of 450,000 in the active army and the pessimistic totals of 360,000–288,000. Probably the cause was the necessity of maintaining a certain group of soldiers at strategic points along the seacoast and in the system of fortifications. In November, 1866, the figure needed for this purpose was set as high as 229,000. (AN: "1er projet," documents sent by the Minister of War to the Minister of State in connection with the proposed army reforms, November 6, 1866 [45 AP14, cahier 2].) This was undoubtedly a maximum estimate, since it was made at the time the government was trying to justify a massive increase in the fighting force, against obstacles whose strength we have already seen and which had been only slightly diminished by the anxiety aroused by the Prussian victory.

[67] Randon, II, 347.

[68] Randon, II, 146.

the far from flourishing state of public finances. Bismarck's trump card throughout this period was the threat that in case of French intervention, he could appeal to German national feeling and rally the small states solidly behind him. The information reaching the French government during the spring and early summer of 1866 tended to substantiate this claim,[69] and the trend continued in this direction in the first days of the war.[70] Sadowa marked a turning point, however. The appeal of German patriotism continued to be strong in some sectors of the population;[71] but there now arose, through fear of Prussia, a feeling that France represented the only "anchor of safety." [72] This sentiment can be traced in a number of small states.[73] Its presence casts doubt upon the likelihood of a "holy war." Another, and more precise, argument in the same tenor is based on the opinions of contemporary observers. Although the possibility of full-scale involvement was mentioned by Napoleon after the fact as a reason against the posting of an observation corps,[74] statesmen closer to the situation believed that the gambit could have succeeded. Gramont urged the French government to intervene in the assurance that the Prussians would be unable to challenge the move and thus the plan for French mediation would be greatly strengthened.[75] Bismarck himself, in a speech of 1874, admitted that a very small French demonstration could have turned the scale against him.[76] He still believed this when Friedjung interviewed

---

[69] See Appendix B.

. [70] For examples, see Reculot to Drouyn de Lhuys, June 22, 1866 (*Origines,* X, 249–50) and Méloizes to Drouyn de Lhuys, June 26, 1866 (*Origines,* X, 280).

[71] See Méloizes to Drouyn de Lhuys, July 11, 1866 (*Origines,* XI, 7); Cadore to Drouyn, July 11, 1866 (*Origines,* XI, 5–6); Reiset to Drouyn, July 18, 1866 (*Origines,* XI, 104).

[72] Reculot to Drouyn de Lhuys, July 6, 1866 (*Origines,* X, 334).

[73] See AN: Colmar, Report of July 12, 1866 (BB^{30}376, Colmar 1865–66); Bondy to Drouyn, July 11, 1866 (*Origines,* XI, 6); d'Astorg to Drouyn, July 15, 1866 (*Origines,* XI, 62).

[74] PRO: Cowley to Stanley, July 11, 1866 (F. O. 519/233); see also d'Harcourt, *Les Quatre Ministères de M. Drouyn de Lhuys,* pp. 340–1.

[75] Gramont to Drouyn de Lhuys, July 17, 1866 (*Origines,* XI, 92–3).

[76] D'Harcourt, p. 345.

him in 1890.[77] After all, as long as the Austrians continued a holding
action and as long as the small states did not unite against the
foreigner, the Prussians would be fighting on at least three fronts.
Since the entire Prussian army had numbered only about 520,000 at
the beginning of the war, a French army of even 180,000 would have
been more or less adequate numerically. The conclusion is inescapable: the French army was large enough to intervene; the War
Ministry was not profoundly anxious about the advantage conferred
on the Prussians by the needle gun; and so the mood of optimism in
military circles, which many observers note, was probably sincere and
firmly based. It is doubtful that French military weakness can have
decisively influenced Napoleon against armed mediation.

Finally, there is Lynn Case's explanation of the change from military to diplomatic action. He contends that the almost universal
desire for peace made a policy of force well-nigh impossible. Several
excellent studies of public opinion in this period suggest that this
argument was indeed potent. The public reaction in the hours after
Sadowa testifies to a widespread desire for peace which colored and
eventually overcame partisanship of any one of the belligerents. Most
of the sources say that the reaction to the Prussian victory was one
of "consternation." [78] According to Case, anxiety was so general that
Napoleon felt it necessary to play up as much as possible the Austrian
invitation to mediate, in order to quiet people. Unfortunately, the
public formed an exaggerated hope for the success of mediation,
which was embarrassing for the government.[79] Armengaud paints
the same picture in greater detail. He declares that even the pro-
Prussian newspapers greeted the news of Sadowa without enthusiasm, emphasizing that the Prussians must stop at the Main

[77] Friedjung, p. 390.
[78] Case, *French Opinion on War and Diplomacy,* p. 205. Only Albertini in
"Frankreichs Stellungnahme zur Deutschen Einigung," p. 336, says that the French
received the news with joy, and it is noteworthy that his study is cast in far more
general terms than the work either of Case or of Armengaud ("L'Opinion publique
en France et la crise nationale allemande en 1866").
[79] Case, *French Opinion on War and Diplomacy,* pp. 205–6.

River. The anti-Prussian journals were vociferous in pointing up the Prussian menace. This impression is corroborated by the testimony of eyewitnesses, who maintained that the mood in Paris directly after the battle was decidedly glum. However, all was changed when the news of mediation was received. Armengaud describes a scene related in the *Temps* of July 7 as one in which, within a half-hour after the news was known, many shopkeepers in the rue Montmartre and throughout the center of the city had draped their shops with flags. The members of the Corps Législatif were so excited that they were almost ready to pay Napoleon a visit in his palace as a group. The stock market rose, as did the cotton market at Le Havre. The reaction in the provinces was also enthusiastic, especially in the large commercial and manufacturing towns. Armengaud concludes from these details reinforced by the attitude of the press, that the joy over mediation sprang largely from the fact that the public in general believed that peace was now assured. If so, this is impressive evidence of the pacifist tenor of opinion.

Further corroboration of the breadth and depth of popular pacifism is the fact that the desire was strong enough to survive, without fundamental damage, the checks which marked the later progress of Napoleon's mediation. To be sure, the public was poorly informed about this phase of the negotiations, but many people realized that the very lack of information was a bad sign. The natural result was a certain uneasiness.[80] It reached significant proportions in some circles; Prévost-Paradol wrote: "I wonder sincerely . . . whether it was we who lost the battle of Sadowa." [81] One solution, considered at length in ministerial circles, was the posing of a firm demand for compensations. Despite the anxiety already noted, however, the public did not seriously require that the government gain compensations because there was a general fear that such a policy would lead to war. The French people preferred acceptance of humiliation

---

[80] Armengaud, pp. 94–110.

[81] Prévost-Paradol, *Quelques Pages d'histoire contemporaine: Lettres politiques,* IV, 135.

to engagement in a conflict.[82] This public desire for peace could not fail to influence the thinking of the Emperor. Case, who emphasizes the serious, indeed disastrous, consequences of the decision to give up armed mediation, assigns great importance to popular pacifism as one of the determining, if not the determining, factor in the decision.[83] Armengaud agrees that the Emperor lacked adequate backing for an active policy, but he does not feel that public opinion was as significant in the renunciation of the use of force as does Case.[84] Despite Armengaud's emphasis on the eagerness for peace which was widely expressed immediately after Sadowa, he believes that the public attitude changed fairly quickly, so that by the middle of July, it was no longer an obstacle to intervention. Case himself gives impressive evidence of Napoleon's skill in guiding public opinion at the time of the Italian War.[85] Finally there is the cautious evaluation by Albertini which emerges in the course of a discussion of compensations: Albertini believes that an initial desire for compensations right after Sadowa cooled off rather rapidly as people became increasingly conscious of the difficulties involved.[86] This would suggest a fluctuating but ultimately negative reaction to the possibility of intervention. However, both Armengaud's and Albertini's assessments would tend to modify Case's theory that the condition of public opinion ruled out armed action immediately and conclusively. Furthermore, there is no direct evidence that La Valette based his case during the evening of July 5 upon public opinion; there is merely the strong probability that as Minister of the Interior he would have emphasized this aspect. Finally, it is not clear that

---

[82] Albertini, pp. 342–3. Armengaud (p. 135) gives a striking example of this reaction among the manufacturers from the prefectural report from the Haut-Rhin, September 1, 1866.

[83] Case, *French Opinion on War and Diplomacy,* pp. 209–10; Case, "French Opinion and Napoleon III's Decision after Sadowa," *Public Opinion Quarterly,* 13:460 (1949).

[84] Armengaud, pp. 199–201.

[85] Armengaud, pp. 192–3; Case, *French Opinion on War and Diplomacy,* pp. 51–68.

[86] Albertini, pp. 338, 342–3.

the conversation with La Valette changed Napoleon's mind. Plon-plon's activities after talking to the Emperor earlier in the day sug-gest that the Emperor had already weakened; while both Plon-plon's arguments and the apparent cooperativeness demonstrated in the Prussian and Italian telegrams would have tended to dissuade Napo-leon from a pro-Austrian demonstration if he felt sympathy for the Prusso-Italian cause.

We may conclude, then, that neither the Emperor's physical weak-ness, nor doubts about French military preparedness, nor the state of public opinion offer a sufficient explanation of Napoleon's failure to aid the Austrians after Sadowa. Such traditional interpretations become more unsatisfactory the more emphasis is laid on Napoleon's concern with events in Central Europe. One example among many is the work of Hermann Oncken, by all odds the most complete discussion of Napoleon's policy available. Oncken believes that Napoleon's major aim, which he carried almost to the point of obses-sion, was the return of the Rhine provinces to France. Oncken tries to show that all Napoleon's diplomatic activities were calculated to facilitate this goal. He states that Napoleon expected a stalemate and even declares that Napoleon deliberately tried to create a stalemate by balancing off his encouragement to the Italians to accept Prussia's treaty offers with encouragement to the small Ger-man states to join the Austrian side. In bringing about a military draw, Napoleon's objective was to lay the groundwork for his mediation; but he was not content to trust entirely to the chances of the military campaign. He attempted to reinforce his position with agreements with both the Austrians and the Prussians which would entitle him to a voice in the eventual peace settlement. The treaty signed on June 12 with Austria fits quite well into this pattern. There was, of course, nothing comparable between France and Prussia, but Oncken could and did point to the almost consistently parallel nego-tiations with the two German great powers as evidence in support of his theory. In following this line, Oncken maintains, Napoleon's thinking was strictly traditional. He envisaged the future organization of Central Europe in terms of the old French plan of three Germanies and regarded the supposed safeguarding of the independence of the South German states as the one advantage of the Nikolsburg settlement. His favorite idea, however, was the restoration of the honor and prestige of the Bonapartes through the cession of the Rhineland to France. According to Oncken, this was the goal which underlay all Napoleon's twists and turns and all his complex negotiations; throughout all his conversations with the Austrians and the Prussians, he was seeking this prize. Oncken covers himself skillfully before the obvious objection that Napoleon, if he were really clear about his price, should have quoted it definitely to Austria and Prussia; he argues that Napoleon feared that a premature revelation of his true aims might frighten his opponents into a reconciliation. Hence it was only at the eleventh hour that he insisted on promises with regard to the Rhenish buffer state plans for the Austrians in connection with the June 12 treaty,[87] while only in May did he abandon his equivocal attitude toward the Prussians. Although it would have been convenient to reach an agreement before the war, the most opportune method of achieving such ambitious plans was to wait until a stalemate had exhausted his opponents. Then he could produce his schemes as a rider to a solicited mediation.

This interpretation has been repeated virtually unchanged in most modern accounts which touch on the crisis. The present study takes issue with this assessment of Napoleon's motives on two major grounds. First of all, although it is difficult to understand why Napoleon did not intervene after Sadowa if he was interested in the traditional structure of the balance of power and Austria's historical status, it becomes even harder to comprehend if one believes that he was actuated by an enormous hunger for compensations. Secondly, Napoleon's tactics throughout this period, while they never finally precluded compensations, do not seem to have been based on that wish. Compensations were not a sine qua non of an acceptable settlement. There is no reason to ascribe to the Emperor superhuman

[87] See Oncken, *Napoleon III and the Rhine*, pp. 38–67.

disinterestedness. Doubtless he would have been happy to accept compensations if a practicable plan had been offered to him. But there were significant moments during the crisis, for example at the time of the negotiations for a congress, when he seems to have been sincere in rejecting annexations for France, while there were other occasions, such as the Auxerre speech, when his desire for compensations is clearly traceable to the wish to enlist public opinion in support of his plans. By and large it can be said, as Gerhard Ritter has pointed out, that if Napoleon had been profoundly committed to gaining the Rhine provinces, he would have gone about the negotiations of 1865–66 in a different manner. Ritter makes a strong case against Oncken by pointing out that Oncken's thesis becomes excessively complicated, while a tenable interpretation can be achieved merely by accepting more or less at face value the statements which Oncken attempts to explain or explain away. For example, Ritter maintains that Napoleon would have liked to retrieve Landau and Saarbrücken, areas which he had been told were of considerable strategic importance; but he realized that this dream was dangerous. Its realization would have called down the popular opposition of liberal and nationalistic circles in Germany as well as the diplomatic hostility of the powers, with England and Belgium to the fore. There was also the danger, noted by Oncken, that if his price was too high, King William would give up the idea of war entirely or, alternatively, Bismarck would bring off a reconciliation with the Austrians. Caution about international repercussions made Napoleon hesitate about the annexation of even non-German territories, such as Belgium. When the Emperor confided to Goltz early in March that he would like to designate an area for compensations but did not know where to turn, he was not being Machiavellian but was simply voicing an uncomfortable truth.[88] The result was that the crux of Napoleon's policy was not an unshakable determination to win the

---

[88] Gerhard Ritter, "Bismarck und die Rhein-Politik Napoleons III," *Rheinische Vierteljahresblätte,* 15–16: 358–67 (1950–51).

Rhine provinces, but a desire to see Germany reorganized in a manner which would suit French diplomacy.[89]

In conclusion, we may ask what effect the revisions proposed here would have upon the picture of Napoleon III as a diplomat. Napoleon has often been portrayed as a statesman who was influenced primarily by the principle of the balance of power. By the same token, he has been castigated because of the failure which attended his efforts when judged in strict balance-of-power terms, as advocated, for example, by Thiers. The interesting work of C. W. Hallberg advanced the hypothesis maintained here that Napoleon's policies were not wholly shaped by considerations of power in the sense of classical balance-of-power diplomacy; they were also determined by ideological factors. Hallberg declares that Napoleonic France and the Austrian Empire represented two different and fundamentally opposed systems: tradition versus revolution and a powerful monarchy versus Caesarian democracy. An unbridgeable gap existed between the foreign policies of the two countries, since Napoleon, whether in cynicism or sincerity, had made himself the champion of the principle of nationalities, whereas the nationalistic ideology threatened the very bases of the Austrian state.[90] Although Hallberg's study terminates in 1864, his conclusions seem equally applicable to the two years immediately following. It seems highly probable that Napoleon III consciously promoted the cause of German nationalism as represented by Prussia in the best tradition of the *Idées napoléoniennes* and on the model of his Italian policy. In the same vein, Napoleon affirmed his loyalty to his revolutionary and Bonapartist heritage by working for the destruction of the

[89] Ritter, p. 339. Ritter emphasizes Napoleon's interest in a dualistic organization of Germany in contrast to the weight laid in the present study on the principle of nationalities. As will be shown below, the two considerations appeared complementary to Napoleon and the question of their relative importance seems rather insignificant as well as difficult of resolution. It does seem worth noting that since Napoleon did proclaim an interest in nationalism, conduct which harmonizes with that concern might logically have some ideological basis.

[90] C. W. Hallberg, *Franz Joseph and Napoleon III, 1852–64*, pp. 342–4.

German Confederation, the handiwork of the conservative Congress of Vienna. But Napoleon was sufficiently in touch with the realities of his day to give these ideals a practical formulation which was structured on the maintenance of the balance of power. He saw the two approaches to diplomacy not only as reconcilable, but even as complementary. To be sure, he would have liked to see a German national state unified under Prussian leadership. But nationalism to Napoleon was not an answer to the world's ills; it was merely one aspect of the units in a system designed to achieve a balance of power. It was in accordance with this political philosophy that Napoleon limited his championship of Prussia to support of her unification of Germany in the area north of the Main River. The new nationalist state would be counterbalanced, not only by the South German states, the bulk of the traditional Third Germany, but also by the Austrian Empire, whose diplomats would be forced to turn their attention to German affairs with renewed keenness, once the distraction of Venetia had been removed by the completion of the unification of Italy.[91] So Napoleon schemed to further the cause of nationalism and adjust the balance of power at the same time. But as events were to prove, he had helped to institutionalize a force far greater than he realized. The conjunction of nationalism and balance of power was ultimately either impossible or possible only after the most sweeping changes in the world situation. The first result was the diplomatic revolution occasioned by Bismarck's triumphant creation of a German state which was formed along nationalist lines and included the entire non-Austrian German area, north and south of the Main.

[91] Cf. Bush, "Napoleon III and the Redeeming of Venetia." Bush emphasizes Napoleon's concern for Italian nationalism and his desire to integrate an Italian national state into the balance of power system.

APPENDIXES
BIBLIOGRAPHY
INDEX

APPENDIX A

An additional factor which should be noted in evaluating the army itself is the intangible effect on morale. Reduction was bound to be unpopular per se in a career army. Probably typical was the attitude of Marshal Canrobert, who commanded the garrison at Paris. During the fall of 1865, when the law was under consideration, Canrobert took care to tell Napoleon that he had only a skeleton force, and he even complained that it was barely possible to carry out the traditional, small-scale maneuvers at Vincennes (Bapst, *Le Maréchal Canrobert*, IV, 22). Presumably in order to soften the blow, Randon made public on the day the decree was passed a raise in pay for army officers which would total 3,558,850 francs. This increase was to be financed from funds already voted by the Corps Législatif (Randon, *Mémoires*, II, 117). It is conceivable that this measure stemmed the discontent among the officers retained in service; but there was also the problem of the 1,193 officers who lost their jobs [Vincennes: *Guerre*, "Organisation et Recrutement. Réduction des cadres de l'armée. 2ᵉ Epreuve, 22 Janvier 1867," p. 3 (Mémoires et Reconnaissances: 2139, dossier 1866)]. The War Ministry worked out plans on paper which should have taken care of everyone. "Compensations" were granted to those officers who had been with the army long enough to win the right to a pension if they wished to return to work in civilian life [Vincennes: *Guerre*, "Effectif de l'Armée. Réduction des cadres," p. 11 (Mémoires et Reconnaissances: 2139, dossier 1865)]. In many cases, such men were placed in minor posts with the railroads, surely a glorious culmination to an officer's career. Other officers, who needed to stay in the army in order to finish earning the right to a pension, were allowed to do so, but were transferred to other units [Vincennes: *Guerre*, "Organisation et Recrutement. Réduction des cadres de l'armée. 2ᵉ Epreuve, 22 Janvier 1867," p. 3 (Mémoires et Reconnaissances: 2139, dossier 1866)]. The biggest problem with the whole blueprint was the inevitable slowness of its execution. For example, in January, 1866, at the time the decree was first going into effect, there were 336 extra officers in the infantry whose status would have to be changed [Vincennes: "Infanterie: Etat des Officiers en excédant au 11 Janvier 1866" (Mémoires et Reconnaissances: 2139, dossier 1866)]. Nearly a year later, in December, 1866, the destination of eighty-four of these officers remained to be settled [Vincennes: "Infanterie. Situation des officiers à la suite à la date du 24 Décembre 1866" (Mémoires et Reconnaissances: 2139, dossier 1866)]. In practice, this meant that throughout 1866 the army was burdened with officers who had lost their posts and had not as yet been given new jobs. Clearly this group must have been thoroughly discontented and must have lowered the morale of the army as a whole and reinforced the opinions of men like Canrobert who had opposed the decree in the first place. To the extent that an atmosphere of chagrin can lower the effectiveness of an army, the French army's effectiveness was lowered. But, on the other hand, the prospect of a good military campaign should have reduced or nullified this disgruntlement. It is hard to see how this dissatisfaction amounted to more than a temporary, peacetime handicap which would have been rapidly dispelled had France gone to war in 1866.

APPENDIX B

It seems worth considering briefly Bismarck's freedom of action with regard to French demands for the Rhineland. Bismarck himself claimed throughout this period that cession of the Rhine provinces was impossible because the inhabitants of the area felt themselves to be Germans and because the abandonment of this territory would outrage national feeling, both in the provinces themselves and throughout the Confederation. Since German nationalism was the sole popular foundation for Bismarck's unification policy, such an insult to it, according to Bismarck, would destroy all chance of fulfilling his plans. An examination of opinion in the Rhineland and in the small German states tends to confirm this argument. Reports from the Procureurs Généraux at Colmar and at Metz, despite their authors' best efforts to encourage Napoleon's hopes, indicated considerable reluctance to join France in the German areas adjacent to their posts [AN: Colmar, Special report of June 5, 1866 (BB^{30}376, Colmar 1865–66); Metz, Report of July 7, 1866 (BB^{30}380, Metz 1865–68)]. Various people who had traveled recently in Germany reported similar sentiments, and, if we are to believe Goltz, their testimony impressed Napoleon [Goltz to William, May 22, 1866 (Oncken, I, 227)]. Finally, there were stories of anti-French demonstrations in the Bavarian Rhineland. Although there were some attempts in French official circles to pass these off as anti-Bavarian, this interpretation hardly seems convincing [d'Astorg to Drouyn de Lhuys, June 1, 1866 (*Les Origines diplomatiques de la guerre de 1870–71*, IX, 357); d'Astorg to Drouyn, June 6, 1866 (*Origines,* X, 51)].

The state of opinion in the Rhine provinces is only half the story. One should consider also the feelings in the small German states vis-à-vis France and French ambitions. Here again, the evidence seems to bear out the Prussian government's insistence that any cession of German soil would awaken the most violent nationalistic antagonism. Napoleon's plan for a congress, for example, was received with suspicion because it included dicussion of the reform of the Confederation, a provision which was interpreted, in some quarters, as veiling a new French intervention in German affairs [Reculot to Drouyn de Lhuys, May 29, 1866 (*Origines,* IX, 312); d'Astorg to Drouyn de Lhuys, May 29, 1866 (*Origines,* IX, 311); Méloizes to Drouyn de Lhuys, May 30, 1866 (*Origines,* IX, 325)]. Another revealing insight into German sentiment is provided by the answers to a request for information on the subject of German reactions to France sent out by Drouyn de Lhuys on June 8 [Drouyn de Lhuys to the French representatives to Austria, Prussia, Württemberg, Hanover, Bavaria, Saxony, Cassel, Weimar, the Confederation, Darmstadt, Baden, and Hamburg, June 8, 1866 (*Origines,* X, 67)]. The answers superficially varied a good deal, with reports from Bavaria, for instance, of a declaration voted by the Chambers which carried strong anti-French implications [Annexe to Méloizes to Drouyn de Lhuys, June 10, 1866 (*Origines,* X, 108); Méloizes to Drouyn de Lhuys, June 11, 1866 (*Origines,* X, 128–30); Bondy to Drouyn, June 11, 1866 (*Origines,* X, 125)], while at the other end of the scale, Damrémont reported from Württemberg an attitude of "admiration" for Napoleon, although he admitted that the French nation was regarded with "fear, suspicion, jealousy" [Damrémont to Drouyn, June 9, 1866 (*Origines,* X, 96)]. Reculot at the headquarters of the Confederation Diet in Frankfurt confirmed the latter part of this judgment; he believed that France was widely suspected of aggressive designs. [Reculot to Drouyn de Lhuys, June 9, 1866 (*Origines,* X, 90).] Many of the ambassadors took a compromise position which did little to disguise a conviction of France's unpopularity. They declared that the distrust of France had lessened in recent months, but attributed this happy result to French maintenance of a hands-off policy vis-à-vis Germany. They cautioned that the slightest false move would activate the hostility which still existed in latent form [Cadore to Drouyn de Lhuys, June 8, 1866 (*Origines,* X, 79); Belcastel to Drouyn de Lhuys, June 8, 1866 (*Origines,* X, 87); Cintrat to Drouyn, June 9, 1866 (*Origines,* X, 91); d'Astorg to Drouyn, June 10, 1866 (*Origines,* X, 103–4)]. Even a rather optimistic survey, such as that presented by Reiset from Hanover, mentioned the congress, generally viewed as a sincere, pacifist gesture, as lulling suspicions of France [Reiset to Drouyn, June 9, 1866 (*Origines,* X, 92–5)]. The same reactions were to greet

Napoleon's statement to the Corps Législatif presented on June 11, 1866; in some quarters, the document was condemned because it was believed to contain a disguised statement of aggressive designs [d'Astorg to Drouyn, June 14, 1866 (*Origines*, X, 172)], while in other places, for instance, Bavaria, where the Emperor's words were interpreted as a disclaimer of ambition, it greatly improved French standing. [Méloizes to Drouyn, June 16, 1866 (*Origines*, X, 191); Méloizes to Drouyn, June 17, 1866 (*Origines*, X, 208); cf. also Reculot to Drouyn, June 14, 1866 (*Origines*, X, 173)]. It may be noted in passing that the same suspicions which hampered the cession of German land to France also rendered problematical any attempts by the French to deal with the small states as allies in German affairs. In early June, only two ambassadors, Damrémont in Württemberg and Bondy in Cassel, felt that relations with France were sufficiently easy that they could advocate direct dealings. [Damrémont to Drouyn, June 9, 1866 (*Origines*, X, 96); Bondy to Drouyn, June 11, 1866 (*Origines*, X, 125).] In actuality any such project would have been almost impossible, for the small states were in no sense a united group in June, 1866 [Benedetti to Drouyn, June 10, 1866 (*Origines*, X, 98–9)]. Despite a certain amount of quiet support indicated by France after the war broke out for closer ties between these governments (Oncken, *Napoleon III and the Rhine,* pp. 55–6), they remained separated until the end. But the crucial point at the moment is the existence of this attitude of profound suspicion and its effect on proposals for the cession of the Rhine provinces. Although the foregoing remarks cannot pretend to be an exhaustive discussion of a very intricate subject, it seems evident that all the signs point to the presence of a dangerous situation. If French ambitions were so widely disapproved, if the mere suggestion of the possibility of a Prusso-French bargain sufficed to multiply the fears [see Reculot to Drouyn, June 9, 1866 (*Origines*, X, 90); Cintrat to Drouyn, June 9, 1866 (*Origines*, X, 91); Reiset to Drouyn, June 9, 1866 (*Origines*, X, 93–4); Méloizes to Drouyn, June 11, 1866 (*Origines*, X, 129)], it is not hard to imagine the reaction to a cession of the Rhine provinces, and it must be admitted that, on this score as well as on the score of sentiment within the provinces, there was a very real justification to Bismarck's oft-repeated argument that he could not abandon this area to France because he would turn against himself the current of German national feeling.

BIBLIOGRAPHY

I. DOCUMENTS

A. *Unpublished Documents*

Berlin—Deutsches Zentralarchiv, Abteilung Merseburg.
> Consulted: Letters relating to the Kiss Mission from May and June, 1866.
> (Cited Merseburg)

London—Public Record Office.
> Consulted: From the Cowley Papers, dispatches of Cowley from August, 1865, through July, 1866; reports of Claremont (England's military attaché); and miscellaneous letters from members of the French government.
> (Cited PRO)

Paris—Archives du Ministère de la Guerre, Château de Vincennes.
> Consulted: Annual reports to Napoleon III for 1865 and 1866 and miscellaneous statistics on French military strength; budgets from 1863 through 1867; general correspondence from July, 1865, through July, 1866; five-day reports from January, 1866, through June, 1866; reports of Merlin (military attaché in Vienna) from April, 1866, through July, 1866; reports of Clermont-Tonnerre (military attaché in Berlin) from November, 1865, through June, 1866; material dealing with Italian affairs including reports of Schmitz from April, 1866, through July, 1866.
> (Cited Vincennes)

Paris—Archives des Affaires Etrangères, Ministère des Affaires Etrangères.
> Consulted: Rouher's Papers.
> (Cited Quai d'Orsay)

Paris—Archives Nationales.
> Consulted: From the Archives Privées, Rouher's Papers, especially his notes on the meetings of the Council of Ministers from Septem-

ber, 1865, through July, 1866, and his collection of military statistics gathered at the time of the army reforms of November, 1866; miscellaneous letters from personages particularly concerned with the German crisis preserved in other private collections (very little here); reports of the Procureurs Généraux in Amiens-Angers, Colmar, Dijon-Douai, Metz-Montpellier, and Nancy from July, 1865, through October, 1866; miscellaneous financial papers dealing with commercial relations with Prussia and the Zollverein and with the affairs of the Crédit Mobilier.
(Cited AN)

Paris—Bibliothèque Nationale, Salle des Manuscrits.
Consulted: Correspondence of Thiers during 1865 and 1866.
(Cited BN)

Vienna—Haus- Hof- und Staatsarchiv.
Consulted: Correspondence to and from the Paris Embassy from August, 1865, through July, 1866.
(Cited HHSA)

B. *Published Documents*

Annales du Sénat et du Corps Législatif (1866), vols. 1–10, Paris, 1866. See for the debates on foreign policy.
(Cited *Annales 1866*)

Benedetti, Vincent, *Ma mission en Prusse*, 3rd ed., Paris, 1871. This book, Benedetti's self-defence written during the Franco-Prussian War, consists mainly of long extracts from his dispatches, now available in the *Origines*.

—— *Studies in Diplomacy*, New York, 1896. Alludes briefly to events in 1866.

Berdrow, Wilhelm, *Alfred Krupps Briefe 1826–87*, Berlin, 1928. Much correspondence, of little significance here, between Krupp and von Roon.

Bismarck, Otto von, *Die gesammelten Werke*, ed. Friedrich Thimme, 19 vols., Berlin, 1924–35. Admirable as an insight into Bismarck's plans and procedures; as a collection of documents relevant to the period it is less useful, partly because of the lack of an index, partly because of the exclusive concentration on Bismarck, only slightly relieved by the editor's excellent introductions. Contains some documents missing in the *APP*.
(Cited *GW*)

Eugénie, *Lettres familières*, 2 vols., Paris, 1935. Nothing of interest.

D'Hauterive, Ernest, "La Mission du Prince Napoléon en Italie (1866) —Lettres inédites," *Revue des deux mondes*, 27:83–120 (May 1925). Useful for negotiations with Italy during July and August, 1866; adds little however to the *Origines* as to over-all French policy.

————— ed., *Napoleon III et le Prince Napoléon: Correspondance inédite*, Paris, 1925. D'Hauterive is almost alone among scholars in having been permitted to see the tantalizing collection preserved by Prince Napoleon and his family from which these letters (and those published in the *Revue des deux mondes'* article) are excerpted. As the only considerable body of papers from Napoleon's own hand, these documents might prove a great deal, but probably don't. Unfortunately the emphasis here is on letters which will reveal the character of Napoleon and of Prince Napoleon; consequently there is very little material about the German crisis or any aspect of politics in 1866. D'Hauterive gives a strong but now demonstrably erroneous impression that Napoleon did not discuss politics with the Prince in the period between the fiasco of the Ajaccio speech in 1865 and the reconciliation on the eve of the war.

Historische Reichskommission, *Die auswärtige Politik Preussens 1858–71*, 10 vols., Berlin, 1932–45. Obviously a very important collection. An excellent index. Some duplication with Oncken and with Bismarck's *Die gesammelten Werke* is credited in a somewhat confusing system of cross-references. (Cited *APP*)

Ministère des Affaires Etrangères, *Les Origines diplomatiques de la guerre de 1870–71*, 29 vols., Paris, 1910–32. Indispensable. (Cited *Origines*)

Moltke, Helmuth von, *Militärische Werke*, 13 vols., Berlin, 1892–1912. Gives important insights into Prussian military planning in 1865–66.

Napoleon III, *Des Idées napoléoniennes*, Paris, 1860. Useful as an exposé, although admittedly a confused one, of Napoleon's ideas, written long before his rise to power. The relationship between theory and practice has long been a matter for debate.

Oncken, Hermann, *Die Rheinpolitik Kaiser Napoleons III. von 1863 bis 1870*, 3 vols., Berlin, 1926. (English ed. of Introduction, *Napoleon III and the Rhine*, trans. Edwin H. Zeydel, New York, 1928.) Valuable as the only extensive publication of documents on this subject from the Haus- Hof- und Staatsarchiv. Although there is much evidence here for Oncken's thesis, as presented in his introduction, the collection, despite careful selection, does not conclusively prove his point. His interpretation revolves mainly around the compensations issue and bears marks of a desire to prove that France was not the innocent victim of German aggression in 1870 and 1914 (see the highly favorable introduction to the English edition by Ferdinand Schevill). Oncken's analysis, which carried much earlier work to its logical conclusion, has remained widely accepted; it is the closest thing to a monographic treatment of Napoleon's policy in 1865–66, although it covers a much longer time span. (Cited Oncken)

Papiers et correspondance de la famille impériale, 3 vols., Paris, 1870– [72?]. A very mixed draw and inadequately indexed. Nonetheless, a few scattered documents of interest will repay the specialist, while for the more general reader, the very variety of the collection gives a vivid impression of the Second Empire.

Papiers secrets brulés dans l'incendie des Tuileries, Brussels, 1871. The most interesting thing about this work is its title.

Les Papiers secrets de l'Empire, Brussels, 1871. A far less scholarly collection than the *Papiers et correspondance*, evidently drawn up by anti-Bonapartist editors.

The Paris Embassy during the Second Empire: Selections from the Papers of Henry Richard Charles Wellesley 1st Earl Cowley, ed. Colonel F. A. Wellesley, London [1928]. Selections from the dispatches of the astute and experienced but very deaf English ambassador, edited by his son. Does not replace the collection preserved in the Public Record Office.

Poschinger, H. von, ed., *Fürst Bismarck: neue Tischgespräche*, 2 vols., Stuttgart, 1895–99. One or two points of interest.

Quellen zur deutschen Politik Österreichs 1859–66, ed. Oskar Schmid and Heinrich Ritter von Srbik, 5 vols., Berlin, 1934–38. Some important documents about Franco-Austrian negotiations not to be found in the Haus- Hof- und Staatsarchiv. (Cited *Quellen*)

Roon, Waldemar, Graf von, ed., *Denkwürdigkeiten aus dem Leben des General-Feldmarschalls-Kriegsminister Grafen von Roon*, 3 vols., Berlin, 1905. Not very illuminating except on German matters.

Steefel, Lawrence, "A Letter of Francis Joseph," *Journal of Modern History*, 2:70–1 (March 1930). Gives Beust's instructions in July, 1866.

Stolberg-Wernigerode, Otto zu, *Robert Heinrich Graf von der Goltz,*
Berlin, 1941. Includes an extensive documentary section: much of
the material relates to the Prussian internal situation and to Goltz's
worries about his own status, but there are some valuable points
about foreign policy.

Vautier, G., "Au-delà et en-deçà de nos frontières de l'est en 1866," *La
Révolution de 1848,* 25:112–22 (1928). Reprints a few procureurial
reports.

II. BOOKS

A. Accounts by Contemporaries

Berthet-Leleux, François, *Le Vrai Prince Napoléon,* Paris [1932]. A
chatty and partisan work done by the prince's secretary. No mention of the 1866 crisis.

Chiala, Luigi, *Le Général La Marmora et l'alliance prussienne,* Paris,
1868. The memoirs of La Marmora's great military rival.

Dosne, Eurydice Sophie, *Mémoires,* ed. Henri Malo, 2 vols., Paris, 1928.
This book, the journals kept by Thiers' mother-in-law, gives a brief
but remarkably interesting and colorful account of Thiers' role in
1866. A violent partisan of Thiers, she brings his experiences to life
most vividly.

Eugénie, *Memoirs,* ed. Comte Fleury, 2 vols., New York, 1920. Dis-
appointingly omits Eugénie's own views in favor of Napoleon's
later statements about his opinions and policies, all pretty undependable since they were enunciated after Sedan. Sentimental, re-
trospectively deferential tone used toward Napoleon.

Eulenburg, Botho Wend August, Graf zu, *Zehn Jahre innerer Politik
1862–72,* Berlin, 1872. Sheds a little light on Eulenburg.

[Ferrero del] la Marmora, Alfonso, *Un peu plus de lumière,* trans. Niox
and Descourbès, 4th ed., Paris, 1874. La Marmora's own story and
self-justification; frequently untrustworthy.

Fleury [Emile Félix], Comte, *Souvenirs,* 2 vols., Paris, 1897–98. Some
relevant personal glimpses.

Hansen, Jules, *Les Coulisses de la diplomatie,* Paris, 1880. Undependable.

D'Harcourt, Bernard, *Les Quatre Ministères de M. Drouyn de Lhuys,*
Paris, 1882. Nearly useless now that the Quai d'Orsay correspondence has been published. D'Harcourt's interpretation is focused

strictly upon Drouyn de Lhuys and represents an unquestioning endorsement of his policy.

Le Moyne, J.-V., ed. and trans., *Campagne de 1866 en Italie,* Paris, 1875. A greatly enlarged French version of Chiala's memoirs.

Loë [Friedrich] Freiherr von, *Erinnerungen aus meinem Berufsleben 1849–67,* 2nd ed., Stuttgart, 1906. Pleasant and sober in tone, this work gives an impression of accuracy from the constant use of Loë's contemporary reports. Strongly critical of the French military situation and of Randon, Loë gives himself, possibly with an element of hindsight, full credit for having reassured the Prussian government on this point.

Mérimée, Prosper, *Lettres à M. Panizzi,* 2 vols., Paris, 1881. Mérimée was in fairly close contact with imperial circles; his many fascinating and useful descriptions, both of individuals and of incidents, provide valuable background information about the atmosphere of events and the cross-currents of opinion.

────── *Lettres à une inconnue,* 6th ed., 2 vols., Paris, 1874. This collection is far less directly helpful than the *Lettres à M. Panizzi;* however it does give an amusing picture of the social and literary life of the times.

Ollivier, Emile, *L'Empire libéral,* 18 vols., Paris, 1895–1918. A monumental but disappointing account. Although Ollivier was concerned in the German crisis as an active and articulate member of the Corps Législatif, he almost invariably eschews personal reminiscence in favor of "historical" narration, including lengthy summaries of purely German events, marred by insufficient or inaccurate information.

Persigny [Jean], duc de, *Mémoires,* ed. H. de Laire, Comte d'Espagny, 3rd ed., Paris, 1896. A lively, stimulating, and thoroughly untrustworthy account. Unconsciously, Persigny reveals himself cruelly: he is full of ideas, the validity of which he never questions, profoundly conceited, and vitriolically contemptuous of others. His devotion to Napoleon and to Bonapartism is, of course, enormous.

Plener, Ernst von, *Erinnerungen,* 2 vols., Stuttgart, 1911. A most charming book with sketches of leading figures and lively reminiscences of court and Parisian life. Valuable information about the Austrian loan negotiations.

Prévost-Paradol [Lucien], *Quelques Pages d'histoire contemporaine: Lettres politiques,* 2nd ed., 4 vols., Paris, 1862–67. A collection of his contemporary articles reprinted from the *Courrier du dimanche:*

very interesting and quotable. There is much material about the German crisis from mid-April on; it is largely slanted, however, toward Prévost-Paradol's paramount concern, the struggle for the Liberal Empire. This angle, although sometimes unhelpful, is at least instructive.

Radowitz, Joseph Maria von, *Aufzeichnungen und Erinnerungen,* ed. Hajo Holborn, 2 vols., Stuttgart, 1925. Brief and very generalized account of the negotiations between Goltz and Napoleon; excellent picture of contemporary life in Paris. Some interesting information about relations between Goltz and Bismarck.

Randon [Jacques], Maréchal, *Mémoires,* 2nd ed., 2 vols., Paris, 1875–77. A vindication of Randon and the army, this book contains many statistics and much information about French military preparations; little insight into Randon's personality.

Rothan G[ustave], *L'Affaire du Luxembourg,* n.p., 1883. Very brief.

—— *La Politique française en 1866,* Paris, 1879.
Valuable as the first important attempt by a Frenchman at writing the history of the crisis. Emphasizes French military inadequacy.

Vitzthum von Eckstädt, Karl Friedrich, Count, *London, Gastein and Sadowa,* Stuttgart, 1889. Some perceptive insights; little information.

B. Scholarly Accounts

Albertini, Rudolf von, "Frankreichs Stellungnahme zur Deutschen Einigung während des zweiten Kaiserreiches," *Schweizerische Zeitschrift für Geschichte,* 5:305–68 (1955). A thorough, closely written, and highly informative study of French public opinion, especially useful (though at times bewildering) because of the careful relating of ideas to groups and individuals. Although Albertini agrees with Armengaud in his belief that French public opinion in 1866 was primarily pacifist, his further conclusions, which emphasize the prounification trend of opinion, contrast strongly with those of Armengaud.

Armengaud, André, "L'Opinion publique en France et la crise nationale allemande en 1866," unpubl. thèse complémentaire, Faculté des Lettres de Paris, Paris, 1958. A thoroughly competent and comprehensive account of public opinion in the spring and summer of 1866; suffers only (and remarkably little) from the author's relative lack of grounding in the political history of the period.

Bapst, Germain, *Le Maréchal Canrobert,* 5 vols., Paris, 1898–1911. A pleasant and informative study; although Canrobert was not initiated into high politics, his biography does give a sample of opinions and expectations among the rank and file of the officers plus some useful incidental military information. Evidently Bapst knew Canrobert; he also made full use of his papers.

Beer, Adolf, *Die Finanzen Österreichs im XIX. Jahrhundert*, Prague, 1877. Very brief but fairly detailed account of the Austrian loan.

Beiche, F., *Bismarck und Italien*, Berlin, 1931. Little new information.

Berdrow, Wilhelm, *The Krupps*, trans. Fritz Homann, Berlin, 1937. A rather good survey which, however, adds little to the present study.

Bernstein, Paul, "The Economic Aspect of Napoleon III's Rhine Policy," *French Historical Studies*, 1:335–47 (1960). Brilliant but not entirely convincing.

—— "Les Entrevues de Biarritz et de Saint-Cloud (Octobre-Novembre 1865)," *Revue d'histoire diplomatique*, 78:330–9 (1964). Provocative discussion.

—— "The Rhine Policy of Napoleon III: A New Interpretation," *Lock Haven Bulletin*, 1:47–67 (1962). A superficial account which adds nothing to his earlier article.

Bertaut, Jules, *L'Impératrice Eugénie et son temps* [Paris, 1956]. A few points of interest; the study is marred by quick and impressionistic sketches of political events.

Bonnal, H[enri], *Sadowa*, Paris, 1901. Emphasizes deployment of manpower rather than technological advances.

Bush, John W., "Napoleon III and the Redeeming of Venetia, 1864–66," unpubl. diss., Fordham University, 1961. The most helpful and thorough study of the Italian side of the 1866 crisis.

Case, Lynn M., "French Opinion and Napoleon III's Decision after Sadowa," *Public Opinion Quarterly*, 13:441–61 (1949). Later condensed, toned down, and included in *French Opinion on War and Diplomacy*.

—— *French Opinion on War and Diplomacy during the Second Empire*, Philadelphia, 1954. Only a chapter on 1865–66, but it is clearly argued and well substantiated.

Chrétien, Paul, *Le Duc de Persigny*, Toulouse, 1943. Inadequate treatment of Persigny's role in 1866.

Clapham, J. H., *The Economic Development of France and Germany 1815–1914*, 4th ed., Cambridge, England, 1936. A good introductory text but contains little information on international finance.

Clark, C. W., *Franz Joseph and Bismarck*, Cambridge, Mass., 1934. Excellent survey of Austro-Prussian relations to the outbreak of the war in 1866 based on wide reading and extensive archival research. Sane and often penetrating treatment of French policy, but the focus on Austria does not permit detailed development of French plans. Emphasis on the primacy of the Italian problem as a determinant in Napoleon's calculations.

Corti, Egon Caesar, Count, *The Reign of the House of Rothschild 1830–71,* trans. Brian and Beatrix Lunn, New York, 1928. Adds little; heavily based on secondary sources.

Cowan, Laing Gray, *France and the Saar, 1680–1948,* New York, 1950. A rather general study, of necessity too general to be very helpful. Written from the viewpoint of the inhabitants of the Saar, Cowan stresses the French desire throughout the sixties to annex the Saar and the inhabitants' desire to remain German. Does not have the scope to analyze or differentiate French aims in any depth.

Craig, Gordon, *The Battle of Königgrätz* (Philadelphia and New York, 1964). Helpful study.

Doutenville, J., "La France, La Prusse, et L'Allemagne au lendemain de Sadowa," *La Nouvelle Revue,* 51:349–69 (1921). Deals almost entirely with the period after Sadowa.

Durieux, Joseph, *Le Ministre Pierre Magne,* 2 vols., Paris, 1929. Scanty treatment of the German question devoted mainly to Magne's reaction to the final settlement at Nikolsburg.

Esslinger, Elisabet, *Kaiserin Eugenie und die Politik des zweiten Kaiserreichs,* Stuttgart, 1932. An adequate summary of Eugénie's role in 1865–66 based almost entirely on the documents published by Oncken.

Falls, Cyril, *The Art of War,* London, 1961. A very generalized discussion, in the Home University Library.

———— *A Hundred Years of War,* London, 1953. More detailed than his later *The Art of War.*

Farat, Honoré, *Persigny* [Paris, 1957]. A pretty chatty effort.

Feis, Herbert, *Europe the World's Banker 1870–1914,* New Haven, 1930. An indispensable text on international finance, although not concerned with the Second Empire directly.

Fester, R., "Biarritz," *Deutsche Rundschau,* 113:212–36 (1902). Outdated, but still impressive for logic and shrewdness.

Fohlen, Claude, *L'Industrie textile au temps du Second Empire,* Paris, 1956. Excellent background work on conditions and unrest in one of France's major industries, but developed almost entirely from the economic point of view. Useful bibliography.

Frahm, Friedrich, "Biarritz," *Historische Vierteljahrschrift,* 15:337–61 (July 1912). A careful article, marred by the fact that Frahm just missed the publication of the relevant sections of the *Origines.* Advances the widely held contention that the Biarritz meeting was a failure; emphasizes the central importance to Bismarck of the French danger.

Friedjung, Heinrich, *The Struggle for Supremacy in Germany 1859–66,* trans. A. J. P. Taylor and W. L. McElwee, London, 1935. The translation, although also an abridgment, gives an adequate impression of Friedjung's thesis, since the material omitted is mainly military history. Writing from the Austrian viewpoint, Friedjung emphasizes both Napoleon's illness and his desire for compensations.

Fuller, J. C., *War and Western Civilization, 1832–1932,* London, 1932. A good, general account.

Gavin, James M., "Civil War: Great Advances that Changed War" [Part IV], *Life,* 50:66–82 (February 17, 1961). An amusing and instructive sideline; good pictures.

Geuss, Herbert, *Bismarck und Napoleon III,* Cologne, 1959. Interesting summary.

Girard, Louis, *La Politique des travaux publics du Second Empire,* Paris, 1952. Useful bibliography with helpful and very complete indications on research on economic subjects.

Guiral, Pierre, *Prévost-Paradol,* Paris, 1955. A solid, scholarly account of Prévost-Paradol's life; for the present purposes, adds little to Prévost-Paradol's own writings but does give some background about the reaction of the government and of Prévost-Paradol's colleagues.

Hallberg, Charles W., *Franz Joseph and Napoleon III, 1852–64,* New York, 1955. An impressively documented survey of the first half of Napoleon's reign; conclusions about his aims in this period give an extremely interesting comparison and analogy with the later years.

Herly, Robert, *Les Conditions de production de la métallurgie sarroise depuis 1815,* Paris, 1926. Many useful facts about the industrial situation in the Saar; rather generalized but quite adequate treatment.

Kulessa, Adolf, *Die Kongressidee Napoleons III. im Mai 1866,* Giessen, 1927. This book is seriously weakened by the fact that Kulessa was entirely dependent upon printed sources. Particularly when he moves away from his special subject, he is inclined to lean heavily upon Oncken and he adds little or nothing to Oncken's interpretation, which he sometimes applies with questionable logic.

La Gorce, Pierre de, *Histoire du Second Empire,* 7 vols., Paris, 1899–1905. Despite disclaimers of any ability to understand Napoleonic policy (which the reader can only echo), La Gorce produces an interpretation couched mainly in terms of French desire for compensations. Acidic comments on practically everyone connected with the 1865–66 crisis.

Long, Dwight C., "The Austro-French Commercial Treaty of 1866," *American Historical Review,* 41:474–91 (April 1936). A competent and well-balanced study; although the focus is on the economic aspects, political factors are considered. A clear and helpful footnote to the present subject.

Maurain, Jean, *Un Bourgeois français au XIXe siècle: Baroche,* Paris, 1936. A competent, well-documented study of an important but undynamic figure. Section on the German question is well done, with many quotations; but since Baroche was little concerned with foreign policy at this time, the study principally reveals the view of the crisis seen in the outer circles of the government.

Moss, Herbert James, "Napoleon III and Belgium 1866–70," unpubl. diss., Harvard University, 1937. A fairly good study, done from the Belgian viewpoint. Most of Moss's work deals with events after the Austro-Prussian War.

Mosse, W. E., *The European Powers and the German Question, 1848–71,* Cambridge, England, 1958. An attempt, not entirely successful, to restate the history of the early Bismarckian period from the European, rather than the Prussian viewpoint. Although based on a definitive survey of the archives, this study does not change the broad outlines of the picture. Mosse does make important contributions by suggesting that the powers in general were less hostile, and the Russians more hostile, to unification under Prussia than has been thought.

Plenge, Johann, *Gründung und Geschichte des Crédit Mobilier,* Tübingen, 1903. Doctoral thesis at Leipzig. Since Plenge knew the Péreire family, they made private papers available to him. Although he deals with the Crédit Mobilier as an economic rather than a historical phenomenon, there is a useful bibliographical essay and some helpful details about the areas in which the organization was financially interested.

230   BIBLIOGRAPHY

Poirson, Philippe, *Walewski, fils de Napoléon,* Paris [1943]. A lively, rather popularized, but adequately documented account.

Pomaret, Charles, *Monsieur Thiers et son siècle* [Paris, 1948]. A lovingly thorough study, but almost ludicrously pro-Thiers.

Renouvin, Pierre, *Le XIXe siècle I: De 1815 à 1871* (vol. V of *Histoire des Relations Internationales,* ed. Pierre Renouvin), Paris, 1954. Brief but lucid analysis of Napoleon's policy viewed in terms of traditional balance-of-power diplomatic goals.

Riker, T. W., *The Making of Roumania. A Study of an International Problem 1856–66,* London, 1931. A solid work of diplomatic history. Some points of interest with regard to the interaction between the powers' stand on Moldavia and Wallachia and their stands on other issues.

Ritter, Gerhard, "Bismarck und die Rhein-Politik Napoleons III," *Rheinische Vierteljahresblätter,* 15–16:339–70 (1950–51). An able refutation of the Oncken thesis by one of the best contemporary authorities on the period. In opposition to Oncken's emphasis on compensations, Ritter maintains that Napoleon was primarily interested in promoting and, if possible, perpetuating Austro-Prussian rivalry.

Ropp, Theodore, *War in the Modern World,* New York, 1962. A helpful summary.

Salomon, Henry, *L'Ambassade de Richard de Metternich à Paris,* Paris, 1931. A brief, rather generalized account.

Schnerb, Robert, *Rouher et le Second Empire,* Paris, 1949. A recent and well-documented study. Brief but important treatment of events in 1865–66.

Srbik, Heinrich Ritter von, *Deutsche Einheit,* 4 vols., Munich, 1935–42. Brilliant treatment.

——— "Der Geheimvertrag Österreichs und Frankreichs vom 12. Juni 1866," *Historisches Jahrbuch,* 57:454–507 (1937). A few points of interest. Srbik's principal contribution here is the integration into the story of the secret letters of Metternich to Mensdorff about the May overtures. These had been found among Mensdorff's private papers and had been published by Srbik in the *Quellen.* They had not been available to Clark, who had used the general correspondence in the Haus- Hof- und Staatsarchiv.

Stadelmann, Rudolf, *Das Jahr 1865,* Munich, 1933. Deals almost entirely with Germany.

Steefel, Lawrence, "The Rothschilds and the Austrian Loan of 1865,"

Journal of Modern History, 8:27–39 (March 1936). Very helpful coverage.

Stern, Alfred, *Geschichte Europas [1815–71]*, 10 vols., Berlin, 1894–1924. Many factual inaccuracies. Interpretation emphasizes Napoleon's poor health as a factor in his indecisiveness.

Sybel, Heinrich von, *The Founding of the German Empire*, trans. Marshall Livingston Perrin and Gamaliel Bradford, Jr., 7 vols., New York [1890–98]. A remarkably thorough and accurate account considering its publication not long after the event and before many of the documentary collections had been made available. Sybel did have the advantage, however, of access to the Prussian archives. His pro-Prussian bias does lead him astray occasionally, notably in his interpretation of Franco-Prussian relations.

—— *Napoleon III*, Bonn, 1873. Deals mainly with the fifties.

Zeldin, Theodore, *The Political System of Napoleon III*, London, 1958. An interesting but tantalizingly brief analysis. Useful background.

INDEX

Aal, 96
Adriatic Sea, 162
Ajaccio, 139
Albertini, Rudolf von, 205
Algeria, 97, 167, 197–9
Alsace, 34
Arese, Count Francisco, 78–9
Armengaud, André, 122–3, 204–5
Artillery, French, 38–9
August 29 circular, 16–23, 28, 41, 68
Austria: Foreign Office, 63, 77, 112, 114–6, 134, 136, 153, 162, 172, 177; Convention of Gastein, 8, 13–4, 42–3; exclusion from Germany, 8, 165, 167, 170–3, 175, 177, 181–2; relations with France, 10, 15, 20, 22–3, 33, 42–63, 72–7, 104–16, 126–36, 142–61, 166–82, 185–90, 206–10, 216; French loan, 42–8, 52, 186; commercial treaty with France, 47–9, 186; commercial relations with Italy, 49–52, 56; political relations with Italy, 54–8, 72–6, 80, 82–3, 104–6, 109–16, 126–9, 134–6, 142–6, 149–53, 158–62, 172, 177–9, 181–2, 185–90; internal situation, 93–4; military position of, 82–94, 101–4; relations with Third Germany, 103, 129, 146–7, 173, 176–7, 206; congress, 129–30, 142–3. *See also* Prussia; Seven Weeks' War
Austro-Italian War of 1859, 81, 97, 118, 205
Austro-Prussian War, *see* Seven Weeks' War
Auxerre, 117, 122
Auxerre speech, 117–8, 120–7, 136, 141, 188, 208
Avenir National, 148

Baden, 216
Balance of power, 6–7, 18, 67, 71–2, 81–2, 110–1, 117, 126, 144, 146–9, 189, 207, 209–10
Ballplatz, *see* Austria
Bank of France, 123
Bapst, Germain, 82
Baroche, Jules, 157–8
Bavaria, 40–1, 51, 70, 89, 103, 113, 147, 153, 176, 215–7
Belfort, 38
Belgium, 18, 27, 29–33, 40–1, 70, 113, 141, 185–6, 208
Benedek, Field Marshal Ludwig von, 93
Benedetti, Count Vincent, 61–2, 77, 79–80, 103, 163, 172–5, 179–80, 182–4
Berckheim, General Sigismond-Guillaume de, 84
Berlin, Congress of, 75
Beust, Count Friedrich von, 167–8, 170
Biarritz meeting, 17, 19, 21–2, 24–33, 59–60, 185–6
Bismarck, Prince Otto von, 1–2, 8, 40–1, 66–8, 185–6, 188, 190, 201–3, 208, 210, 215–7; Convention of Gastein, 8–14, 17–22; Biarritz meeting, 24–34; Austrian loan, 45–6; March proposals to France, 60–3, 69–73, 104–5; relations with Italy, 11, 51, 70, 79–81; view of military situation, 81, 88–9; Thiers' speech, 110, 112; May discussions with France, 116, 121, 125–6, 136–42, 144; Seven Weeks' War, 148–51, 158–9, 164–5; peace negotiations, 172–6, 180, 182–4
Black Eagle, Order of the, 51
Bohemia, 89, 102, 164, 193

HARVARD HISTORICAL STUDIES

OUT OF PRINT TITLES ARE OMITTED

22. *Howard Levi Gray*. English Field Systems. 1959.

32. *Lawrence D. Steefel*. The Schleswig-Holstein Question. 1932.

33. *Lewis George Vander Velde*. The Presbyterian Churches and the Federal Union, 1861–1869. 1932.

37. *Roland Dennis Hussey*. The Caracas Company, 1728–1784: A Study in the History of Spanish Monopolistic Trade. 1934.

38. *Dwight Erwin Lee*. Great Britain and the Cyprus Convention Policy of 1878. 1934.

39. *Paul Rice Doolin*. The Fronde. 1935.

40. *Arthur McCandless Wilson*. French Foreign Policy during the Administration of Cardinal Fleury, 1726–1743. 1936.

41. *Harold Charles Deutsch*. The Genesis of Napoleonic Imperialism. 1938.

48. *Jack H. Hexter*. The Reign of King Pym. 1941.

60. *Robert G. L. Waite*. Vanguard of Nazism: The Free Corps Movement in Postwar Germany, 1918–1923. 1952.

62, 63. *John King Fairbank*. Trade and Diplomacy on the China Coast: The Opening of the Treaty Ports, 1842–1854. One-volume edition. 1964.

64. *Franklin L. Ford*. Robe and Sword: The Regrouping of the French Aristocracy after Louis XIV. 1953.

66. *Wallace Evan Davies*. Patriotism on Parade: The Story of Veterans' and Hereditary Organizations in America, 1783–1900. 1955.

67. *Harold Schwartz*. Samuel Gridley Howe: Social Reformer, 1801–1876. 1956.

68. *Bryce D. Lyon*. From Fief to Indenture: The Transition from Feudal to Non-Feudal Contract in Western Europe. 1957.

69. *Stanley J. Stein*. Vassouras: A Brazilian Coffee County, 1850–1900. 1957.

70. *Thomas F. McGann*. Argentina, the United States, and the Inter-American System, 1880–1914. 1957.

71. *Ernest R. May*. The World War and American Isolation, 1914–1917. 1959.

72. *John B. Blake*. Public Health in the Town of Boston, 1630–1822. 1959.

73. *Benjamin W. Labaree*. Patriots and Partisans: The Merchants of Newburyport, 1764–1815. 1962.

74. *Alexander Sedgwick*. The Ralliement in French Politics, 1890–1898. 1965.

75. *E. Ann Pottinger*. Napoleon III and the German Crisis, 1865–1866. 1966.

76. *Walter Goffart*. The Le Mans Forgeries: A Chapter from the History of Church Property in the Ninth Century. 1966.

77. *Daniel P. Resnick*. The White Terror and the Political Reaction after Waterloo. 1966.

78. *Giles Constable*. The Letters of Peter the Venerable. 1967.

79. *Lloyd E. Eastman*. Throne and Mandarins: China's Search for a Policy during the Sino-French Controversy, 1880–1885. 1967.

80. *Allen J. Matusow*. Farm Policies and Politics in the Truman Years. 1967.

81. *Philip Charles Farwell Bankwitz*. Maxime Weygand and Civil-Military Relations in Modern France. 1967.